JIM O'BRIEN

BUCKING THE ODDS

BY
RALPH PAULK

SPORTS PUBLISHING L.L.C.
SPORTSPUBLISHINGLLC.COM

Director of production: Susan M. Moyer
Dustjacket and photo insert design: Kenneth J. Higgerson
Editor: David Hamburg

ISBN: 1-58261-313-3

SPORTS PUBLISHING L.L.C.
www.sportspublishingllc.com

Printed in the United States.

To Hubert Knight (1935-1972)
An inspiring uncle with an endearing personality,
who was the sunshine of our lives.

ACKNOWLEDGMENTS

This book could not have been written without Coach Jim O'Brien sharing his time and thoughts with me. The players on the Ohio State men's basketball players, particularly Scoonie Penn and Michael Redd, were always gracious gentlemen in both victory and defeat.

It's hard to imagine that this project would have been completed without the inspiring words of my wife, Marilyn, and my oldest son, David, whose work ethic is inspiring. Thanks to all my kids—Manny, Brittany, Terra, and Amber—for their encouraging words.

Thanks to a good friend, Carl Chancellor, a truly talented writer who didn't spare my feelings with his critical analysis and suggestions. He was annoying even on the golf course, the only place I could get even. Thanks to David Hamburg, a meat-and-potatoes book editor whose contributions were immeasurable.

Thanks to Dan Wallenberg, Ohio State's assistant sports information director. Thanks to Jack Schrom, Coach O'Brien's good friend. The time they afforded me was invaluable.

Thanks to the Ohio State assistant coaches—Dave Spiller, Paul Biancardi, and Rick Boyages—and director of basketball operations Randy Shrout. And to OSU's men's basketball secretary, Debbie Cacchio.

Thanks to Andrew Stuart, a tireless agent whose handling of the mounds of paperwork enabled me to focus on writing.

CONTENTS

FOREWORD

Bob Cousy, a Hall of Fame basketball player, coached Jim O'Brien at Boston College in the late 1960s after helping lead the Boston Celtics to several NBA world championships.

It was somewhat of a surreal experience for me to recruit Jim O'Brien to play basketball at Boston College in the mid-1960s. I found myself identifying with a young man who was a throwback to the old days, when I was growing up on the playgrounds of New York City's ghettos in the 1930s and 1940s.

I admired the way he played, his dogged determination, his instincts for the game and his overall approach to playing point guard. Even at an early age, he established a basketball philosophy of his own. He was intensely hungry to win. He was coachable. His ego was under control.

O'Brien possessed great vision for a young player. He had remarkable court awareness, and his unselfishness complemented his passing and shooting skills perfectly. Today, many observers are often overly generous when they say that a player has the total package. O'Brien was the total package, especially during my last season at Boston College in 1968–69. He led us to the finals of the National Invitation Tournament at Madison Square Garden in New York. He and Billy Evans formed what was arguably the best backcourt duo in college basketball that year.

O'Brien was also a student of the game, which explains why he develops good point guards like Scoonie Penn and Howard Eisley. His laid-back personality off the court allows him to communicate and develop a genuine relationship with today's players. He solidifies these bonds with his sincerity and basic integrity.

He doesn't engage in spin, and the result has been an outstanding coaching career—which *Bucking the Odds* chronicles beautifully—that makes all of us who have played a role in helping to develop this wonderful husband, father, coach, and friend very proud.

— Bob Cousy

STARTING OVER

1

A S JIM O'BRIEN MADE HIS WAY DOWN to the arena level of Value City Arena on November 13, 1998, he heard the echoes of basketballs pounding relentlessly on the hardwood court. He smelled the buttered popcorn that crackled like dry wood burning. He felt the anxieties of another college basketball season building like a rumbling volcano.

O'Brien, usually unflappable and unperturbed, was nervous. His heart had seldom skipped beats like this before. This was not a typical season opener for the long-suffering Ohio State Buckeyes. They were about to embark on their centennial season—100 years of basketball—in a brand-new home.

It did not matter that OSU had won only eight of its 30 games during O'Brien's first season in Columbus; the expectations were greater for the 1998-99 campaign. For some fans, reaching the 15-win plateau would be a monumental achievement. For others, success would be gauged by how the Buckeyes competed, especially in the Big Ten Conference. Besides, they had lost 20 of their last 21 conference games.

O'Brien, looking as if he had stepped off the cover of *GQ* magazine, peeped out from beyond the north entrance staging area to watch his players during the pregame shoot-around. A few fans wished him good luck. He smiled—albeit uneasily. His companion, Mary, gave him an encouraging smile. O'Brien blushed.

O'Brien had been a head coach for 16 years. He had had his share of ups and downs. He had enjoyed good seasons, mostly at Boston College, when little was expected of his teams. He had endured hard times at both Boston College and St. Bonaventure, when the promises of success were supposed to be fulfilled.

Yet, in all of his experiences, O'Brien never had encountered a challenge like that of revitalizing the once-tradition-rich basketball program at Ohio State. After five consecutive losing seasons, everyone in Columbus looked toward the Brooklyn, New York, native to turn things around. He stared back at the Ohio State fans and assured them better days were ahead. Still, the Buckeyes had to prove themselves. They had to win to fill the 19,100-seat arena. On this night, with Oakland (Michigan) University making its Division I debut, only 11,533 fans showed up for the first-ever regular-season game at Value City Arena.

This was a curious crowd, really. Many of these fans had seen the Buckeyes in action in two exhibition games, but they hadn't seen enough of what O'Brien promised would be Ohio State's foundation—backcourt mates Michael Redd and Scoonie Penn. Redd was the daring 6-6 sophomore swingman who rarely shied away from a shot. Penn, a 5-10 transfer recruited by O'Brien while at Boston College, was the fearless junior point guard who was supposed to restore some semblance of order to a chaotic team.

O'Brien huddled with his coaches an hour before tip-off to discuss the game plan. He did not want to complicate things—not on a night when he figured the Ohio State fans would be watching with more than passing interest. He knew the fans were anxious to see what kind of team he would put on the floor at the start of his second season.

The Buckeyes impressed the home crowd almost immediately. They jumped all over the shell-shocked Golden Grizzlies to take a 58-25 lead at halftime and cruised to an 89-61 victory. The Buckeyes shot 65 percent in the first 20 minutes and knocked down 12 treys. By the time O'Brien called off the dogs, Redd had tallied a game-high 29 points and Penn had chipped in 17 points and eight assists in his Ohio State debut.

After being slapped silly by their Big Ten brethren since winning the conference championship in 1992, any Ohio State victory seemed worth celebrating. The Buckeyes' fans were thrilled. However, there were some skeptics among them, considering the Buckeyes' checkered history during much of the 1990s. The OSU faithful didn't want to be teased. They wanted to believe the Buckeyes were the real McCoy—a feel-good comeback story.

Two days later, O'Brien was nervous—again. This time, he had reason to be on edge as the Buckeyes hosted the Alabama Crimson Tide, a quality Southeastern Conference opponent. O'Brien looked around before tip-off to see a much larger crowd—16,763 fans. The news spread quickly throughout

Columbus that OSU had two talented players, Penn and Redd, who could potentially steer the troubled basketball program in the right direction.

Penn stole the show, scoring 23 points in 37 minutes to lead the Buckeyes to a 78-70 win. Redd put up a game-high 19 shots and scored 17 points in 28 minutes. Forward Jason Singleton stepped into the spotlight and scored a career-high 19 points to give O'Brien confidence that the Buckeyes might be more than a two-man team.

"If we keep improving, we'll be fine," O'Brien said with a reluctant smile moments after the Buckeyes improved to 2-0. It was the first time Ohio State had won back-to-back games since beating the University of Southern California and Tennessee-Chattanooga nearly a year earlier.

O'Brien, though, was hesitant to trumpet the Buckeyes' early-season success as a declaration of Ohio State's return among the Big Ten elite. In reality, he would have rather the media not make a big deal of it. O'Brien didn't make any promises when he signed on to replace the fired Randy Ayers in the spring of 1997. He figured it would take four to five years before the Buckeyes evolved into conference contenders. O'Brien, though, had never been that patient. He wanted to win. He wanted to win yesterday.

"We want to win all the time," O'Brien said. "We never accepted having a bad season. We don't all have it happen for us right now, but we want to win right away."

The obstacles were many for O'Brien. He resisted the temptation to walk away from coaching after unceremoniously leaving his alma mater, Boston College, following the 1996-97 season. Admittedly, he lacked the usual zest for life and coaching that defined his personality before his wife, Christine O'Brien, died of complications from Hodgkin's disease on a cold, dark winter morning in 1991. It seemed, he said, no dream was worth chasing without his college sweetheart.

"It's unfair, really," O'Brien said. "She was there for all the terrible times, the crappy years, and then to miss all the good times."

Christine O'Brien followed her college sweetheart from coast to coast, thus sharing his every dream. She, too, shared his fears as well as his successes. It seemed life couldn't have been better for the O'Briens after his alma mater, Boston College, welcomed them back to Chestnut Hill in the spring of 1986.

In a made-for-fantasy script, O'Brien landed his dream job. He had ascended the college-coaching ladder quicker than he had ever imagined. As an assistant at Connecticut under Dom Perno, O'Brien acquired immeasurable knowledge of the game. His stay at St. Bonaventure taught him invaluable lessons about basketball and life. He also polished his people skills and learned to cope with adversity.

Yet all the lessons learned couldn't prepare O'Brien for his greatest disappointment—the death of Christine O'Brien.

At 41, Christine O'Brien collapsed at the O'Briens's Westwood, Massachusetts, home after returning from a short walk. Christine O'Brien, who devoted much of her life to charity work, had a history of heart problems and had undergone open-heart surgery for a pacemaker implant. Suddenly, O'Brien was left alone to raise the couple's two teenage daughters, Erin and Amy. O'Brien did not coach the Eagles in their Big East Tournament first-round game. Still, as he grieved, he took time to send a note to his players, imploring them to give their best effort against Villanova at Madison Square Garden.

O'Brien, now less than a month away from his 41st birthday, was about to assume the most demanding role of his life. He was now a single father. It's a task familiar to many other men in America, so he wasn't about to feel sorry for himself. Amy and Erin wouldn't allow that to happen, either. They needed each other to be strong. O'Brien had spent a lot of time at the gym and on the road, so this was an adjustment that would affect his family's life far more than those uncertain days when his playing career ended with the San Diego Conquistadors of the American Basketball Association in 1975.

"When my wife passed, I asked myself, 'What do I do now?'" O'Brien said. "How else do you respond to it? You have all these emotions, but you have two girls who need parenting. How do you just walk away? There was more than an obligation to what I'm doing for me. I had two kids who needed to be taken care of. There was no other alternative. I had to do it. I just don't know what Plan B would have been. You just have to do it. You fight your way through it. You struggle through every day.

"After awhile, the sun started to come out. The days became a little brighter. We found a way to deal with it. There was no solution. It was about living."

The O'Briens were tough emotionally. Erin and Amy pulled themselves together to lead their high school basketball team to victory in a state tournament game just days after their mother's passing. Christine O'Brien inspired them with her presence. She seldom missed one of her daughters' basketball games. She was always there at the Conte Forum to cheer on the Eagles.

"Chris was one of the greatest people you could imagine," Connecticut coach Jim Calhoun recalled. "How Jim handled that, going through a tumultuous time and raising two daughters, speaks to what kind of man he is."

Admittedly, O'Brien hadn't always been at home. That, though, is the nature of his job. He couldn't function as an absentee coach. He was always a hands-on guy. He had to oversee everything, yet delegated authority and responsibility whenever appropriate. He couldn't, however, hand the responsibility of raising his two teenage daughters to anyone else. He would have to make this situation work. At the same time, he had to respond to the pressures of turning around the Boston College program.

"I'm very fortunate in that both of them were very well-grounded kids with good heads on their shoulders," O'Brien said. "I'm not sure it was I who got them through it or they who got me through it. I think I was more dependent on them than they were on me. It's something I think a lot of parents have to go through."

O'Brien manipulated ways to spend more time with Amy and Erin. He traveled to road games the morning after his team departed to allow for an extra day at home. He learned to listen to his daughters. He talked about boys. He went shopping for prom dresses. He did the kinds of things that brought them closer together. "We've become a lot closer since my mom's passing," said Erin O'Brien, who played college basketball at Stonehill College in Northeaston, Massachusetts. "My sister and I and Dad, we have a much stronger bond now. I don't think a lot of daughters can say they really can talk about anything with their father. We can do that."

O'Brien did more than just talk. He listened. He took his daughters by their hands, and together they moved on.

"There are two million people in America who do the same thing," O'Brien said. "They have lost. They tighten their belt. They go do what they have to do. How do I tell people to raise two kids? You roll the dice and hope it comes up good. You hope they make good choices and hope you make good choices for your kids. There is no blueprint.

"I don't want to be painted as a guy who did some magnificent deed because he raised his two kids. Who in my situation wouldn't have done the same thing? There is no alternative. Whether you are a plumber or a college basketball coach, kids want to know 'What's next?' If you don't raise your kids, it's not going to get done. You are who you are. You're not what you do."

O'Brien did just fine. Erin is now an administrative assistant at Vanderbilt University. Amy is the varsity coach of the girls' basketball team at a suburban high school in Boston. When O'Brien's daughters went off to college, he spent hours on the phone talking with them about most everything. He encouraged them to improve their basketball skills so they could compete at the collegiate level, but he wasn't demanding. He would remember that his father encouraged, but didn't push.

As he does with his players, O'Brien drew a line with his daughters when they went off to play college basketball. Admittedly, he was somewhat naïve to think that his daughters would be the atypical college athletes. They would never question authority, particularly that of their basketball coach.

After all, hadn't their father told them the stories of the defiant athletes? They knew where the line was drawn. At least, he thought so.

"As a typical college athlete, after her first two years, Erin said, 'I don't know what's wrong, the coach isn't playing me.' " O'Brien recalled. "She kept saying, 'I should be this and I should be that.' Hold it. Stop. I said to her, 'You got a problem with your coach, go sit down and talk with your coach. I will support you 100 percent, but don't come in here bitching and moaning.' I asked her did she work on her game during the summer or did she go to the beach every day. This is a young woman who I suggested work on her game if she wanted to play college basketball. She would say, 'I'm going to, but a bunch of us are going to the Cape today.' I asked again 'What did you do last summer? You went to the beach every day and hung out with your friends. So I don't want to hear it. Go back and talk to your coach. You know why you're not playing.' "

O'Brien has spent a lifetime teaching his daughters and young men about being responsible and accountable. He talks a lot about being resilient. He talks, too, about bouncing back from adversity. A few weeks after his wife's funeral, O'Brien, still trying to mend a broken heart, forced himself to return to the job. He and his assistant coaches had to prepare for the impending recruiting wars. The Eagles finished the 1990-91 season at 11-19, including an emotionally charged 74-73 loss to Villanova in the first round of the Big East Tournament that left them with a 16-game conference losing streak.

There was a sense of urgency about O'Brien after his fifth season. The Boston College alumni were patient, but the won-lost numbers weren't good. The Eagles won 60 games, but lost 89—including 20 losses during the 1989-90 season. After his wife's death, talk circulated throughout Chestnut Hill that perhaps O'Brien couldn't coach after his personal tragedy.

"There was a discussion at Boston College about me not coaching there anymore at one point, and this is after a week or 10 days after my wife died, and I couldn't believe that that was being brought up to me," O'Brien said. "But I don't know if they didn't want me to coach there, or they thought it was going to be too difficult. I got to a point where I said, 'If you don't want me to coach here, you have to fire me.' I was not quitting. I was not going to walk away."

O'Brien began to dream again, as Amy and Erin matured into resourceful and independent women—like their mother. They inspired their father by igniting the flame of emotion that had driven him during his early coaching days as an assistant at Connecticut in the late 1970s.

When O'Brien arrived in Columbus to face a gathering of curious reporters at a press conference on April 3, 1997, he had a determined fire burning within as he was named the Buckeyes' 12th coach. He hoped to salvage what remained of Ohio State's dysfunctional basketball program during the last year of play in an aging St. John Arena. O'Brien's hopes of an immediate turnaround were dashed when the Buckeyes finished his first season (1997-98) with an 8-22 overall record, including a 1-15 mark in the Big Ten.

At the start of the 1998-99 season, O'Brien was still in the process of rebuilding a program that had all but crumbled to pieces since winning back-to-back conference championships in 1991 and 1992. He also had to restore pride within a program that was once among the basketball in crowd during the early 1960s. Back then, the Buckeyes advanced to three consecutive Final Fours, winning the national championship in 1960 before losing to the Cincinnati Bearcats in the 1961 and 1962 finals. Then, 30 years after their remarkable run, the Buckeyes hit rock bottom. Ohio State stumbled to six consecutive losing seasons in the Big Ten. They were the victims of bad recruiting, bad players, and, some say, bad luck.

In 1992, O'Brien's predecessor, Randy Ayers, led Ohio State to within a victory of the Final Four. But he was let go almost immediately after Ohio State practically sleepwalked through an uneventful 10-17 campaign—including a 5-13 record in the Big Ten—during the 1996-97 season. Ayers's demise may have started long before his final season began.

Ayers's fate, however, was sealed on March 9, 1997, when 12,570 fans packed St. John Arena for the regular-season finale with conference rival Michigan. Even though the Buckeyes had lost six in a row to the Wolverines, their followers hung tight, pleading for a victory. After all, nothing is sweeter for an Ohio State fan than beating Michigan—even in basketball. With 19 seconds remaining on the clock, the Buckeyes were leading by five points, 74-69. Their impending triumph, it seemed, would represent some measure of redemption for a university whose football team had lost to the hated Wolverines for the seventh time in nine seasons.

Ayers, despite all of his team's problems, could breathe a little easier if the Buckeyes could protect their lead over Michigan. Rumors of his imminent dismissal had spread rapidly around Columbus. It was a near certainty that if the Buckeyes finished the 1996-97 season with six straight losses, Ayers would be left out in the cold. The school's athletics director, Andy Geiger, sat in the mezzanine across from the Ohio State bench with a concerned look on his face. He knew—or at least that was the perception—it did not matter whether Ohio State won or lost; Ayers was history.

Ayers knew, too. Yet he never let on.

Ayers kept coaching with an irrepressible zeal, always looking secure. If only his team could gut this one out, all else would be forgiven, maybe forgotten. There were four consecutive losing seasons; attendance dropped like a bad penny stock; and there were the transgressions and troubles of a basketball team whose top recruits often made more of an impact on the police blotter than on the box score. At some point, winning wasn't nearly as relevant as the program's desire to improve its image.

If Geiger wasn't in a forgiving mood, then the fans seemed willing to forgive and forget—at least this time, especially with a win over Michigan in the offing. The fans didn't heckle Ayers unmercifully, as they had most of the season. When Ayers chastised the officials, the fans cheered him. Ayers had never been the volatile, animated type, casting his emotions publicly. At times, his critics claimed he was too laid back, sometimes seemingly disinterested. He allowed his assistants, Jerry Francis and Randy Roth, to keep the players in check. The Buckeyes stepped boldly over the line so often that Francis and Roth were easily overrun. At some point, Ayers had to put his foot down and demand a change.

Some were defiant. Some seemed belligerent. In a public display of rebellion, point guard Damon Stringer, a sometimes moody, inharmonious cocaptain from Cleveland, inexplicably defied his coach's orders, taking countless off-balance shots against Michigan's zone, infuriating even his startled teammates.

Ayers no longer commanded his wayward vessel. It didn't matter because the castaway Buckeyes were already shipwrecked. By the time Michigan made the three-hour drive from Ann Arbor to Columbus, the debris of a splintered Ohio State program was scattered about St. John Arena, with a cleanup crew, led by Geiger, ready to dispose of the mess.

Ayers, who had come to Ohio State from the U.S. Military Academy, tried gathering up the pieces in hopes of ending the season on a positive note. He somehow convinced his usually uninspired team to play as if there were no tomorrow. There would be no tomorrow for Ayers—nor for many of his players. Even if they could withstand a Michigan rally, the landscape of Ohio State basketball was about to change.

Geiger, with his massive arms folded, maintained an unchanging poker face. He looked like a man who desperately wanted to put an end to this horrific five-year stint of bad basketball in the Big Ten. He may not have had his short list of coaches in the pocket of his scarlet coat, but he only needed to walk up a short flight of stairs in St. John Arena to dig the list out of his desk drawer. When asked to comment on Ayers's future at Ohio State, Geiger was always noncommittal. He would only say, "We're going to do what's best for the program, and right now Randy Ayers is our coach."

Geiger, an imposing and engaging 6-foot-4 Syracuse University graduate, was determined to turn the entire athletic department around when he took over for James L. Jones in 1993. In the minds of some observers, Geiger had been surprisingly patient with Ayers. He accepted the fact that every program has a string of bad breaks and bad recruits. He liked Ayers, too. He wanted him to succeed. Yet, as the Wolverines began to mount a stunning rally in the final 19 seconds, the pained expression on Geiger's face revealed that Ayers had finally tested his patience. Ayers's dismissal was no longer in question; it was just a matter of when.

"I thought it was really important for me to do a good job of establishing myself and to get a good sense of the place before I made a whole bunch of changes," Geiger said. "My patience with Randy was born of my high regard for him as a person. I was hoping that we were going to move forward without much trouble once we got some stability in the program, but it didn't work out. I never figured out what the problem was. I don't know what it was that couldn't be turned around here. I don't know what the intangible was or what was the missing link. It was clear that it wasn't turning around, and that is when we decided we needed a fresh start."

Geiger, who had an unsteady relationship with former Ohio State coach Gary Williams while at Maryland, was hesitant to change coaches. He brushed off demands of disgruntled Ohio State fans to fire football coach John Cooper, who in 13 years compiled a 2-10-1 record against Big Ten rival Michigan. Cooper, unlike Ayers, won far more than he lost, taking the Buckeyes to 11 bowl games—including a Rose Bowl victory in 1997.

"I didn't add up the losses," Geiger said. "I'm not so much a statistician as I am one who gets involved with process. I'm more concerned with the experience the students are having at the university than I am wins and losses. Wins and losses will tell you something about the program from a systematic point of view. It's better trying to get the situation corrected before you go throwing coaches out. I was trying to find a way to help the [basketball] coaching staff instead of having them feel as if they were going out the door the next minute.

"The negativism that surrounded the program is one of the reasons we changed coaches. It was time to get a new face, a new personality into the system. It was clear that whatever ability Randy had to move his players in a different direction wasn't there. I found myself in the same meetings having the same conversations before I decided that wasn't productive. It was time for us to do something different."

Geiger had stood pat with Ayers as if he were clinging to a pair of aces, hoping someone wouldn't trump them. Yet, with every loss, Geiger's hand was weakening. It became increasingly difficult to fend off Ayers's critics, some of whom were on the board of trustees, others of whom were influential, powerful alumni.

"Surprisingly, there wasn't much pressure to fire Randy," Geiger said. "People here are much more patient in their approach to things than it appears on the outside. My phone doesn't ring off the hook when things don't go well. I think people know, for the most part, I try not to operate the athletic department as if it's a revolving door. If something can be done to improve the situation, I would rather do that than fire the coach. I think that's an appropriate way to conduct an intercollegiate program."

As if Geiger needed more evidence to excuse Ayers, the Buckeyes contributed to the ouster of their soft-spoken coach by falling flat on their faces. Against Michigan, they squandered what appeared to be an insurmountable lead in the time it takes sprint champion Michael Johnson to cover 200 meters. It was becoming clear that no measure of damage control was going to change the situation in Columbus.

The Buckeyes missed two potential game-clinching free throws and threw away an inbound pass that allowed guard Louis Bullock to hit a three-pointer that tied the game at 79-all with 8.3 seconds left to force overtime. Suddenly, there was a haunting hush amid the crowd. It had exhausted itself in its exuberance. There were whispers among the doubting faithful, who could sense this game slipping away to Michigan like so many football games had during the 1990s.

Ayers, with a rolled-up program in his hand, began riding his players as if they were thoroughbreds trying to maintain their stride in the final, agonizing furlong. Ayers could never use his whip during this 10-17 season. He believed a few encouraging words were enough to keep the Buckeyes from fading, as the Wolverines reeled them back in with a furious kick down the stretch.

Now, with the game going into overtime, Michigan coach Steve Fisher —who had led the Wolverines to the national title in 1989 and back-to-back title-game losses to Duke and North Carolina in 1992 and 1993, respectively—instructed guard Travis Conlan to pressure Damon Stringer. Stringer was putting on a show, tying his career high with 27 points. Fisher knew Stringer was vulnerable to half-court pressure, so he deployed a half-court trap that enabled Conlan to force Stringer to commit a momentum-shifting turnover. Conlan picked him clean, scooping up an errant bounce pass before dishing the ball off to a streaking Brandon Hughes. Hughes, who had gotten behind Shaun Stonerook, scored a layup as a frustrated Stringer raked him across the face, allowing Hughes to convert a three-point play that gave Michigan an 82-79 lead with 11 seconds left.

For Ayers, these would be among the most agonizing 11 seconds of his coaching career. Ultimately, they were his last at Ohio State.

The Buckeyes let a sure thing get away, losing 86-81. As the mumbling crowd walked out the exit doors into the cold, Ayers followed his players into the locker room. He continuously pounded himself with his tightly rolled program. If only he had lashed his players with the whip, Ayers might have gotten out of St. John Arena with a victory.

For five seasons, the Buckeyes had developed a consistent pattern of defeat. If not for a 73-67 win over Indiana on January 30 at St. John Arena, the 1996-97 Big Ten season would have netted nary a consolation prize. The Buckeyes' once-proud basketball program had become a wasteland for hot-heads, underachievers, and malcontents.

At the final buzzer, Geiger walked slowly from his courtside seat and across the court. He never looked Ayers's way. It would be difficult for Geiger to look into the eyes of a man he genuinely admired, then suggest, without saying a word, that it's time for a change. Ayers walked briskly toward the interview room. He looked like a fired man walking. Eight years after replacing Gary Williams as Ohio State's basketball coach, his clock had run out. No way could he turn back the hands of time, rekindling the enthusiasm and promise of his earlier years in Columbus. His fate had already been sealed. All that was left was to clean out his locker and undress the office walls of the fine paintings and plaques.

As the bright, blinding lights of the television cameras beamed into his eyes, Ayers stood at the podium, searching for the right words. It was a terribly awkward moment, he admitted, having to explain how the Buckeyes came unglued in the final 19 seconds against the hated Wolverines. There were no answers, no excuses. He questioned his late-game strategy, but never the effort of his players. Ayers, with a habitual stroke of his thick black mustache, defended the Buckeyes even when it was apparent to everyone in the arena that his players had folded—and let him down—as the Wolverines stormed from behind.

Ayers, who starred at Miami University in Oxford, Ohio, after a stellar high school career at Springfield (Ohio) North High School, could not survive this season-ending collapse. Bad recruiting and poor judgment had managed to tarnish his once-golden image. Ayers had not envisioned his departure this way. He may have left with his honor intact, but his coaching career had taken a severe beating. It would be hard for him to get another Division I job, considering most athletics directors frown on the kinds of problems that had permeated Ohio State's basketball program.

As Ayers made the drive back to his suburban Columbus home, there was time enough to reflect on better days. The Buckeyes had advanced to the NCAA Tournament in three of his first four seasons—including the finals of the 1992 Midwest Regional in Lexington, where they narrowly lost to eventual national-championship-game finalist Michigan. There had been three 20-win seasons, an encouraging sign that Ayers had all the building blocks necessary to construct a championship team.

The Buckeyes had become perennial national-championship contenders in the early 1990s. It was like old times, when Jerry Lucas and John Havlicek had helped Ohio State battle Cincinnati in one of the most memorable and intense intrastate rivalries in the history of college basketball some three decades earlier. Lucas and Havlicek had managed to lead the Buckeyes to one national title, a 75-55 win over California in the 1960 Final Four. Ayers's teams seemed destined to make a run at proclaiming themselves the kings of the decade. Besides, his program was attracting some of the nation's top high school players.

In 1989, Ayers was largely responsible for recruiting two-time All-American Jimmy Jackson, who was the cornerstone of Ohio State's success in the early 1990s. In fact, Ayers landed the job, in part, because of his ability to communicate effectively with prospective blue-chip recruits, sometimes luring some of the nation's top talent to Army while serving as the Cadets' assistant coach and recruiting coordinator.

When Jackson entered the NBA draft after his junior season in 1992, Ayers needed to find someone to replace him, preferably the No. 1 high school player in Ohio. He began working his recruiting magic, outhustling other Big Ten coaches in securing signatures on national letters of intent from three *Parade* All-Americans—including Greg Simpson, Ohio's two-time Mr. Basketball. Simpson, a 6-1 guard from Lima, averaged 35 points a game as a high school senior.

The Buckeyes had the third-rated recruiting class in the country. It was by far the best in the Big Ten. Ayers worked day and night trying to keep Simpson in Ohio, outmaneuvering Michigan State's Judd Heathcote, Purdue's Gene Keady, and Michigan's Steve Fisher. He also signed the state's No. 3-rated player, Nate Wilbourne of Columbus. Even more impressive, Ayers was such a persuasive recruiter that he dared to cross the border to challenge Rick Pitino of Kentucky, Lou Henson of Illinois, and Bobby Knight of Indiana for their best in-state players. Ayers walked away from foreign turf with his chin up and the commitments of the three *Parade* All-Americans: 6-6 Derek Anderson of Louisville, Kentucky; 6-11 center Gerald Eaker of Bellwood, Illinois; and 6-6 forward Charles Macon of Michigan City, Indiana.

Ayers had assembled a great collection of athletes to play alongside 6-9 forward Lawrence Funderburke, who many considered one of the best players in the Big Ten. It was a roster that included two-sport star Ricky Dudley, who as a tight end would later become the top draft pick of the Oakland Raiders in 1996. "We had all the talent in the world," Dudley said. "We didn't doubt for a minute that we were going to tear through the Big Ten and win the national championship. We certainly had the look of champions."

However, Ohio State was a facade, its looks deceiving. The Buckeyes teased their faithful with promises of dominance. They had plenty of talent, but were lacking the vital team components—character, leadership, continuity, and chemistry. These were the qualities necessary for fulfilling the promise of advancing to the Final Four for the first time since 1968, when Ohio State lost 80-66 to North Carolina in the national semifinals and defeated Houston 89-85 in the consolation game. Supposedly, this Ohio State team had everything. In actuality, it turned out to be a loosely organized fraternity of disenchanted basketball players whose mental shortcomings overshadowed their extraordinary physical talents. Consequently, the Buckeyes slipped to 15-13 and seventh place in the Big Ten with an 8-10 record, then lost 56-53 to Ayers's alma mater, Miami of Ohio, in the first round of the NIT.

Ayers didn't even blink after the Redskins (now RedHawks) eliminated Ohio State from the postseason tournament. He figured the Buckeyes' six super freshmen were just having a difficult time adjusting. In reality, most were slow to mature. It was enough to frustrate Derek Anderson, who promptly went home to Kentucky to play for Rick Pitino's Wildcats. Anderson had seen the future and wanted no part of the forthcoming malaise that would put an insufferable grip on an Ohio State program that slammed on its brakes while seemingly in cruise control.

In many ways, Ayers was far more of a disciplinarian than O'Brien. He opposed his players walking about campus wearing headsets. He wanted his players neat and tidy, insisting they wear coats and ties on charter flights.

The departure of Anderson, who experienced only frustration in Columbus, was only the beginning of the problems that cascaded over the troubled Ayers. Suddenly, for Geiger the past and future had collided. He remembered what a wondrous job Ayers had done making the Buckeyes one of the most successful teams in the country. However, not even his loyalty and patience could tolerate another embarrassing season.

For Geiger, it wasn't solely the disparity between wins and losses, although that certainly was troubling. Instead, there were fears—some real, some imagined—that the hole the Buckeyes had dug would bury the program even deeper into the abyss.

Admittedly, Geiger wanted to start anew, now that Ohio State would be moving into its new home, the $110 million Value City Arena at the Schottenstein Center for the 1998-99 season. Therefore, he had to rid the team of its complacency. It took less than 24 hours after Ohio State's loss to Michigan for Geiger and university president Dr. E. Gordon Gee to confirm the worst-kept secret in Columbus—that Ayers's contract would not be renewed. Geiger made it a clean sweep by firing longtime women's coach Nancy Darsch, who would later resurface in the WNBA as coach of the New York Liberty.

"I wasn't hesitant at all about taking this job," O'Brien said. "On paper, a lot of people whose judgment I value talked about the potential of Ohio State. I didn't totally appreciate what they meant, because I spent all my time in the Big East. I didn't pay a lot of attention to a lot of other jobs. Everybody talked about the enormous potential and being one of the best jobs in the country. People say if you have a chance to get the job at Ohio State, you would be crazy not to try to get it. I could sense there was a commitment to do well here when I began to research the school, but especially after I met Andy Geiger.

"No one builds a building like the Schottenstein Center without enormous commitment. Even though there were some down years, the commitment was obvious. There was a collection of people only a step away from turning this thing around. Then, you think in terms of that sophomore class that included Stringer, Stonerook, and Tate, and you had in those three guys three double-figure scorers.

"On top of that you had Jason Singleton and Neshaun Coleman. I really felt, without knowing much about those guys, maybe there is a chance to build the program quickly. I didn't think I was inheriting a program in which the cupboard was bare. I knew there was some losing, but there were some good, talented kids. I didn't know anything about Michael Redd, Ken Johnson, or Shamar Herron. There were some pieces in place and there was some potential. All of those things never had me second-guessing my interest or my desire to come here."

Geiger was as much under the microscope as O'Brien. With all the talk about the possible candidates to replace Ayers, Geiger wanted to get this one right. For Geiger, this was more than about hiring a basketball coach. In reality, he was making a corporate-like decision that would affect the entire university, considering the millions of dollars invested in renovation projects, particularly the construction of several new athletic facilities.

"I think there's a lot of analogy to being a CEO in some management sense, and in some management sense, it's nothing like that at all," Geiger said. "We don't make widgets. We are not a manufacturing entity. We are an intercollegiate program, and we're about human development. I try hard to keep that in focus, and hope I don't lose that perspective as I'm making decisions about people or about programs or about decisions to spend money. I'm a builder. I tend to try to promote and lift rather than tear down.

"When I'm dealing with Jim O'Brien or Randy Ayers or John Cooper, it's more in terms of me understanding their problems," said Geiger, who eventually fired Cooper on January 2, 2001, a day after Ohio State suffered an embarrassing 24-14 loss to unranked South Carolina in the Outback Bowl in Tampa, Florida. "I know more questions than I used to, but I don't necessarily know more answers. Anybody who tells you they know how to do all this has not sat here before. I've learned that my ego isn't very important. How we do what we do is far more important. There is no room for arrogance. You have to be innovative; if not, you are helpless."

Geiger spoke to the media during an afternoon press conference, while Ayers quietly prepared to leave town. Only then did Geiger admit that the search for Ayers's replacement had already begun. "I have a list [of coaches], but I've always had a list," Geiger said. "I haven't talked to anyone yet. But I'll be talking to all sorts of people over the next couple of days to get the search under way."

Ayers had won 124 games, lost 108, and made four postseason tournament appearances. That, however, wasn't impressive-enough resume material to motivate athletics directors elsewhere to come calling. It wasn't good enough to earn him a place on the coaching carousel from where discarded coaches land safety elsewhere. With no job lined up and few prospects in sight, Ayers accepted the position as strength and conditioning coach with the Philadelphia 76ers. Philadelphia coach Larry Brown promoted Ayers to assistant coach after one season. It was a career boost for Ayers, who in 1992 had appeared to have all of Columbus in his hands.

Ayers's job began to slip from his grasp after four of his five 1991-92 recruits—guard Greg Simpson, forward Charles Macon, forward Derek Anderson, and center Nate Wilbourne—were either dismissed for disciplinary reasons or transferred. Center Lawrence Funderburke, an Ohio native who transferred from Indiana, was the lone survivor. It was the beginning of an alarming trend that would result in 22 of Ayers's 31 scholarship recruits failing to complete their allotted four years of eligibility.

During the next five years, scholarship after scholarship was tossed away like a bad piece of fruit. For Ayers, nearly every bite of the recruiting apple was bitter. He had entrusted his career—and the program's stability—to the young men for whom he worked diligently to persuade to wear scarlet and gray. As the losses mounted, the bodies kept dropping from an already-thin roster that was gradually filled with walk-ons.

Simpson was perhaps the biggest disappointment. The former two-time Mr. Basketball in Ohio was touted as the best shooting guard in his class. Simpson ran afoul of the law a couple of times, which clearly became a distraction for a team desperately seeking any semblance of focus. Ultimately, Ayers was forced to dismiss Simpson after his sophomore season.

The Buckeyes, it seemed, could deal with Simpson's expulsion from the program. However, Anderson's departure left a crack in the foundation. As it turned out, Anderson would help the Kentucky Wildcats win the national championship in 1996. With Simpson and Anderson gone, Ohio State was a team with marginal talent, at best. The defections and suspensions continued at an alarming rate as Ohio State tried to keep up in an increasingly powerful Big Ten conference.

Most everyone wondered who would be left standing in the ring when the madness reached its climax. In a roll call of highly touted blue-chippers, the list kept getting longer and longer:

- Joe Reid: The 6-8 center transferred to Ohio Northern before playing any significant minutes.
- Damon Flint: The 6-5 guard enrolled at the University of Cincinnati after the school reported 17 violations during his recruiting in 1993.

- Marlon Minifee: The 6-6 forward transferred from Olney Junior College, then transferred to NAIA Division II Urbana University.
- Robert Shelton: The 6-3 guard played one year before sustaining a career-ending foot injury.
- Jami Bosley: The 6-1 guard started 18 games as sophomore, but was dismissed from the team when he was arrested for breaking into cars at a campus garage. He made the most of a second chance, leading the University of Akron in scoring during the 1998-99 and 1999-2000 seasons.
- Damon Stringer: The 6-0 guard, a former Mr. Basketball in Ohio, was charged with assaulting a motorist following a minor fender-bender, then left the team in early 1998. He transferred to Cleveland State.
- Jermaine Tate: The 6-8 center had a heart problem that forced him to miss most of the 1997-98 season. He was later kicked off the team for violating team rules, then transferred to the University of Cincinnati, where he helped lead the Bearcats to a No. 1 seed in the 2000 NCAA Tournament.
- Shaun Stonerook: The 6-7 forward was ruled ineligible for the first quarter of the 1997-98 season after leading Ohio State in rebounding the season before. He later transferred to Ohio University.
- Mark Howard: A 6-10 center, he never played a minute of regular-season basketball after being diagnosed with hemophilia.
- Scott Gradney: The 6-9 forward played one season before he was dismissed, along with Bosley, after being charged with breaking into parked cars at a campus garage. He transferred to Texas Christian, where he was a reserve.
- Ed Jenkins: The 6-9 center transferred from Sullivan (Kentucky) Junior College. He never fully recovered from a knee injury and then failed to survive academically.
- Trent Jackson: The 6-4 guard was tossed off the team after he and Stringer were involved in a barroom brawl near campus.
- Sean Tucker: The 6-7 forward had an up-and-down career before a knee injury slowed his progress. Then, after violating team rules shortly after O'Brien's arrival in 1997, he was dismissed from the team.
- Jon Sanderson: The 6-7 forward was arrested shortly before his freshman season for allegedly resisting arrest and for public intoxication. He was a two-year starter, but transferred after losing his starting job to Brian Brown prior to the 1999 NCAA Tournament.
- Shamar Herron: The 6-9 center played only sparingly in two seasons before transferring after the Buckeyes' Final Four run in 1999.

Ohio State's problems would be magnified some by the fact that six of its eight 1995 recruits—Stringer, Bosley, Gradney, Howard, Stonerook, and Tate—couldn't make it to their senior seasons. Bosley and Gradney had stepped out of line during Ayers's watch, while Stonerook, Stringer, and Tate were precariously walking the narrowest of tightropes as their embattled coach struggled with his own balancing act—with his job in jeopardy. Stonerook, Stringer and Tate would leave the program as it prepared to make an about-face.

When it became clear that Ayers was being ousted, many of his former players rallied around him. They couldn't understand why Ayers, a national and two-time Big Ten Coach of the Year, was being fired. After all, Ayers had been successful earlier during his tenure at Ohio State.

"I came to Ohio State because of Randy Ayers," said Jimmy Jackson, a first-round NBA pick in 1993. "He and I hit if off immediately, and I knew he was someone I could talk to about things other than just basketball. I learned a lot about basketball, but I also learned a lot about life, just listening to Coach Ayers. He stands for all the right things."

In the business world that is college basketball, Ayers was a nice guy who was turned away as the finish line became a blur. Historically, Ohio State fans had been far more patient, if not lenient, with the basketball program's failures. Ayers, though, had tested their patience, too, after Ohio State strung together five consecutive losing seasons in the Big Ten. During that period, the Buckeyes compiled a 32-72 record—including a dismal 16-56 showing in conference play. The numbers, of course, didn't add up for Ayers.

2

ON THE REBOUND

T HE OHIO STATE MEN'S BASKETBALL head-coaching job is considered among the most attractive in college athletics, yet Andy Geiger knew it wouldn't be easy finding the right man —one who could maneuver his way through the debris. So even though Jim O'Brien wasn't Geiger's first choice, he ultimately was the best choice for the program.

O'Brien had to rebuild the program recruit by recruit. By the time O'Brien finished drawing his blueprint, there remained only six of Randy Ayers' recruits—forward Jason Singleton, guard Neshaun Coleman, forward Jon Sanderson, center Ken Johnson, Michael Redd and forward Shamar Herron.

O'Brien assumed he would have more to build on when he signed up for the job. He figured that with Shaun Stonerook, Jermaine Tate, Damon Stringer, Sanderson, Johnson, and Redd, he had the makings of a potentially competitive basketball team. The task of competing in the Big Ten was diffi- cult, however, considering the Buckeyes' youth and inexperience. O'Brien, too, had taken over a team that had had its confidence shattered at the end of the 1996-97 season. The Buckeyes had lost their last six games—including that disheartening 86-81 overtime setback to Michigan.

If O'Brien desired a challenge, this was it. Climbers have their Mt. Everest. Swimmers have their English Channel. Runners have their Boston

Marathon. O'Brien needed repelling gear and fins to navigate his way through Ohio State's troubled waters. It was one thing to battle the Boston College administrators over the admission of recruits which had been a nagging problem during his tenure there; it was another trying to convince prospective recruits across the country that things in Columbus weren't as bad as they seemed—and that he would fix the problems.

"The biggest obstacle was to change the perception and the image of the program," O'Brien said. "It's not pointing fingers at anyone, but the fact of the matter is, the perception was one of a troubled program with bad guys that were always getting in trouble. So we were out recruiting, and guys were saying, 'I'm not sure about Ohio State, and I don't know if that's where I want to go.' If you are a parent, you're saying, 'I'm not sure if I want my kid to go there.' So part of what we were attempting to do was to get by all of that. The actions always speak louder than words. You can go in and tell somebody what you're going to do, but you have to actually show people the kind of guys you want and the type of program you're interested in having. It's not always easy to accomplish.

"It was a more difficult sale to the kids who were here already. It wasn't that big of a deal to the newcomers, kids like Michael and Sharmar. We put our stamp on the new guys. Our stamp had already been on Scoonie Penn to a certain degree. It was difficult for the junior and senior classes when they found out we wanted to go in a different direction.

"This was a big coaching challenge. But when I took the job at Boston College, it was very hard job because of the very stringent academic restrictions. Our first couple of years we really struggled. We had to play our conference games in the Boston Garden my first two years there, which wasn't a real benefit to us. They were building a place that would sit about 9,000, and we were playing in a place that seated about 4,000. The first couple of years, the academic responsibilities tighten up like you can't believe. It was a very difficult job at the time. To turn that thing around took awhile. That was real hard. Ohio State had the potential to turn it around a little bit quicker than we did at Boston College. I was very confident we could get it done [at Ohio State].

"We had to overcome an image problem in Columbus. We wondered what people were thinking about the Ohio State program. As coaches, we had to sell ourselves to coaches and parents, mostly in Ohio.

"We don't enjoy our kids getting into trouble. Really, no one wants that. Unfortunately, it happens. Most college coaches are only one phone call away from having huge headaches. You talk to kids about what's right and what's wrong, but there's always going to be headaches. It's the way it is with our society. These young men are going to make bad choices, and some of them are going to get themselves in trouble. But that has to be the exception, not the norm."

Admittedly, OSU's new coaching staff conceded it didn't have a quick fix. First, it would take time adjusting to a campus atmosphere that was totally unlike Chestnut Hill. Whatever decision O'Brien and his coaching staff made would draw attention. It was front-page news in the sports sections, particularly in the Columbus area. There were no Boston Celtics, Boston Bruins, Boston Red Sox, or New England Patriots to overshadow the basketball program. It will take some time for the Columbus Blue Jackets, an NHL expansion team, to establish a fan base similar to that of Ohio State basketball. In essence, the Buckeyes wouldn't have much competition, except for the Ohio State-Michigan football game in late November.

"After all that stuff happened," O'Brien said, "I went through a period when I was saying, 'Man, this is going to be hard. It's going to be really hard.' I felt we weren't going to be real good that first year. I came here initially thinking we had a good chance because of what was here. It became very clear early on that we had to make some changes with some of the guys. It wasn't about just cleaning house. It was apparent it wasn't going to work."

Even before O'Brien's debut, a 73-67 win over Kent State, yet another string of unwanted incidents were surfacing while O'Brien was on a golfing vacation in Scotland. Three Buckeyes—Stringer, Trent Jackson, and Sanderson—had run-ins with the law. The police reports indicated that all three had tested positive for alcohol consumption. Stringer and Jackson were arrested outside a campus bar, but both pleaded not guilty to charges of disorderly conduct and resisting arrest. Sanderson, an incoming freshman from Lexington (Ohio) High School, faced a felony count of assaulting a police officer and a misdemeanor charge of underage drinking and public intoxication after an incident at the University of Dayton. He, too, pleaded not guilty.

But the verdict was already in. The basketball program had suffered another black eye. Only this time, O'Brien, not Ayers, had to polish an already tarnished image. It didn't matter that these were Ayers's recruits; O'Brien had the unenviable task of disciplining players he hardly knew.

"We never got to the point where we coached Tate, Stonerook, or Stringer," O'Brien said. "That kind of fell apart before they even suited up for practice. The talent level was down, and we weren't going to be as good as the other teams. We were trying to establish a style, a work ethic, and a philosophy about how we wanted to practice.

"It was important to set the groundwork for how we hoped things would become at Ohio State. You have to start someplace, and we were starting from the basement. We were emphasizing things like the importance of going to class and monitoring class attendance. We talked about being on time for things and the importance of working in the weight room. We addressed all of the things you take for granted and even how we wanted them to act. We talked to them about how to handle themselves in certain situations, how to speak with the media and how to deal with autograph seekers.

"The hardest part was asking those guys to leave. I hoped and prayed that things worked out for all those guys at their respective schools. It was very hard because we were outsiders asking kids who grew up in this state to leave Ohio State. I thought that was hard. It was a very difficult time for us. We asked kids to leave who were potentially the best players in the program. When we bottomed out, we bottomed out big time. Then, we started saying we're going to be better, but who's going to want to come here."

It was smooth sailing for the Buckeyes early in the 1997-98 campaign. They easily defeated Robert Morris and Rider in nonconference games, before losing 64-54 to Vanderbilt. Yet, the Buckeyes didn't look like a team built for the long haul. They were a collection of quarter horses, trying to keep up in a mile run. They were without a true center, and their power forward, 6-8 John Lumpkin, was a starting tight end who played basketball mostly for recreational purposes. The Buckeyes, too, had lost their best quarter horses—Stonerook and Tate.

Tate's loss seemed most damaging. He was clearly the most promising of Ayers's recruits. He was physical and daring, though sometimes erratic. Ohio State offered to honor the remaining two years of Tate's scholarship. But O'Brien didn't want to risk having him play again after he was limited to playing 16 games during the 1996-97 season because of a heart problem.

It wasn't Tate's heart that influenced O'Brien's decision. Instead, it was Tate's actions off the court that concerned O'Brien. Tate, according to sources close to the team, allegedly threatened to attack an Ohio State assistant coach. The incident occurred shortly after the Buckeyes dropped back-to-back games to Southern Cal and San Diego State in late December 1996. That, of course, was the proverbial last straw for a coaching staff that prided itself on running a disciplined program.

As Tate prepared to transfer to Cincinnati, a raw, inexperienced 6-11 center was thrust into the starting lineup. The growing pains were immense for Ken Johnson, a thin, gentle giant who wasn't nearly as eloquent on the court as his fingers were on the keys of a piano. Johnson's personality is reflected in his songs. He plays music that is as easy as his smile. While many of his childhood friends were hanging out in the gym, Johnson was taking piano lessons. He spent time perfecting a Mozart concerto instead of the half hook he needed to complement his offensive skills.

Johnson doesn't have the look of a man willing to mix it up in the low post. He has more of a game face on the piano bench than he does on the court. "I think Kenny has an easy, cool nature," Scoonie Penn said. Johnson has an easy, deliberate style. It doesn't matter whether he's running the floor or battling for position inside the paint; he never seems to sweat much. Early on, his skills, particularly on offense, were limited, yet he progressed rapidly on defense, becoming somewhat of an intimidating force in the paint during his sophomore season.

The Buckeyes leaned mostly on their freshman swingman from Columbus West High School. Michael Redd led the charge as Ohio State defeated Southern Cal and Tennessee-Chattanooga. But after the Buckeyes finished toying with their Christmas gifts, it was lights out. The reality hit O'Brien like a cold slap to the face. Ohio State's 7-3 start was a tease, a temporary reprieve from the inevitable collapse that had been forged by years of bad luck, bad timing, bad recruiting, and bad karma.

There was some sunshine amid the clouds. At least, the Buckeyes were afforded a trip to Honolulu, where they played three games in the Rainbow Classic. They lost them all, including a 69-56 setback to then-No. 2 Kansas. The Buckeyes played relatively well against the stronger, more experienced Jayhawks. Then the inconsistency and letdowns that are familiar with most struggling teams were visible during a 73-46 loss to New Mexico State. Ohio State wanted to get out of Hawaii with something more than souvenirs, but Brigham Young dashed its hopes with a 72-57 win two days before New Year's Eve.

"I remember being down and disappointed after the Brigham Young game because maybe I was dreaming that something good was going to come out of the effort we had against Kansas," O'Brien said. "I was disappointed that we lost those last two games the way we did. It kind of set the tone for a lot of losing."

Hardly anyone noticed that the Buckeyes had fallen to 7-6. It simply wasn't that important, considering the Ohio State football team was in California preparing to play in its first Rose Bowl since 1985. The Buckeyes defeated Arizona State 20-17, giving them their first Rose Bowl win since a 42-21 thrashing of Southern California in 1974. The Ohio State basketball team was a wire-service footnote in most of Ohio's newspapers. If nothing else, the football team's conquest of the Sun Devils in Pasadena kept the media from bashing the basketball team. However, as the sun set on the football season, the curious, at least, wondered how O'Brien was doing in his inaugural season. But even the kindest and gentlest of fans weren't prepared for the insufferable stretch of growing pains that followed.

The Buckeyes lost 17 games in a row. They lost 20 Big Ten games in a row—including their last six conference games of the 1996-97 season. They lost in every conceivable way. They routinely snatched defeat from the jaws of victory. Mostly, they were never within shouting distance—except for a 74-72 loss to the Indiana Hoosiers before a lively crowd of 13,276 at St. John Arena.

The Buckeyes overcame a nine-point, second-half deficit to scare the Hoosiers, but Indiana prevailed when Luke Recker stole a pass with 10 seconds remaining and then slam-dunked Ohio State's upset hopes. This defeat didn't hurt nearly as much as the loss to Michigan a year earlier, partly because the Buckeyes had already lost 15 straight games. The fact that they were competitive was good enough—considering that blowouts had become the norm.

O'Brien smiled as he and Indiana coach Bobby Knight shook hands afterwards. He could sense that the tide had turned. The Buckeyes still lacked the know-how to win, but they were learning to fight. They seemed now to walk with their heads up. The partisan, yet sometimes skeptical Ohio State fans began to appreciate their efforts. The Buckeyes had exchanged blows with Indiana before narrowly losing to a team that would eliminate them in the first round of the inaugural Big Ten Tournament less than a month later.

Finally, there was a feeling that O'Brien was putting the pieces together. For the first time in five years, the Buckeyes' future overshadowed their dubious past. They played with more intensity, and their errors were the result of uncontrolled enthusiasm instead of the absentminded carelessness that had originally created the disparity between themselves and their Big Ten rivals.

Still, the Buckeyes couldn't cheat their twisted fate. They put up a good fight at Northwestern, but the losing streak reached a school-record 17. Neshaun Coleman, one of Ayers's surviving recruits, gathered his teammates together shortly after the defeat, challenging them to put an end to the losing. He reminded them that the Buckeyes were once a proud program, one that had produced a long list of college basketball legends—John Havlicek, Jerry Lucas, Herb Williams, Jim Cleamons, Dennis Hopson, Clark Kellogg, and Jimmy Jackson.

"No one wants to go through a situation where you are going to lose," O'Brien said. "You are going to come into a pressure situation where there better be an expectation to win. The bottom line is that if you don't win, you probably are going to get fired. At this level, that's the way it is. If you're not willing to accept that, then don't attempt to get a job such as this. I really felt we could turn it all around. I felt there was an opportunity to go out of the state to possibly interest some kids in coming here. When we started doing our recruiting, it was clear this was going to be even more difficult than we initially thought, and that's what opened my eyes to some of the headaches the program had to endure."

The Buckeyes were a dominant team with legendary coach Fred Taylor on the bench. Ohio State was ranked in the Top 10 of both the Associated Press and UPI polls from 1960 to 1963. They were ranked No. 1 in both polls in 1961 and 1962, but lost to Oscar Robertson and Cincinnati in the 1962 NCAA title game.

Ohio State's dominance wasn't as complete or as long as that of the UCLA Bruins, who won 12 NCAA titles from 1964 to 1975. The Buckeyes weren't as feared as, say, Kentucky or North Carolina, but they were consistently among the best teams in the Big Ten, often keeping pace with Indiana, Michigan, Michigan State and Wisconsin—the only other Big Ten schools to win national championships. The Buckeyes have appeared in nine Final Fours, which ranks them sixth behind only UCLA (14), North Carolina (13), Kentucky (12), Duke (12) and Kansas (10). Ohio State also has more Final Four appearances than any other Big Ten school—including Indiana, which has qualified for the national semifinals seven times.

Since losing to Cincinnati in the 1962 championship game in Louisville, Kentucky, the Buckeyes had endured only four losing seasons before they began this string of five consecutive losing seasons—beginning with the 1993-94 season, in which they were 13-16. The Buckeyes didn't have a winning season in Taylor's final three years, and Eldon Miller's Buckeyes went 9-18 after Miller replaced Fred Taylor in 1976.

Miller was fired after the Buckeyes finished the 1985-86 season with a 19-14 record, a season capped with a 73-63 win over Wyoming in the National Invitation Tournament championship game in Madison Square Garden in New York. Gary Williams, who was O'Brien's predecessor at Boston College, had two 20-win seasons in three years before relinquishing the head coaching duties to Ayers. However, Taylor, Miller, and Williams didn't have to deal with the myriad distractions that led to Ayers's departure in the spring of 1997.

Unlike Ayers, O'Brien inherited only marginal talent. What he had were an imaginative, fearless freshman, Michael Redd, and a sharp-shooting Neshaun Coleman.

It was Redd and Coleman who provided some hope. The Buckeyes finally broke through in Madison, Wisconsin, beating the Badgers 61-56 at the Kohl Center before a stunned crowd of 16,042. Coleman, Redd, and Sanderson combined to make eight free throws in a row in the last 57 seconds to end yet another forgettable streak: 19 straight road losses. Ironically, the Buckeyes' previous road win had come on Jan. 2, 1997, at Crisler Arena in Ann Arbor, a 73-71 win over No. 8 Michigan—the day after Ohio State came from behind to beat Arizona State in the Rose Bowl.

Now, the stage was set for Ohio State to leave a lasting impression in the Buckeyes' final game at St. John Arena. If they could beat Penn State in their regular-season finale, the Buckeyes would convince most everyone that they had turned the corner and were ready for a successful 1998-99 season.

This, though, seemed the most unlikely of scenarios, considering how complex a puzzle O'Brien had to piece together. The Nittany Lions weren't interested in becoming a footnote to Ohio State's basketball history. They needed this game to get the attention of the NCAA Tournament selection committee.

With Fred Taylor sitting courtside in a wheelchair and 127 former Ohio State players watching from their courtside seats, the Buckeyes threw everything at Penn State. Redd scored a career-high 32 points to become the first freshman ever to win the Big Ten scoring title. Carlos Davis, an unheralded senior guard, played way over his head in scoring 14 points and handing out seven assists.

Amid the unrelenting cheers, the Nittany Lions slowly chipped away a 14-point Ohio State lead. The Buckeyes led 55-41 with 14:18 to go, but Penn State staged a 15-2 run to narrow the deficit to 57-56 with 9:49 to play. The Buckeyes had been here before with Michigan, but this time they didn't surrender the lead without delivering their best shot. They countered with a 13-3 run to take a 69-60 lead. The Nittany Lions, though, were motivated by the fact that a loss would damage their postseason tournament aspirations. Penn State tied the game 76-all and forced overtime on a baseline jumper by 7-foot center Calvin Booth—a Columbus native whom Ayers had mildly courted during the recruiting wars.

Coach Taylor, who had embraced O'Brien moments before the tip-off, watched joyously as tears streamed down his face. John Havlicek and Jerry Lucas watched anxiously, hoping that the last game in this 42-year-old arena would be as memorable as the ones they played during the early 1960s.

An Ohio State victory in the last of 577 games at St. John Arena would have made for good theater. But the Nittany Lions crashed the party and spoiled a perfectly good ending by beating the Buckeyes 89-85. Guard Joe Crispin netted two three-pointers, and guard Pete Lisicky made six free throws in overtime to secure a berth in the National Invitation Tournament for the Lions. Penn State eventually advanced to the NIT title game, where it lost to Big Ten foe Minnesota.

While the crowd cheered them, even in defeat, the Buckeyes walked slowly to their locker room with anguished looks on their faces. They wanted this game badly. They wanted to prove that things had changed. Yet, they earned the respect they coveted most of all. The Buckeyes also put a smile on the face of an ailing Taylor, whose 297 wins are the most in school history. Taylor, surrounded by Havlicek and Clark Kellogg, whispered softly, "This team will get better."

The Buckeyes didn't look good in losing to Indiana in the first round of the inaugural Big Ten Tournament at the United Center in Chicago. After trailing by as many as 24 points to Indiana, the Buckeyes put on an inspiring stretch run before falling 78-71.

"Winning wasn't the single biggest thing," O'Brien said. "We never verbalized it to the kids. We tried like crazy to win every single game. When you get through 17 consecutive losses, to get the kids to buy into that and keep coming back for more—that was a tremendous challenge.

"We were very concerned about the psyche of the young guys because we were being beaten down. I kept encouraging them that we have to come back to practice and keep getting better. There were some head games being played that year. We all knew that we were going to lose many games, but we couldn't lose our cool."

As the season unfolded, the Buckeyes' practices were spirited. They were learning something every day, most of it remedial work on fundamentals. O'Brien rolled up his white short-sleeve shirt and donned his Nike cap like a construction worker putting on his hard hat. All that was missing on days like these was a lunch box. He would break the Buckeyes down without breaking their spirit.

"The day after you lose, you walk into the gym and guys are moping," O'Brien said. "They have long faces and they are tired. We had four or five guys playing 30 minutes a game. When we lost on Tuesday, then Wednesday's practice would be down. We would climb back on Thursday. On Friday, it was 'We could win this game.' The guys were upbeat again. We go play on Saturday, and we would get beat again."

The Buckeyes would mope again in practice. It was a disturbing routine, a challenging hurdle for O'Brien and his staff to clear. The Buckeyes showed up at practice early in the afternoon with their feet dragging and their heads hanging. Still, O'Brien didn't let up. The Buckeyes ran wind sprints and scrimmaged until they finally got right whatever they had been doing wrong.

"We wondered how we were going to get them back," O'Brien said. "It was about building motivation and getting these guys to believe in what we were doing. That first year was as tough a year as any of us have ever gone through. To lose that many consecutive games was hard."

In the days before the Big Ten Tournament game against Indiana, the Buckeyes were as relaxed as they had been all season. O'Brien yelled only as the constant pounding of the basketball echoed throughout the practice gymnasium. It was time to pull back and begin preparing for the next season, even though at least one more game remained.

"We didn't want to embarrass our guys," said O'Brien, an avid reader who lost himself in his books to take his mind off the losing. "Just keep working at it. No matter what, this was going to be hard. While we were pushing and pushing, that first group of guys [in 1997-98] deserved a lot of credit. It's not always about the Xs and Os. It's about getting guys who want to play. When you lose 17 straight, and you don't win a game from December —before Christmas—to the middle of February, you're looking at each other every day, realizing those kids wanted to win. We just weren't good enough."

The Buckeyes weren't supposed to compete. Michael Redd was the only legitimate star on a team that had 10 Ohioans and two Michigan natives; and that was mostly because of recruiting failures that left them with four former walk-ons—Eric Hanna, Byron Wilson, Kwadjo Steele, and John Lumpkin. O'Brien and his staff had gone on the recruiting trail, trying to beef up Ohio State's frontcourt with basketball players—not a two-sport athlete who had to split his time—and commitments. None of these players produced any significant numbers, but they were invaluable in practice.

"In our last game [against Indiana in the Big Ten Tournament], we're losing by 18 points with six minutes to go in the game, and every single game, I would ask the guys on my staff, 'Are we going to be able to come back from this? How much can these kids give us?' With six minutes to go in Chicago, we cannot get anything going, so we call time out. We talked to the kids in the huddle, and I said to my staff, 'This is it.' This is going to be our last game; it's too bad we're going to finish the season like this."

O'Brien, with the season already lost, looked like a trainer entreating a beaten fighter to keep throwing punches no matter how many times he was knocked to the canvas. The Hoosiers had delivered enough blows to leave the Buckeyes spinning. O'Brien kept telling the Buckeyes not to pack it in. He told them the Hoosiers would drop their guard, giving them one more chance to fight back.

"They didn't have to worry about practicing," O'Brien said. "The season was almost over."

But this was a team, despite all the losing, that was developing a new attitude. They slammed the Hoosiers' backs against the wall. Redd hammered down a slam dunk, Singleton drove baseline for a layup, and Coleman drove Indiana coach Bobby Knight mad when he dropped a three-pointer to ignite a rally that enabled Ohio State to trim the Hoosiers' lead to four points. Suddenly, this did not look like the same Ohio State team that had been embarrassed in an 84-58 loss to Michigan State a month earlier.

"That showed me what was inside these guys," O'Brien said. "They kept coming back for more. They kept getting beat, but they kept coming back. We kept pleading why they have to do this. We have to try to get better. For them to finish the way they did, to put a brief, little scare into Indiana at the end. The kids played hard and didn't have anything to show for it."

The Buckeyes did show a change of character. They defied a temptation to concede when defeat was imminent. O'Brien knew the Buckeyes weren't going to nip Indiana at the wire, but he wanted to see how they would respond when all that was at stake was pride and self-respect.

"We had a chance to beat Indiana in a season when we had not beaten anyone [except Wisconsin]," said O'Brien, sounding like the angler who had let the catch of the day wriggle off the hook. "We had a chance with a last-second shot, but Luke Recker steals the ball and we lose.

"After the season was over, there were reasons for optimism. The key thing at the end of the year was that Ken Johnson had the best game of his career in the loss to Indiana in the first round of the tournament. Michael Redd was establishing himself. He got away with murder because he had the green light. He benefited from being on a bad team.

"We knew we had a lot to look forward to, even though we had just lost a zillion games. We felt we were a little more competitive, and now, if only we could carry that over to next year . . . but it was going to be a very different team. At that point, we didn't think of it as having something good going on here. We got better toward the end of our first season. If anyone had seen us in October, no one would have believed our improvement."

The Buckeyes' resurgence at season's end was a testament to the coaching staff's persistence and the players' incalculable drive to elevate their game to such heights as to compete with the likes of Purdue and Michigan State. The Spartans had distanced themselves from most everyone in the conference, partly because of their depth, but mostly because of point guard Mateen Cleaves and forward Morris Peterson. The Buckeyes had lost a promising point man in Stringer and their shooting forward, Tate, who would become the perfect complement to All-America center Kenyon Martin at Cincinnati.

At Boston College, O'Brien didn't have a Cleaves-Peterson combination with which to build a championship-caliber team. He had role players with marginal skills, but he seemingly always had a better-than-average point guard to execute his offense. Howard Eisley and Dana Barros were both All-Big East performers. The Eagles' title aspirations were dashed because of the absence of both a feared shooting guard and a slashing small forward who could weaken an opponent's interior defense with his ability to score in the paint.

In Columbus, O'Brien had waiting upon his arrival a creative, slick ballhandling swingman who possessed a feathery touch around the basket and a delicate, yet unrefined shooting touch from the perimeter. Redd, an overlooked prep sensation, would be the perfect complement to the point guard O'Brien left behind at Chestnut Hill. Scoonie Penn, who was generally considered the best guard in the Big East during the 1996-97 season, sat out a year after transferring to Ohio State in the fall of 1997.

When Penn and Redd stepped on the floor for the Buckeyes' first practice in 1998, the Buckeyes had the perfect mix—a duo that would help bring the Buckeyes in from out of the cold.

"In the back of our minds, we knew help was immediate," O'Brien said, referring to Penn. "There [Penn] was, sitting next to us during all those games in our first year. Nobody else in Columbus really knew that we knew what we were going to have the following year."

In the waning seconds of the tournament loss to Indiana, Penn sat on the bench with a painful expression on his face. He was helpless and restless as he slid up and down the bench. His rich New England accent bellowed along the bench as he encouraged the Buckeyes to play on. O'Brien needed that kind of personality on the floor, and he could see it materializing with Redd as the season progressed.

O'Brien had always been confident, but not overconfident. He figured with Penn and Redd, the Buckeyes could win 16 games and contend for an NIT bid. The Buckeyes had won only eight games in his first season, and now he was talking about winning 16 in his second season.

"Sixteen wins doesn't seem like a whole lot," O'Brien said. "It would be a great year for us. It's almost incredible to believe, but we felt we were going to be better. I knew we would be able to play a lot differently. We knew we could win some of the close games we lost last season because Scoonie understands what happens at the end of games.

"As a coach, you have to convince yourself that you don't have to take shortcuts. You don't have to roll the dice in an area that might not be the right thing because you want the success to happen right away. That is why coaches talk in terms of tenure and in terms of long-term contracts, because it takes time to do these things. There is an impatient attitude among some administrators. If it doesn't happen right now because everybody else is getting it done, then we have to make a change. We have to get somebody else in here because this is not going the way we want. No one other than your team understands this does not happen overnight."

Andy Geiger understood perfectly. Geiger figured Ayers would turn things around eventually. Maybe he would get lucky. Ayers, though, had no such luck.

"You've got to be pretty lucky to get this thing going," O'Brien said. "It's why you have this thing where coaches are trying to get as much security as they can. This has become a crazy business, but Andy Geiger has been good here in that he has repeatedly told me to build it the right way.

"When you come into a situation and you ask a few kids to leave, then you're taking another step back. There was a flicker of hope with that sophomore class, but now you're going to put out that flicker of hope. That's why I think our fans were tremendous. They were patient, at least in that first year. They came out to cheer. They stayed behind us. They encouraged the kids. It's not easy to sit through some of the games they had to. Some of those games were bad, but it was a learning experience for us all."

The Ohio State fans, like the Ohio State players, kept coming back for more. A few had given up, but most came to St. John Arena hoping that O'Brien had finally pushed the right buttons. At times, they would see something good in their team. They were enthusiastic and energetic, but invariably the energy level dropped midway through the second half of many games as the Buckeyes surrendered to the opposition a lead too big to overcome.

The Buckeyes were so used to being in this position, they responded the same almost instinctively. Even if they were winning, the Buckeyes couldn't avoid looking over their shoulders. They would stop traveling the road that nearly carried them to victory. They would take shots they hadn't hit all night. They would run when the half-court offense had been most effective.

"I sensed we were all waiting for something bad to happen," O'Brien said. "That became a little bit of a mind-set also. How do you get them to be confident in the end? There's only one way to do it. They have to go out and do something good. You cannot tell them to feel good about this, because bad things have happened every time they've gone through this.

"You hear players say all the time, 'He took my confidence away from me.' The player has to get something done to get confidence from a coach. I want to sit there and say, 'I have a lot of confidence in this guy, because he is going to get something done. He'll make a play. He'll make his free throws. He will not turn the ball over. Maybe he'll make a shot at the end.' You have confidence in that guy. If another player consistently makes mistakes, how is the coach going to have confidence in him? The players have to understand where the coach is coming from. You build confidence by encouraging and promoting the good things they do. Instead of saying you cannot do this or that, we are more inclined to say go ahead and do what you do well.

"We kind of piece together some things. Frankly, there were some things said to us that we were real happy with. There were incidents during the course of the year, and I am sure it had to do with the frustrations during the season. We knew there were some headaches, but we were willing to overlook some of it. We were hoping that maybe it would be different with us.

"We said to the kids, 'Hey, fellas, you don't know us and we don't know you, we need to get this thing going.' I don't care what happened in the past. I don't care who played in the past. It was time to turn this thing around."

3

MORE THAN
A GAME

THE BUCKEYES APPEARED TO BE HEADED in the wrong direction when Robert Morris came to Columbus on November 18, 1998. They were seemingly overconfident after starting 2-0 with wins over Oakland and Alabama. The Buckeyes were supposed to handle the Colonels like buck privates. Instead, their knees buckled before a crowd of 15,364 at Value City Arena.

O'Brien clutched his hands behind his head as Ohio State staggered out of the starting blocks like three-legged greyhounds. The Buckeyes played a game that was ghostly familiar to the ones their fans had been used to seeing for much of the previous six seasons. They made only one of 16 shots from beyond the three-point arc. They committed 19 turnovers.

The Buckeyes were bad. It was déjà vu.

Finally, midway through the second half, O'Brien put his arms around his new floor leader, Scoonie Penn, and demanded he take control. Penn responded by scoring 17 points in leading the Buckeyes to an uninspiring 61-49 victory and a 3-0 record before opening their 1998-99 Big Ten season against Penn State on November 20.

Penn had become a reflection of O'Brien's past. O'Brien admired how hard his diminutive point guard had worked on his game while sitting out the entire 1997-98 season after transferring from Boston College. Penn would spend countless hours in the practice gym, working on his crossover dribble.

He took as many as 500 jump shots a day, in hopes that OSU's opponents would be hesitant to focus primarily on his backcourt mate, Michael Redd.

In the summer of 1968, amid the prevailing absurdity, violence, and nihilism gripping a country at war with the North Vietnamese, an 18-year-old Jim O'Brien tried focusing mostly on his promising basketball career at Boston College. He spent that tumultuous summer trying—as Penn had—to develop a definitive shot. He went back home to Brooklyn, playing sometimes from sunup to sundown. It didn't matter how hot or how cold, he kept lofting shot after shot until the trigger on his shooting hand locked.

O'Brien did not return home as some conquering hero because he was playing big-time college basketball. Whenever he spun baseline or ran behind a pick at the top of the key, he would stare into the face of a childhood chum who wasn't nearly as impressed with his game as the folks back at Chestnut Hill. He had to prove that he could beat them off the dribble or run with them from baseline to baseline.

On the outdoor courts and in the YMCA, O'Brien faced the kind of competition that would sharpen the dull edges of his game. The former All-New York City high school player was slapped in the face. He took a knee to the thigh and a blow to the head. He bled. He limped. He carried on. On these courts, where the rules were either bent or ignored, O'Brien didn't cry foul. Only wimps did such a thing. So he learned to administer his own brand of justice in pickup games where the players hesitantly police themselves.

If nothing else, O'Brien returned for his sophomore season at Boston College with a new resolve. He was stronger, quicker—and he had a shot.

During Boston College's preseason scrimmages, a confident O'Brien blew on his fingertips like some hired gunman. With All-America center Terry Driscoll demanding the ball in the paint, O'Brien pulled up from 18 feet, then unblinkingly drilled a jumper. He jogged back down the court with a confident swagger. Now, defenses couldn't sag inside; they had to respect his outside shot. In the past, he would be left alone on the perimeter because the opposition knew he didn't have an itchy-enough trigger finger to fire at will.

Still, O'Brien had not distinguished himself from the country's most flamboyant and publicized guards—three-time All-American "Pistol" Pete Maravich of Louisiana State, Calvin Murphy of Niagara, and Jo Jo White of Kansas. He remained a relatively unfamiliar figure, overshadowed by Driscoll, who was the fourth player taken in the 1969 draft. In those days, when UCLA reigned for a decade as the most dominant college basketball team in the land, it was hard to notice anyone wearing colors other than UCLA's blue and gold.

The Eagles were the ninth-ranked team in the country during O'Brien's freshman year in 1967. With Driscoll and O'Brien, Boston College was supposed to make some noise during the 1968-69 season. But the Ivy League shouted the loudest, as Princeton and Columbia both were ranked in the Top 10, along with another Eastern power, St. Bonaventure.

The Eagles didn't have enough to make a run through the NCAA Tournament. O'Brien, though, elevated his game and forced himself into the spotlight as he put up some impressive numbers. Ultimately he led Boston College in scoring in both his junior and senior seasons. He would finish his collegiate career with 1,273 points, which places him 14th on the school's all-time scoring list.

O'Brien was hardly one-dimensional, setting a school single-game record with 18 assists against Le Moyne on December 16, 1970. It's a record that has lasted, eluding three premier guards—Scoonie Penn, Howard Eisley and John Bagley—all of whom earned All-Big East honors while playing for O'Brien at Boston College. Despite his accomplishments as a college player, O'Brien's aspirations were greater. He wanted more from the game. He wanted a championship. But he had to be realistic. Boston College had never been a major basketball power, and it hasn't produced a single first-team All-America selection.

While the Boston College basketball program struggled to find itself, O'Brien longed to be an independent thinker, even as he traveled through a maze created by the pressures of being both a student and an athlete at an academically demanding school. In 1968, a growing curiosity among politically involved students influenced O'Brien and others to separate themselves from the establishment and their typically conservative parents—all the time trying to understand the turmoil that surrounded them.

O'Brien wasn't completely comfortable fitting in like another brick in the wall. In a decade in which freedom of expression became fashionable, O'Brien began to think independently of his father, a gung-ho Marine whose persistence pushed O'Brien from the crowded streets of Brooklyn to a secluded, suburban Boston university. O'Brien wasn't sure if he was a mirror image of his father or his father's antithesis.

"I was part of the [military] draft when the lottery came out," O'Brien said one afternoon as he thumbed through some old pictures of his college days inside his office the day before Penn State arrived. "I remember all my friends sitting around listening to the radio when they were coming up with those draft numbers."

O'Brien waited, too. He carried his transistor radio from the dorm to the student union, pinning his ear against it, listening for his number.

O'Brien, though, didn't consume himself with the draft. His fate rested in the luck of the draw. He did have the odds in his favor, however, because he was a college student who was born on April 9, 1950—putting his number somewhere near the bottom of the draft pile. He could afford to turn his attention to the heated American League pennant race in 1968. Even with the rioting and protesting over the Vietnam War, the Tigers, Red Sox, and Orioles continued to engage in a pennant battle that would last well into September. While Detroit pitcher Denny McLain closed in on his magical 30th victory, O'Brien, if only in the recesses of his mind, knew he, too, was closing in on his magic number. It happened to be 217.

"I was lucky because my number was still down and I was still in school," O'Brien said. "That was one of the lucky things. I never had to face the decision of being part of the draft. My dad played sports in the Marine Corps. He seemingly had his life well in hand and wasn't in very many dangerous situations. It's not something he talked about. You could never find another guy prouder to have been in the Marine Corps.

It was an ambiguous time for O'Brien, an antiwar proponent who reasoned that the conflict in Vietnam served only to distract the country from its social ills—racism, sexism, and economic disparity—which helped to create the great social divide in America.

In this age of Aquarius, an electrifying stage production of *Hair* and singers such as Simon and Garfunkel and Joan Baez stirred emotions with lyrics and poems meant to unite, then carry, America's people over troubled waters. Still, O'Brien could not distance himself from kinships and friendships that had shaped his personality. In the suburban sprawl of Chestnut Hill, with its perfectly aligned and manicured lawns, O'Brien was still a gritty blacktop city boy at heart.

Basketball had brought him to this place. He learned the game in Brooklyn, where the melting pot was vastly different from the campus' lily-white culture.

O'Brien could not ignore all that was happening around him. As the country tried to steady itself two months after the assassinations of the Rev. Martin Luther King Jr. and Robert F. Kennedy, America was left staggering aimlessly and groping for solutions to resolve the madness.

As the Tet Offensive escalated, student rebellion and protest in a budding age of flower children, O'Brien decided basketball could somehow, if only transparently, transcend winning and losing. It could become a means toward mending the fiber of a morally vacant America.

Thus, O'Brien was an idealistic college student whose value system was instilled by a meticulous, sagacious father who opposed New Age parenting that encouraged teenage sons and daughters to seek independence – distancing themselves from the cradle, sometimes prematurely.

Jim O'Brien Sr. didn't rule with a heavy hand, but a firm one. "My father never pushed me athletically," O'Brien said. "He was a thorn academically more than anything. I remember situations when he knew how much playing sports meant to me, and he used that as a source of discipline."

As a high school junior, O'Brien dared to slip in the classroom. His father was unforgiving, delivering both a stinging blow and a resounding message by refusing to let him play in one of New York's most prestigious amateur basketball tournaments – an event in which O'Brien was determined to prove he belonged on the hardwood with the big boys.

"I grew up playing with older guys all the time," O'Brien recalled. "I would always play in the tournaments higher than my age group. I could compete with those guys, but I was never the best player. When I got to this one tournament where I was the best player on my team, maybe the best player in the tournament, I played a lot. In two games, I had scored 35 and 40 points. I'm thinking I'm going to get MVP in this tournament. And that had never happened to me before.

"Then, my grades come out. My father has this thing about school. In my school, 75 percent was passing, but in some other schools it was 60 percent. I got 70 in Latin, or something like that. The rule was that if I got an F on my report card, I wasn't allowed to go out of my house from marking period to marking period. I couldn't go out on weekends to play pickup games. I couldn't go out at night. The only thing I could do was go to practice with my high school team. There was no social stuff or extracurricular activities.

"When the next report card came out, I got this F in Latin. My father wouldn't let me play the rest of the tournament. I remember begging him, and I'm like, 'I'll do anything you want. Don't feed me. Beat me. Don't give me any money. I don't care what happens, but please don't take away basketball. Don't take away my chance to experience something that might be pretty special.'

"So, I end up not going. I was steaming. It was all about academics. It was about my father standing up for something he believed in as a parent. I learned to respect that when I went off to college.

"When I was on my way to college, he reminded me about avoiding the temptations to drink and smoke. He pushed me like crazy to get good grades. I was just an average student who wanted to play ball. I wasn't really tuned in to the academics. I did what I had to do. I had some bumps in the road. My father knew that, and that's why he kept pushing the academics. It's why I've always pushed my kids at St. Bonaventure, Boston College, and Ohio State."

O'Brien, the second-oldest of Jim and Katherine O'Brien's seven children, said one of his biggest disappointments in his life was that his father didn't live to see him walk across the stage to receive his college diploma at Boston College. The elder O'Brien died on a September morning in 1970, two months before his son was voted captain of the Boston College basketball team. His mother died in 1985, a year before he became head coach at his alma mater.

Somewhere in the heavens, O'Brien said, his parents are smiling. They prepared their children—including twins Jeff and Matt, Michael, Kathleen, Eileen, and Colleen—for success by building their self-confidence and using sports as an avenue to acquire self-esteem.

"I was just one of those kids who grew up in the city where that's what we all did," O'Brien said. "We played every sport imaginable, depending upon the season. My father and my uncles were all sport-oriented guys to begin with. So that part was easy."

O'Brien's father coached him in the Christian Youth Organization and Police Athletic League. There was little time for television. O'Brien played on two different baseball teams in different summer leagues. There were doubleheaders on Saturday and Sunday, followed by basketball at night.

O'Brien was considered one of the most versatile athletes at St. Francis Prep in Brooklyn. He wasn't a blazer at receiver, but he had good-enough hands to become a legitimate scoring threat. However, his football career never took flight. He separated his shoulder quarterbacking the freshman team, and then broke his ankle as a sophomore while running a seemingly harmless pass route. With football no longer an option, baseball fueled O'Brien's competitive fire. However, basketball became his passion.

"I was all into playing sports," O'Brien said. "I did it because it made me feel good. I worked hard at being the best in every sport, because I think it gave my father a sense of pride."

O'Brien has that proud papa look on his face whenever his Ohio State players show improvement in class or work themselves onto the dean's list. As he thumbed through his notebook, surveying a list of possible recruits, he remembered how happy he was to find out that his only Prop 48 recruit (in 1998), freshman guard Doylan Robinson, worked hard in the classroom to earn his eligibility.

"I can't ever remember being pushed like this before, except by my high school coach [Harvey Sims]," said Robinson, who assistant coach Dave Spiller recruited out of Akron Buchtel High School. "I feel a sense of urgency about getting my degree. I know no matter what happens with my basketball career, Coach O'Brien will stay on all of us to graduate."

O'Brien is most proud of the fact that all 30 of his players who exhausted their eligibility at Boston College graduated. He is proud, too, that those graduates were an enviable mixture of different cultures—unlike anything he experienced in 1968.

"I took a lot of pride in knowing that the time I was at Boston College, every kid that finished his eligibility graduated," said O'Brien, who was the Boston College Scholar Athlete of the Year in 1971. "I think that is something that is a little special. I think that was a combination of the importance placed on academics at Boston College by the administration and how important our staff viewed those guys getting their degrees. We really wanted our guys to graduate. We emphasize all the time the importance of going to class. I know that we can do a better job here at Ohio State.

"The thing I say to them is, I know the importance of coming to college. Can you just imagine what it's like to be a student and not be able to play basketball? Doylan understands that. I'm always asking them what are they doing with their grades. Maybe there is a little fear. I don't know what drives these guys, but for me, I just loved playing. You go out of your house, and depending on what time of year, it would determine what sport you would be playing. We would play baseball on the weekends, softball during the week in leagues, stickball, and punchball. We played all sorts of games. It was all about a game. We played touch football in and between parked cars on the streets.

"My dad never had to ask me what I wanted to do. I could never imagine not being able to play. I got my grades because I wanted to play. You couldn't do one without the other. The point was made early on. My dad went to college on a GI bill. With my dad it was all about a clean living. I remember getting letters from my dad, and it was never about what I should do basketball-wise. It was always about you will have plenty of time to meet girls and go drinking with your friends. He would tell me not to get caught up in drinking and smoking. All of that stuff hit home.

"I never smoked anything when I was in college. I never put a cigarette in my mouth—ever. I could forget about smoking a joint or anything like that. I would go out and drink a few beers. I wasn't an angel, but there was always that message that this is the right thing to do. It never went away. It's always there. I was into playing ball."

Admittedly, it bothered O'Brien that Boston College did not have an African-American player on its team when he arrived as a freshman in the autumn of 1967. Unlike many of his college teammates, he wasn't nearly as sheltered, having grown up in Brooklyn. He had found friendship and camaraderie from all points in Brooklyn. Basketball had afforded him that opportunity. In an era of civil disharmony, which cultivated distrust between blacks and whites, basketball was color blind—at least in O'Brien's eyes. He was talented enough that on the outdoor courts in Brooklyn, only the game mattered; it overshadowed race and, in some cases, other cultural hang-ups.

"I was always the best player of my group, so I was always looking for other competition," O'Brien said. "A lot of my friends would shy away from playing in the summer leagues. I thought playing in the predominantly black leagues was a little different for me at the time, but it was a great experience."

However, Boston College was a vastly different world. This thriving college town had gained a reputation for being less tolerant of blacks. It wasn't the same liberal-thinking community as many other New England college towns. Or, at least, that was the perception of many black students at Chestnut Hill.

Yet many of Boston's sports heroes were blacks, including Bill Russell, K.C. Jones, and Sam Jones, who helped the Boston Celtics dominate the NBA in the late 1950s and through the 1960s. Russell led the Celtics to 11 NBA world championships, but even his pleas for peace could not deter blacks from rioting in the streets of Boston, as they did in Harlem and Watts in the days following the assassination of Dr. King.

The political and ideological pressures weren't great enough to persuade Boston College coach Bob Cousy, who played with Russell from 1958 to 1963, to make a stronger bid at recruiting minority student-athletes. In reality, Cousy's efforts to create a culturally diverse society within the isolated basketball world of Chestnut Hill were seemingly thwarted by administrative decree. O'Brien would discover later that Cousy's recruiting style was cramped some by a stringent, very selective admissions policy that typically opened its doors only to the affluent and privileged.

"In those days at Boston College, our recruiting budget was basically zero," said Cousy, who coached the Eagles from 1966 to 1969 before embarking on a 10-year coaching career in the NBA. "We did everything on the telephone. We tried to zero in on Catholic kids who were going to be able to qualify and hopefully would be blue-chip players. I would contact the young man, and if he was receptive at all, I would call an alumnus in the area to stay in contact with the young man."

Cousy remembered how difficult it was for black players to assimilate in Boston—and how many Bostonians rebelled against desegregating the Celtics. Cousy remembered when Russell's home in Reading, Massachusetts, was ransacked and the walls splattered with racial epithets. So he wasn't surprised to discover that there were no black student-athletes on the Boston College roster when he took over in 1966.

"The whole time I was at Boston College, I played with only one black guy [Stafford Hillaire, who was a nonscholarship player]," O'Brien said. "Right after I got out of Boston College, a lot more African-American players were coming into Boston College, which I thought was a good thing. But it seemed to come too late.

"We lived in a lily-white environment, really. We had guys who were all from middle-class families. We had everybody from an environment that had both parents at home. Maybe that's why my example isn't a good one. I was surrounded by a much simpler system than the one my players have today. I'm sure there must have been some programs where it wasn't as simple because maybe there were some of those other issues."

O'Brien paused for a moment. He glanced over his shoulder as if he were looking back for an answer. Then, he repeated himself.

"It's amazing to me when I think back at it now that there was only one black guy I played with when I was at Boston College," he said. "It's a new day now. As blind as I must have been, it never dawned on me until I was long out of school to have a black guy on the team. It was never an issue. I never considered it a possibility. It wasn't an issue about not playing with black guys. When Stafford was there, it never became like a thing with any of us."

When O'Brien enrolled at Boston College, it was a school in transition. It had been a largely residential commuter school. Consequently, the campus environment attracted few black athletes in any sport, mostly because Chestnut Hill did not offer a more diverse social climate and support network.

"When I was a senior, Chuck Daly started recruiting some black players, but they were on the freshman team," O'Brien said. "We would practice with those guys, but never play with them. At that point, freshmen had to play on a freshman basketball team. Stafford was a very bright man, but I don't know if he ever felt comfortable. When I look back at it, I don't know if we ever made him uncomfortable or if we would have been aware if he was uncomfortable.

"You become so oblivious to everything and so tuned in to what you are about; the selfishness of young adults is sometimes amazing. Stafford was just like one of the guys. He was one of us. Now, when you start to analyze it, you say it must have been really hard for him. You have to be a little older and a little smarter to understand what happened years ago that you weren't tuned in to it. I think that is the case with me. I wasn't smart enough to really appreciate somebody else's headache.

"I remember hearing people criticizing John Thompson for not recruiting enough white basketball players at Georgetown. Brigham Young University has had few black student-athletes. You don't consciously recruit numbers and quotas. For the most part, it works out because you are hoping to find a young man who works for your team. We had only two white kids on our Final Four team, but we've since gotten commitments from other white kids. There was no pressure to recruit them. It wasn't that way at Boston College."

At Boston College, seldom did anyone voice any objections to the racial makeup of O'Brien's teams. O'Brien brought together student-athletes who adjusted easily to college life. In his efforts to find the best talent, O'Brien spent as much time recruiting in the inner cities and rural areas as he did in the suburbs.

"There's never been a discussion about where we had too many black guys or not enough black guys in the program," O'Brien said. "You just go out and recruit whom you can get. You have to make adjustments with personnel. I cannot imagine how you cannot do that today. You would have to be living in the dark ages."

Indeed, the times are changing. The game has changed, transform
ing itself from peach baskets dangling from barn roofs to multimillion-dollar, on-campus arenas such as the Value City Arena at the Jerome
Schottenstein Center in Columbus. It is, in essence, a game in perpetual
reinvention and rebirth. It is far more popular than ever before; only now, at
some tradition-rich basketball schools, it caters to the well-to-do alumni, who
can afford the expensive regular-season and tournament tickets.

There are no more college basketball dynasties, such as that enjoyed by
the UCLA Bruins, who won 10 NCAA championships from 1964 to 1975.
The Duke Blue Devils, though, have flirted with the creation of another
dynasty by winning three national championships in nine years (1992, 1993,
and 2001). Since 1976, only Indiana, Kentucky, and Duke have won three
titles, while North Carolina and Michigan State are the only other multiple
national-championship winners. In this era of parity, repeating as national
champion is far more improbable than in years past, partly because of recruiting limitations. O'Brien hasn't allowed his hands to be tied when it comes
to recruiting. At Ohio State, he has had the freedom to search for talent at
junior colleges, a recruiting avenue closed to him at Boston College. In 1997,
he found a gem in 6-foot-7 forward George Reese, who helped transform the
Buckeyes from perennial losers to Big Ten contenders.

In his search, he found four Serbian recruits—guard Boban Savovic,
forward Slobodan Ocokoljic, and centers Aleksander Radojevic and Cana-
dian-born Velimir Radinovic. Radojevic was later declared ineligible by the
NCAA because he played 19 minutes of professional basketball in Europe.
And Ocokoljic would later transfer out after the 2000-2001 season. O'Brien
admitted to avoiding any ideological uproar by opting not to recruit players
of Croatian descent. There was a need to recognize the friction that existed
between the Serbs and Croatians, proving that sometimes he wears the hat of
a diplomat. It wasn't about being politically perceptive or correct, he said. It
was simply the right thing to do. There is a need, he said, to maintain the
harmonious atmosphere he has created in Columbus. Savovic became a much
more dependable player during the second half of the 1998-99 season. However, the conflict in Kosovo surely affected his performance at the Final Four
in St. Petersburg.

Some college coaches make a conscious effort to recruit players who
are much like them or are best suited for their systems. O'Brien did it with
Penn. Cousy did it with O'Brien. "I was on the lookout for point guards who
had the speed and saw the court well," Cousy said. "Jimmy reminded me a
little of myself. I came out of those New York City ghettos. I was socially
retarded and shy and laid back. Both of us have come a long ways since then."

For the most part, the 12 men who represented Ohio State during the 1998-99 season were unlike their coach, but they were a perfect fit for his system. Their backgrounds were as varied as their tastes in clothes and food. Some were from well-to-do homes, but not affluent ones. Some were from one-parent homes, but not broken ones. For some, the Buckeyes were their family and Ohio State was their home.

O'Brien was all things to all of them.

He was a father figure, a teacher, a disciplinarian, a friend, a confidant, and someone they all respected. Even though their player-coach relationship had its difficulties, O'Brien's insistence on building a familial environment during the 1998-99 season enabled the Buckeyes to overcome the shortcomings and pitfalls that ultimately led to the dismissal of Randy Ayers at the end of the 1996-97 campaign.

O'Brien dealt with most of his players' quirks and idiosyncrasies. However, they could never broker a compromise with music. O'Brien, a self-proclaimed square, wasn't going to cross the line that separated pop legend Neil Diamond and rap master Tupac Shakur.

"I am a big Beatles, Rolling Stones, and Elton John guy," O'Brien said. "When my daughters were younger, I would have them in the car with me listening to all that stuff. Their friends would ask them how they knew that stuff, and they would say, 'I've been listening to it with my father.' Elton John was huge. I like Chicago and the Eagles, Billy Joel and Peter Gabriel, but nothing hard or too loud.

"I don't like the music today. I don't like it all. I have a hard time with the rap music. My players think my taste in music is old-fashioned. I'll walk into the locker room and they'll have this music blasting, and some of it is like, well, nasty. I tell them if this is what you guys want to listen to, fine. When I come in, please turn it off because it's just so, so loud. I don't like it, but that's their taste. They think I'm square in terms of what I listen to."

The truth is, O'Brien is a bore, said guard Scoonie Penn. He's cool, but light years removed from being hip. That might explain why the players' lounge at Value City Arena isn't within shouting distance of the coaches' lounge.

"We just laugh about it," O'Brien said. "There was a kid at Boston College name Brad Christensen who used to listen to a lot of the music I listen to, and we would rap about it. It's not just a cultural thing, but it's a difference in the ages. As a coach, you must give your players space and freedom to express themselves. They teased me, but it has strengthened my sense of humor. It helps them, too, in that they respect what I'm about and understand how I feel about certain things. I would fall out if I caught them listening to Neil Diamond. I wouldn't expect them in 100 years to be listening to that stuff. Occasionally, I will come up with a name of some rap guy, and they will be shocked that I know someone like Dr. Dre, but it's just from watching television. I've got them fooled." Not really.

"Coach doesn't know what's up," said forward George Reese. "We may not speak the same language when it comes to music, but I understand where he's coming from."

O'Brien is still trying to figure out where his players are coming from. Fortunately, he has an idea where they're going. While swingman Michael Redd jumped to the NBA after his junior year, the 1999-2000 season, the rest of Ohio State's underclassmen assured O'Brien that they would remain in Columbus to complete their eligibility.

"We have to make a connection with our players, no matter how bad the music," O'Brien said sarcastically. "I think it forces you to reinforce that we can accept the fact that we can all be different and work toward the same end. I respect what the other guy is all about. We give them their space in the locker room. Something as simple as music reinforces that we can coexist despite the age gap."

O'Brien learned that lesson from his first boss, Dom Perno. Perno reemphasized all those things O'Brien's father had taught him. It influenced how and whom he recruits in his efforts to rebuild the Ohio State basketball program. "You've got to have a combination of good students and good basketball players," O'Brien said. "I'm no different than most coaches who are looking for that great basketball player. Realistically, if a kid is a great student and just a marginal player, you're probably not going to want to recruit him. We look for good players interested in academics and good people who will be a positive influence on the program."

With the current climate of college recruiting being extraordinarily competitive, O'Brien and his staff do not have an off-season. O'Brien squeezes in an occasional round of golf during the summer, but even the clubhouse isn't refuge from the job of recruiting and scouting. At times, he pulls from his golf bag a cell phone and sky pager more often than a driver and wedge.

"It takes a little more time, but you want to get kids who are interested in graduating from college," O'Brien said. "We ask kids all the time, 'How important are academics to you?' If we get the impression that they kind of shrug it off, then you have to make some real hard decisions about if you want to roll the dice. Or do you say, maybe we can take somebody a little bit less talented, but you know who is more tuned in to his academics and be a better guy for you."

In essence, O'Brien looks for someone who would have made his father proud—that someone who commits to both the team and the classroom.

"We have historically done that as a coaching staff," O'Brien said. "I told my guys not to recruit players who we thought weren't what we were looking for. Everybody in the country wants that kind of scenario. We want guys who are pretty well rounded, and that's basically our formula."

As the Buckeyes continue their quest to establish themselves as a college basketball power, O'Brien is convinced the recruiting wars will get nastier. In fact, he said, the battles have already intensified. "Sometimes, I struggle with some of the things that have to be said and done in the recruiting, quite frankly," O'Brien said. "For example, we lost a kid [7-0 center Michael Bradley, who transferred from Kentucky to Villanova] because we didn't make him any promises about playing time."

The Philadelphia Inquirer reported that Bradley, whom O'Brien had gotten a verbal commitment from while at Boston College, was promised he would start and play 35 minutes a game at Villanova. Villanova coach Steve Lappas denied making such a promise, but the *Inquirer* stood by its story. Lappas left the Wildcats after the 2000-2001 season to take over at the University of Massachusetts. Bradley had a sensational 2000-2001 season and was named to the All-Big East first team.

"That kind of put us on notice a little bit that this is the parameter [of recruiting]," O'Brien said. "We don't get Mike Bradley. And I wonder, by not making the same promise, did we hurt ourselves in the recruiting? I keep thinking how Cousy was talking about having other guys while he was recruiting me versus today's coaches making promises and a guarantee of minutes. I know in my heart that I have never promised anybody anything. I said to the Bradley family that it's not a criticism of how others recruit. I didn't promise Scoonie Penn and Bill Curly, both of whom were from the New England area. I showed them the opportunities they would have at Boston College. I wouldn't feel comfortable making a promise that I wouldn't be 100 percent sure that I can deliver.

"I say to young men during the recruiting process that I think you can be a real good player. I think you can play a lot. I think you can be a starter. I think all of that. But I can't make a guarantee. What happens if a kid goes through a stretch of games where he's not playing that well? Then, all of sudden, you don't deserve to play 35 minutes a game. Are you going to come back and say, 'You promised to play me 35 minutes a game'? In that case, he would be right, and I would be wrong. I don't want to have that conversation. I do know that I struggle with the recruiting with some of the things you feel you must say to guys."

O'Brien's primary coaching mission is to lead Ohio State to its first national championship since 1960. But his immediate goal is to improve the school's dismal graduation rate, which in 1999 was among the worst among Big Ten schools and only slightly better than Cincinnati's, which was the lowest among Ohio's Division I-A men's basketball programs.

"Because of the way they evaluate the graduation rates, I think the graduation rates are going to always be reported to be very low," O'Brien said. "I know that we all should be doing a much better job. But I also know that as long as the NCAA is going to base its figures on a particular class, let's say 2000, then ask how many graduated in 2004, the graduation rates will be low because no one is factoring in guys who transferred. If you look at Ohio State as an example, Ayers's 1995 recruiting class [Shaun Stonerook, Jason Singleton, Neshaun Coleman, Jami Bosley, Jermaine Tate, and Damon Stringer] had only two guys, Singleton and Coleman, who actually graduated from Ohio State. The other 1995 recruits transferred after sitting out a year. Stonerook went to Ohio University. Stringer enrolled at Cleveland State. Bosley transferred to the University of Akron. Tate continued his college career at Cincinnati.

"If you took all those other guys, for whatever the reason, those don't get factored into the mind-set of those who calculate these numbers," O'Brien said. "It's not accurate to say they didn't graduate. They just didn't graduate from Ohio State."

The 1999 NCAA Graduation Rates Report accounts only for student-athletes receiving athletic scholarship aid. That report consists of entering freshmen from the 1994-95 school year through 1997-98. Of the eight 1995 scholarship players, only Singleton and Coleman used all four years of eligibility and graduated from Ohio State. Therefore, the Buckeyes had a graduation rate of only 25 percent, which was down from 31 percent in 1997.

"We want our players to have some interest in graduating," O'Brien said. "When we ask a guy what is his academic ambition, we want them to say they want to get their degrees; then they have to make a commitment to go to class and do the things they have to do."

That, of course, is what O'Brien's parents had demanded of him when college scouts began showing interest in recruiting him out of St. Francis Prep in Brooklyn. He and his parents made a pact as they drove onto the campus at Boston College. He promised to focus on academics and not allow himself to think only about basketball, parties, and girls. He was going to class, in part, because that part of the pact was nonnegotiable.

This, though, is not 1967 Boston College. Today, parents don't solely influence student-athletes. There are other, sometimes more powerful, influences luring undergraduates from college.

"Is everybody going to graduate?" O'Brien asked rhetorically. He paused only briefly before answering himself.

"No," he said emphatically.

O'Brien tries to keep things simple with his players. Occasionally, he goes off on a tangent, overemphasizing a point. He hammers it home like a rusty nail, hoping not to bend his players out of shape.

"Does everyone stay for the four years if they're good players?" asked O'Brien, who had never had that problem at Boston College.

"Probably not," he answered without hesitation.

Once, when it appeared that a couple of players had slacked off in class, O'Brien lectured the entire team.

As he sat up in his chair to hammer home another point, he glanced outside his office door at center Ken Johnson, then stepped into his secretary's office to deliver a progress report. Johnson was a nonqualifier when he enrolled at Ohio State in 1997.

Although basketball held his undivided attention as he began his second season at Boston College, O'Brien noticed that the long, hot summer of discontent in 1968 was beginning to cool some. The nation's attention turned to the World Series, which was the one thing that could keep O'Brien off the hardwood—albeit briefly. While there were scattered remnants of the riots that tore at the fabric of Detroit and St. Louis, a sense of calm prevailed in both the Motor City and the Gateway to the West. The Tigers, who had bested the Red Sox in winning the American League pennant, stunned the favored Cardinals in the World Series.

O'Brien used to fantasize about playing in the World Series. He also imagined himself playing in high-stakes basketball games before sold-out crowds; and in the end, his dreams would be complete with a game-winning shot. Cousy, who had fulfilled many of his championship dreams while playing on the parquet floor of Boston Garden, was giving O'Brien his chance to make his dream a reality.

"I probably went to Boston College, and I would say with 90 percent certainty, only because of Cousy," O'Brien recalled. "Back in those days, Bob Cousy was the guy. He was Mr. Basketball. If you were a guard, especially from New York, and you got recruited to play for Bob Cousy, it was like in today's age, like Michael Jordan or Magic Johnson recruiting you. Cousy was a guard. I was a guard. It was flattering having him recruit me. I felt it was the thing for me to do."

O'Brien had considered going elsewhere, including Providence, Holy Cross, Fordham, and St. John's. The University of Miami was an enticing choice: good weather and a program in need of help. Miami wasn't a big basketball town, but Hall of Famer Rick Barry honed his game in Coral Gables. It was an even more attractive offer, considering Cousy hadn't fallen all over himself to sign O'Brien. Deep down, O'Brien wanted Cousy courting his signature. Nevertheless, he didn't want to appear anxious, biting on the first offer without a tease.

"If a recruit's grades were going to be accepted, then I would swoop in if we thought they were going to qualify," Cousy remembered. "They would come to visit, and we would take them to church. The captain would take them to a movie, and the faculty would provide an apartment. That would be the extent of our wining and dining. Now, it's hard to recruit a blue-chipper that way. I'm afraid you wouldn't get your foot in the door."

Cousy offered O'Brien a scholarship just as he was preparing to make an official visit to Miami. But Miami had already sent him his airline ticket. Now, he was being pulled in both directions.

"When he put the thing on the table with an offer for the scholarship, I had plane tickets to visit the University of Miami and I was planning to take some others," O'Brien said. "I had to call everyone to tell them that I was going to Boston College. Lou Carnesecca of St. John's was very good to me. I was at virtually every St. John's home game.

"In my mind, I was going to Boston College, but I wanted to take that trip to Miami, anyway. A couple of coaches indicated that even if I committed to them, they would allow me to visit other schools. Being 16 or 17 years old, I remember saying to myself, 'Let me take this trip to Florida.' Then, my dad got into what's right and what's wrong. Obviously, he was right and I was wrong. He urged that I don't do that. I had to send the tickets back. Instead, I visited Holy Cross, Providence and Fordham.

When O'Brien first met Cousy, he was in awe. He saw him as a legendary basketball player—not as a college basketball coach. It took some time for him to get over the euphoria of being pursued by Cousy. Yet, unlike other coaches who battled for O'Brien's signature on a national letter of intent, Cousy didn't make any promises. He didn't do anything special. He just put the scholarship offer on the table, then said take it or leave it.

Admittedly, O'Brien's ego was bruised. This was not a way to treat a high school hot shot. Take it or leave it. He thought about it for a minute, and then decided to take it. The recruiting war for O'Brien ended the moment Cousy fired his first recruiting pitch.

"I was disappointed," O'Brien said. "He wasn't somebody who liked the recruiting end of being a college basketball coach. I had all these other schools telling me how good I was and what I could do and what I was going to be able to do. That mesmerized me. He basically came in and said we are going to take one point guard."

O'Brien was on Cousy's short list. Cousy had only three players in mind. He wasn't going back and forth, begging, as some coaches do. He waved the scholarship in O'Brien face's and made a take-it-or-leave-it offer that left O'Brien standing with a puzzled look on his face. He expected a better sales pitch.

While O'Brien stood weighing his options, Cousy said, "I'm going to give the scholarship to the first kid who takes it."

Something inside O'Brien wanted to leave it. There would be other offers to consider. He didn't have to succumb to such pressure. He could walk away. Before he could decide, Cousy made one last recruiting pitch.

"We really like you," Cousy said. "We think you are a really good player, but we have these other kids. We would prefer to have you, but if those kids tell us first, then we are going to take them."

It was not what O'Brien wanted to hear. He wanted Cousy to say something that would make him feel more secure about choosing Boston College. "I wanted him to think that I was a pretty good player," O'Brien recalled. "He was nice about it, but he wasn't coming on. He wasn't coming down to my level. Ironically, that's one of the things I enjoyed about being at Boston College with him for two years.

"The other guys on my team felt the same way. Every day in practice, we were playing in front of Bob Cousy. I would go to practice every day thinking I need this guy to believe that I can play. It was so important for me that he felt I was a player. I never, ever wanted to leave the gym with him thinking I wasn't that good. It was like a challenge every day. I wanted this guy's approval so bad. I really wanted him to think that I was his guy. He was always on the pedestal."

O'Brien was still flattered by Cousy the basketball player. He respected him as a coach, yet in the back of his mind, he could see Cousy only as a basketball player.

"Jimmy worshiped Cousy and Cousy loved him," said *Boston Globe* columnist Bob Ryan, a 1968 graduate of Boston College. "O'Brien was another Cousy type. It was hard to imagine a kid from New York being sheltered, but his family life was very old-fashioned. He didn't have the worldly exposure. He wasn't well traveled, not like high school kids are today."

Unlike many of today's coaches, who recognize the necessity of having a solid player-coach relationship, Cousy never felt it necessary. After all, the Eagles were supposed to be looking up to this Boston Celtics icon.

"When you would play well, he wasn't one to come around saying you were great today," O'Brien said. "He would come around with this rolled-up program and tap you on the head and say, 'Good job, Babe.' He called everybody Babe. That was like, oh, my God. It was the ultimate compliment. Then, I would think to myself, 'Just good job, Babe.' If you got that, it was good enough. I would walk out of there thinking I was on top of the world. Now, it's so different. That wouldn't come close to getting anything done today. To me that was part of the attraction."

O'Brien admired Cousy, but they didn't get to know each other in the two years they spent together in Chestnut Hill. Cousy wasn't a resident coach who spent most of his time at the university. In reality, coaching the Golden Eagles was more of a part-time gig, something to do as he adjusted to life without the NBA.

"We had an assistant coach who was there during the day," O'Brien said. "There was no such thing, when Cousy was there, as having [the coaches] around the offices the whole day. Cousy lived in Worchester and would show up at Boston College at noon before three o'clock practices. The assistant coaches were high school teachers. In fact, Cousy never had a full-time assistant coach. If practices were at 3 o'clock, they would come walking in at a quarter to three. We wouldn't see anybody during the course of the day. Today, coaches have many roles and wear any number of hats. We're involved in student support services and other stuff that is absolutely needed."

The atmosphere at Boston College began to change when Chuck Daly took over in 1969. "I was absolutely devastated when Cousy left," O'Brien said.

The Eagles advanced to the NCAA Tournament and finished as the 16th-ranked team in the country in Daly's first season. Only this time, two other Eastern powers—Villanova and St. John's—were ranked ahead of the Eagles. As much as he loved to compete, it wasn't the winning that always mattered with O'Brien. Instead, he was impressed with Daly's organizational skills and commitment to building a basketball program.

For Daly, this was the beginning of a long, successful career as a head coach. After a stint as a basketball commentator, Daly succeeded in leading the Detroit Pistons to back-to-back NBA titles in 1989 and 1990, before coaching both New Jersey and Orlando and later becoming a special consultant with Vancouver.

"Chuck Daly established a program," O'Brien said. "Cousy had only a basketball team."

Cousy was a no-frills type of coach. He was a basketball coach who focused mostly on coaching. Daly, who had been an assistant at Duke, began preparing the Golden Eagles for the long run. He was meticulous in devising game plans, and his practices were long, hard, grueling sessions. He was critical, demanding precise execution on both ends of the floor. This is what O'Brien was used to. It's the way his father used to coach him in the CYO leagues when he was in grade school.

Daly never let up on O'Brien. He altered his game, making him a more complete player. O'Brien would soon become an extension of his coach. He was, Daly said, "our coach on the floor."

"I thought Chuck Daly was one of the best things to ever happen to Boston College," O'Brien said. "As much as I hated Cousy leaving, Daly was into the program. He emphasized how recruiting determines the success and failure of a program. He talked about having the ability to sell your program. Cousy was not into any of that. It was indicative by how he recruited me. The recruiting now is so drastically different than it was in the 1960s. There is a lot that has changed in college basketball. There's a lot that has changed in our society. A lot has changed with young college athletes."

O'Brien's coaching career was greatly influenced by Daly and Cousy. It wasn't so much Daly's methodology as it was his manner. Daly and Cousy treated every player at Boston College as if he were invaluable, but he didn't swell his players' heads with exaggerated praise or by inflating their egos. Daly dressed impeccably. He paneled his office with oak veneer. Cousy had old plastered walls. Daly piped in music—some of which O'Brien actually liked.

There was a feeling among Boston College's players that Cousy was trying to make Boston College mirror the Boston Celtics. Daly, on the other hand, was trying to develop a program that had its own identity. "Cousy and Daly were two drastically different personalities," O'Brien said. "They were drastically different-style coaches. I was able to adapt and exist with both of those guys."

O'Brien learned from them both, too. In an ever-changing society, O'Brien has come to realize that the job of a college basketball coach is far more complex than it was in the late 1960s and early 1970s. "I would think it's a lot more difficult coaching today than it was back then," he said. "I would suspect that back then, Cousy and Daly would have thought it was tough. I don't really think there were as many issues back then that coaches had to deal with as coaches have to today.

"When I was playing, any coach I played for or guys I played with, it was literally true that we would run through a wall to have an opportunity to compete. How many times have we heard that? I think it was a situation where guys were asked to do things on a team and things got done without any questions asked. Our thinking was, he is the coach; we respect him because he is the coach. It was a lot simpler then."

While the demands on coaches have changed, student-athletes are becoming more demanding. Where coaches once threatened to take back scholarships for a lack of effort, many of today's players are threatening revolt—or early entry into the NBA draft—as an expression of defiance.

"Now, some players want to know what's in it for them," O'Brien said. "It's an unfortunate attitude a lot of today's young players have. You don't want your student-athletes to ask themselves, 'How am I going to benefit from this?' I think players have questions that they didn't have a decade or a generation ago.

"The issue of drugs wasn't as prevalent as it is now. It seems as though guys were more interested in understanding the importance of graduating from college because there was a general feeling that most guys weren't going to play in the pros. Now, I don't know how important graduating from college is to a lot of young players today. Now, everybody thinks they are going to play in the pros. You have the temptations and social issues that hadn't surfaced when I was in college. There is a lot more pressure being a student-athlete, too. There are the compliance issues, NCAA conformity, and just a zillion other things.

"It was a simpler time when I played college basketball. We were on our own a lot more. We didn't have anyone baby-sitting us. Now, we watch out for everything that our players do. It's much more difficult to coach in today's environment."

4

ON MY OWN

Before Jim O'Brien was to return to Boston College for his sophomore season in 1968, it was suggested that he spend the summer playing basketball in Los Angeles. For anyone aspiring to play professional basketball, playing in the California summer leagues was a must. The temptation to both travel and improve your game was irresistible, considering the competition included other top collegiate players and young aspiring stars from the NBA and the ABA. It would give O'Brien a chance to enhance his game, maybe enough that his play would be the difference in leading the Eagles into the NCAA Tournament.

The idea of traveling sounded good to O'Brien, considering he hadn't traveled before. He knew, of course, he'd better drop this bomb on his father right away. Jim O'Brien Sr. would compromise occasionally, but he always knew where to draw the line—or hold the line. He had concerns about his kids wandering too far from home. He would have been all right if his son had chosen to play basketball at the University of Miami, but he was thrilled that Boston College was O'Brien's eventual choice.

O'Brien really didn't know how his father would react. Actually, in his heart of hearts, he knew exactly what to expect.

At 18, he had begun to lobby for more independence. He had reached a stage in his life when he could decide for himself what was best for his future. He was his own man. Even the old man had to agree that it was time for his oldest son to make up his own mind. O'Brien bravely approached his father about the idea of making the long trip out west to play in the summer leagues.

"What do you think?" O'Brien remembered asking his father.

O'Brien recalled his father standing there, looking straight into his eyes. He didn't smile. He didn't laugh. He didn't frown. He just stared.

"Well, ..." his father paused.

O'Brien, waiting impatiently, could sense what was coming. Still, he held out hope. Before his father could answer, he felt compelled to explain himself further—to give one final sales pitch before his father answered.

O'Brien had already made up his mind. He wanted to go west. But he trusted his father with his life. But basketball had become more important than it was when he played at St. Francis Prep in Brooklyn. He was taking the game seriously now. He read the newspapers and magazines, like most everyone else. He knew the professional scouts were watching him. They liked his ballhandling skills and the way he ran the Boston College offense. He seemingly always had command of the floor in orchestrating the Eagles' offense almost flawlessly. He knew if he improved his game in a few areas, he would be a virtual lock to be drafted, at least by the ABA. Whenever an opportunity came to improve his game, O'Brien jumped at it without asking many questions.

This, however, was different. He hadn't traveled this far from home.

"What happens is, you're basically on your own," O'Brien said. "Whenever there was a decision to be made, it was like 'What'd you think, Dad?' I was young for my class. Bill Evans, who was a very good college player and a Boston College teammate, was going to play in Los Angeles. We figured we would play in the backcourt together. He really wanted me to go out there and play with him. I had been living at home for one year, so it was important to me what my dad thought. I was comfortable talking with my dad about everything. I didn't know exactly how to present this idea to him. I told him it might not be a bad idea to go out there and play with some very good guys."

Again, O'Brien looked into his father's eyes. He did so because his father had always demanded that he look directly into a man's eyes when he talked. The eyes are windows to the truth, a vision of one's convictions, he would say. There was a look of pride in his father's eyes. He admired the fact that his son had the guts to make such an outrageous suggestion.

In some respect, O'Brien admitted, it was about feeling like a grown-up. The time had come to escape the adolescent trap that had kept him close to home. He now had the chance to explore his curiosities and conquer his fears of being on his own. He had grown to be an unregimented thinker at Boston College. Yet his parents—mostly his father—had always been the safety net that would catch him if he slipped off the high wire in Chestnut Hill. He was expected to be at his very best both in the classroom and on the basketball court. With Cousy and Daly pulling one way and his college professors the other, the demands of meeting everyone's expectations became a delicate balancing act.

Finally, in what seemed like hours to O'Brien, his father uttered the expected.

"There is no way!" his father shouted. "There is no way you are going out to California. You're not going to be hanging out in Los Angeles. There is no way. You're not going."

It wasn't a blow that floored O'Brien. It was, however, a jab at his self-confidence that caused him to rock back on his heels. He wanted to deliver a counterblow, some kind of undeniable argument that his father couldn't dispute. Instead, he put his hands in his pockets, then walked away.

His father didn't necessarily think of Los Angeles as a wretched town. He wasn't worried that his son would get caught up in all that Hollywood craziness. He believed that his son was responsible enough to keep his nose clean. He just didn't trust other folks, especially those 3,000 miles away from home. Chestnut Hill was a four-hour drive from Brooklyn.

O'Brien, as he did most times, took his father's advice. He stayed home. He spent the summer playing in Brooklyn before going back to Boston College.

"My dad made that decision for me," O'Brien said. "The point I'm making is that there is always somebody who is always advising you."

As the leaves on the maple and elm trees turned into many shades of red and brown in the autumn of 1970, O'Brien was about to grow up even more than he ever imagined. He returned to Boston College in late August, only a week before the college football season was in full bloom. It was difficult for him to concentrate totally on his studies. The news back home wasn't good. His father, a vibrant and energetic patriarch, died suddenly of a heart attack at age 49 while reading the newspaper at the breakfast table on September 20, a sobering Sunday for the entire O'Brien family.

"My dad wasn't sick a day in his life," O'Brien recalled. "I remember Chuck Daly called me and asked me to go for a ride. I didn't know what was going on. My dad dying was the farthest thing from my mind. As we were driving around campus, Daly said he had bad news for me. He said, 'Your dad just died of a heart attack.' Chuck Daly will always be connected to me in some way.

"I went home to make sense of my father's death. I couldn't believe it. For about three weeks, I stayed home and actually thought about not going back to school because it was such a confusing time for everybody in the family. I felt there was a need for me to be home.

For much of his young life, O'Brien was motivated by his father's pleas to make something of his life. He didn't have to be a superstar basketball player. O'Brien's father insisted, above all else, that his oldest child set an example for his brothers and sisters. It is why he was unrelenting in his demands that he select a college that would appreciate his desire to learn as much as his desire to develop into an All-America basketball player.

O'Brien had been back in school for only three weeks when Jim O'Brien Sr. died. Suddenly, O'Brien became a man. It was he whom the family turned to, hoping he could help console his grieving mother. He would have to help make the tough decisions, which was a responsibility his father never relinquished.

Suddenly, he had to think for himself. Only he could choose the direction his life would take him.

"When my dad died, I had to make these decisions on my own," O'Brien said. "My mother didn't know much about the stuff my dad and I talked about. She had always let my dad handle it. I remember Chuck Daly being good to me during my senior year at Boston College. He was great. But I missed my dad."

Even now, when certain situations arise with his players at Ohio State, O'Brien often imagines how his father would handle things. He isn't afraid to offer advice, especially to those young men who do not have fathers or surrogates to turn to for encouraging words.

"There have been a lot of young kids on our teams at Boston College and Ohio State who didn't have fathers to help them make it through some difficult times," O'Brien said. "If my dad had still been living, he would probably have had a tremendous impact on how I would have done things. I don't know if anything would have changed much if my father hadn't died. The only thing I regret is that I didn't have an opportunity to share with him my successes."

Five years after his father's death, O'Brien finally made the trip out west. He had fulfilled his promise to his father by earning his college degree from Boston College. He was doing something meaningful with his life. He was working every day—even nights, when necessary.

O'Brien, now a husband and soon to be a father, was still playing basketball. Only now, he was getting paid. He was in his fourth season in the ABA, but it was hardly a secure job. Unlike today's NBA players, even the ones with marginal skills, O'Brien was making chump change in comparison. His take-home pay for one game with the San Diego Conquistadors was about $600 per game—a quarter of a million dollars less than what Michael Jordan made per game during his farewell season in the NBA in 1998.

O'Brien was drafted by the Buffalo Braves of the NBA and the Pittsburgh Condors of the rival ABA in 1971.

At that time, there was a heated bidding war between the two leagues in an effort to sign the top collegiate players. O'Brien had been among the top point guards in the draft, having gone to Buffalo in the fourth round and Pittsburgh in the third round. There were no staggering multimillion-dollar deals being offered, not even to the first-round draft picks of both leagues. But the ABA, in a fight for its very existence, engaged in a signing war that ultimately exacted a financial toll from which it couldn't recover.

"There were certain agents being paid by the ABA to direct their clients to the league," O'Brien said. "The agents were getting a chunk of money from the players, but they were getting money from the ABA's office, too. The league was going to do whatever it took to compete with the NBA. I don't know if that happened with me."

Pittsburgh offered O'Brien a three-year contract for $150,000, much of which was deferred over a period of five years. The Braves, who would later sign first-round picks Randy Smith and Bob McAdoo in successive years, offered O'Brien $35,000, but only if he made the team. There was no guaranteed money. The choice was easy for O'Brien, who took the guaranteed money in Pittsburgh.

"After my third year [in Kentucky] I was traded to San Diego, I negotiated my own contract for $60,000 for one year," said O'Brien, who last played during the 1975-76 season. "It was the most money I ever made in one season. I was on top of the world. I thought I was doing great."

He may not have been rolling in dough, but he and Christine O'Brien had a wealth of sunshine. They lived modestly in an oceanside community only several miles from downtown San Diego. O'Brien was living the dream life. He had high expectations. But playing basketball for a living? It was unfathomable. What would his father think?

Even with hints of the league folding at season's end, O'Brien was having the time of his life. He was an hour and a half away from the influences of Tinseltown. He could breathe and feel the misty breeze that swept inland from the Pacific. He was 90 minutes from Los Angeles, free of the thick, black smog that shaded the blue skies of Southern California. Surely, his father would have liked what he was doing—and that he stayed away from Los Angeles.

For O'Brien, this was as good as it gets. Yet something was missing. He wanted to share this with his father, who had kept telling him time and time again that if he worked hard enough, this would be his destiny. Not that he would be a professional basketball player. Rather, that he would be somebody.

"My dad was really into sports and coaching," O'Brien said. "He was really into my career. When you have a parent like that who follows you your whole life, to play in the pros, it's like the culmination of many things. I was far enough in my development that, even if he were living, my game or career probably wouldn't have changed too much. I probably would have made the same choices.

"I was drafted by teams in both the NBA and ABA. So, again, I had a choice to make. For my dad, it was all about choices. I remember that. The difference was so great in what they were offering; it was easy to choose the ABA. It would have been the opportunity for him to share in what I was doing."

O'Brien didn't have much time to settle down in Pittsburgh. In fact, he didn't play a single game for the Condors before he was traded three months later to the Kentucky Colonels. The Colonels would later deal him to San Diego prior to the 1974 season. O'Brien, now an ABA vagabond, was hesitant to make the move to San Diego, partly because the Conquistadors were a team in constant turmoil. It was anyone's guess as to how long it would be before the owner decided to pull the plug, leaving 12 men standing in the unemployment line.

In fact, the league was struggling, as many of its high-profile players had either bolted to the more established NBA or were threatening to make a move that would be damaging to the ABA. The league, of course, was most concerned with the imminent departure of Julius Erving, who, while with the New Jersey Nets, was the league's marquee player.

O'Brien didn't attract any offers from the NBA as he made the trek from Louisville to San Diego. He was more than a serviceable point guard. He was a solid defender, and his outside shot was good enough to keep teams from packing it in the paint. O'Brien was flattered that the Conquistadors felt he was good enough to make an even trade for him during the off-season.

When he arrived in San Diego, O'Brien discovered San Diego to be among the most loosely organized teams in the league. The entire franchise, it seemed, flew by the seat of its pants. The Conquistadors were like daredevil pilots who didn't bother to pack a parachute, even after narrowly escaping one mishap after another. This wasn't quite the way Daly ran things at Boston College. It was a good thing, he figured, that he loaded up on the caffeine to get that marketing degree.

The owners were watching their pocketbooks. The team's coach, the late Wilt Chamberlain, demanded a good portion of whatever slice of the pie he felt the owners were piling up on their plates.

O'Brien was now playing for his third Hall of Famer. He had settled in quickly with Bob Cousy and Daly at Boston College because he understood their temperament; he knew exactly what they wanted. Daly, who would subsequently lead the Detroit Pistons to back-to-back NBA titles in the late 1980s, got O'Brien's attention with his knowledge of the game. Yet, he was in awe of Chamberlain, a 7-foot-2 tower of power whose personality exuded an impeccable confidence that often bordered on arrogance. He could be a gentle giant, but more often than not, Chamberlain had a volatile persona that made him look upon his players with irreverence. Chamberlain was sometimes abrasive and often avoided even casual conversation.

O'Brien understood Chamberlain as well as anyone. He had read more than one of his autobiographies. The Big Dipper, who won two NBA championship rings and holds 55 NBA records, wore a boulder-size chip on his wide shoulders—in part, because his playing career was tainted by talk that he couldn't win the big games. Chamberlain seldom responded to his critics, mostly because he didn't want to be characterized as the big, bad giant. He didn't smoke. He didn't drink. He did nothing to poison his body.

In his first few days with the Conquistadors, O'Brien had to shake himself. He couldn't get over the fact that he was playing basketball for one of the greatest—if not the greatest—big men ever to play the game. The 7-foot-2 Chamberlain didn't just tower over everyone in stature; he had a commanding, sometimes chilling presence about him. He was easily the most dominant figure in the room. He was as an impressive a figure in person as he had been on the family's black-and-white television set back in Brooklyn.

O'Brien imagined himself doing a great many things, but could never have guessed he would be sharing the same sideline with Wilt Chamberlain. The same man who in one season scored an NBA-record 100 points in a game, averaged 30-plus rebounds and 50 points a game while playing with the Philadelphia 76ers. Chamberlain, with Jerry West and Elgin Baylor as teammates, led the Los Angeles Lakers to the 1972 world championship in a season best remembered for the Lakers' winning a record 33 consecutive games.

In 1973, the former University of Kansas All-American joined the Conquistadors, but was prevented from playing because of a contractual dispute. Chamberlain, who was inducted into the Basketball Hall of Fame in 1978, retired in 1974 before San Diego hired him as head coach.

If O'Brien was going to get to compete for playing time, he had to get over his fascination with Chamberlain. It didn't take long. He wasn't in San Diego a week before he realized that he and Chamberlain differed philosophically. They approached the game differently, too. O'Brien is meticulous and, at times, overly analytical. He wanted to break down film, study the opponents' tendencies, and walk through myriad plays, even if the chances were slim that they would be used. Chamberlain, on the other hand, was satisfied with hour-long practice sessions. In fact, he didn't even bother to show up sometimes. For Chamberlain, coaching the Conquistadors was a logistical nightmare. He lived in Los Angeles, which meant he had to commute by plane to make it to practices and games.

Still, O'Brien was impressed. He was impressed with the fact that unlike anyone else in the ABA, he had played for two NBA legends: Chamberlain and Cousy. "How many guys have done that?" he asked rhetorically. "I've been very fortunate."

Admittedly, playing for Chamberlain was both interesting and bizarre. It also was an awakening for O'Brien, who began to realize the many differences—good and bad—between college and professional basketball. It was unlike anything O'Brien had experienced. The small crowds didn't necessarily come to watch the Conquistadors. Chamberlain was the drawing card. He was, in reality, bigger than both the team and the game. Just as he had redefined the center position in the NBA in the 1960s, Chamberlain challenged the concept of the conventional role of coach in the 1970s. He had a keen sense of the game, yet his ambivalence toward the organization pulled at the fragile fibers of a team already stressed by a shroud of uncertainty.

"Wilt at the time was having some money problems with the organization," said O'Brien, whose office bookshelves are lined with sports books, including some chronicling the abbreviated years of the ABA. "He was complaining they hadn't paid him what he was supposed to get. So he wasn't coming to practice every day. He would only show up at the game. It had gotten to the point that on two different occasions he didn't even come to the games. It was his form of protest or bringing the thing to a head.

"I had been in the league for three years, and I think there were only two guys on the team who had more time in the league than I did. One of them was a guy name Stu Johnson, and the other was Flynn Robinson. Flynn's claim to fame was that he got traded for Oscar Robinson. For the last couple of months I was playing with the Conquistadors, Wilt wasn't coming to practice at all. Because he wouldn't come to practice, we had to take charge of what was going on and decide on how we were going to play. We all had some input on things and we made suggestions about what we would do in practice. I remember having as much say as to what we were going to do in practice as a lot of guys."

In essence, having to help prepare the Conquistadors piqued O'Brien's curiosity about coaching. Unlike Chamberlain, the 24-year-old O'Brien could connect with his teammates. It wasn't lost on Chamberlain that someone was taking charge when he wasn't around. He didn't say much to O'Brien, but privately he admired O'Brien's commitment and dedication. In some respects, he admired O'Brien because he was a knowledgeable fourth-year player who had earned the respect of his teammates, most of whom were older and more experienced.

"I was the one trying to get us organized to do this and do that," O'Brien said. "Wilt would meet us at the game, and we would sometimes do something totally different than what he expected. It was so interesting, because we had just a nice group of guys who needed some direction. We ended up not making it to the playoffs, but it wasn't for a lack of effort. These guys played hard, and they did it without Chamberlain doing much to inspire them.

"We had Caldwell Jones; Bo Lamar, who was from Columbus; and Travis Grant. Grant had played at Kentucky State and was the first-round draft pick of the Lakers. Stu Johnson was just a great scorer. Here I was a point guard on that team and ended up fourth in the league in assists. I wasn't doing anything other than throwing them the ball, and those guys would just jack it up, and they could score like crazy."

It was show time every night in the ABA. The game wasn't nearly as structured as the NBA, but the league's legion of followers appreciated its style. The red, white, and blue basketball symbolized the league's freedom of expression, its daring indifference to and defiance of basketball purism. While its longevity was seemingly always in question, it was hardly a fad like, say, the hula hoop or professional volleyball, a sport Chamberlain tried ushering into west coast culture in the mid-1970s.

O'Brien was hip to the league's style, a basketball genre that appealed to the more open-minded fans who shunned the NBA because it lacked any semblance of parity. The outcome of most NBA seasons was like many predictable movies of the week. The plot was simple: The Boston Celtics were conquering heroes, while the Los Angeles Lakers were the team that would be champion—if only they could conquer their nemesis, the Boston Celtics. Its originality and style points aside, the ABA didn't conform to many of O'Brien's rigid standards of basketball. In reality, he was a purist trying to acclimate himself to a fledgling league that was seeking an identity of its own.

"I remember saying this was supposed to be professional basketball, but something is not right here," O'Brien said. "It's not what I had in mind when people were saying this is the pros."

The Conquistadors were haunted by bad attendance. Even in supposedly big games, attendance rarely exceeded 2,000. Leonard Blum, a hands-off owner, knew Chamberlain wasn't happy. He also knew he could turn to assistant coach Stan Albeck to keep things in order, but when Albeck fled for Kent State University, O'Brien was the only veteran player capable of taking charge of the team.

"When Albeck left, we were coachless on a day-to-day basis," O'Brien said. "There was nobody. I had an understanding of what we were doing. I had a sense of what was effective for us and what wasn't effective. I was one of the more experienced guys. Flynn Robinson broke his jaw, and his mouth was wired shut. So he wasn't saying much of anything. All of the other guys were first- or second-year players."

O'Brien's patience with Chamberlain had been tested. He could no longer look upon him as a basketball hero. All O'Brien knew was that the man he had watched exchange elbows and blows with Bill Russell for years, wasn't getting the job done on the bench.

"We all kind of liked Wilt," O'Brien said. "He was definitely aloof. He was somebody none of us really got to know. Actually, I was always in awe of the guy. I remember having the same feeling about him that I had about playing in college for Bob Cousy. It was important that this guy knew I could play. I felt the same way in college. It was important for me to have Wilt look at me, and say, 'Hey, that kid can play a little bit.'

"I think he had a big ego. But more than anything else, he was his own man first and foremost. He was going to do what he was going to do. He was outspoken as to what he wanted to say."

For the most part, Chamberlain said nothing. "I know on one trip I ended up sitting next to him on one of the flights and having some conversation with him," O'Brien remembered. "Well, at least, I was talking.

"The funny thing is, he lived in Los Angeles in this palatial estate," O'Brien said. "It was just bizarre. I remember there was a flight that left Los Angeles, and if our games were at 7:30 at night, his flight would get him into San Diego at 7 p.m. He would go right to the games, and I can't tell you how many times the game was about to start with them throwing the ball up for the opening tip; then Wilt would come walking into the arena.

"It was a circus-like atmosphere, but nobody really cared. He was Wilt and he did what he wanted to do. If there was any delay in the flight, he would have a guy waiting for him at the airport. When the game was over, he gets back on the flight that night and goes back to L.A. He wasn't living in San Diego, and I don't think he ever planned to move."

O'Brien was used to a more structured environment. He could only imagine what his father would have thought of Chamberlain's coaching style or his lack of commitment to the Conquistadors. It was one thing to dispute his pay, but it was another to practically abandon the team. While O'Brien said he and his teammates liked Chamberlain, some didn't respect him as much, especially when he failed to show up for practices and games.

"The guys who played for my father respected him," O'Brien said. "He was fair, but he was never a guy who yelled and screamed. He never coached in high school, just the Police Athletic League teams. Everybody had some nice things to say about him. I was typically one of the better players, so there was never a question about should I be playing when I played for my dad. Sometimes, when you play for your father, there is that gray area. He had a calmness about him and a caring approach.

"I would like to think that I'm that way. Maybe it's ingrained. He coached me at an early age. You learn a lot by just playing on your own. I played in so many different leagues with so many coaches; you take a little from everybody. Whatever my dad suggested, I would do it. When I think about it, I probably learned more from him about baseball than I did basketball. It never, ever got to the point when I didn't want to hear what my father had to say."

As the 1974-75 season neared its end, O'Brien began to wonder about his future. He had enjoyed his time in the ABA. Now, there were other responsibilities since moving from Louisville, Kentucky, to San Diego. His first daughter, Erin, was born. Suddenly, the strange happenings in San Diego could no longer be tolerated.

"It was a struggling franchise," O'Brien said. "I went from a program of instability in Pittsburgh to one of great stability in Kentucky to one of total instability in San Diego. There were many different emotions. But I knew San Diego was having a tough time when I was traded."

O'Brien did not want to leave Louisville. He was happy playing with the Kentucky Colonels, a perennial championship contender. The Colonels were well organized and well coached. They were more structured than most other ABA teams, playing a more conventional brand of basketball, a more acceptable style for a city without much glitz and glitter. This was a conservative basketball town that had had its culture shaped by late Kentucky Wildcats coach Adolph Rupp.

The Colonels were a star-studded collection of former college all-stars —including guards Rick Mount and Louis Dampier and centers Artis Gilmore and Dan Issel. O'Brien was a victim of bad timing. The Colonels won the ABA title months after he was shipped off to San Diego.

"Those were some pretty good players," O'Brien said. "We went to the league championship game in 1973 and lost to the Indiana Pacers. It wasn't as easy for me—considering I was from New York—and Gilmore to settle down in Kentucky. It was a little more difficult for Artis because he was at a different level. He was one of the premier draft picks in the history of the league. The guys who played at Kentucky, it was easier for them because they all had established themselves through the University of Kentucky.

"For me, it was different. No one had any idea who I was. But it was a nice, comfortable deal because the people were warm and they welcomed me. I became one in the community and a part of the franchise. Those guys were a great group of guys to play with, and that made it a lost easier to play there, too. When you are a young guy in particular and you get traded, now you have to make adjustments to a team where guys are already established in their groups. It's like you are an outsider trying to fit in a little bit. I was able to fit in quickly and be comfortable before too long."

Even though the Colonels were among the most financially stable and successful ABA teams, they were not among the teams (New Jersey, Indiana, and Denver) that merged with the NBA when the ABA dissolved in 1976.

"I'm a little surprised that Kentucky didn't have one of the teams that went into the NBA," O'Brien said. "We were getting great crowds. We were averaging 10,000 fans, and that was great in that league. Indiana was one of the other better teams. It's a basketball-crazy town."

If Kentucky was a basketball haven, Pittsburgh was its polar opposite. It was obvious during the franchise's infancy that the Condors would have a tough time thriving in a city where its sports-hungry fans were spending most of their money on the Pittsburgh Steelers and Pittsburgh Pirates. The University of Pittsburgh basketball team had a far larger following. The Condors, it seemed, were destined for failure. The NBA constantly courted some of the Condors' best players—including center Howard Porter.

Porter was an All-American at Villanova who was taken in the first round by both Pittsburgh and the Chicago Bulls of the NBA. The furor over his dual signings only intensified the bidding war between the two leagues. Typically, the NBA franchise offered the better contract, so Porter opted to play in Chicago and never showed up at Pittsburgh's preseason camp. Porter's absence made second-round pick Levi Wyatt of Alcorn A&M the Condors' highest draft pick. The Condors' troubles weren't over, yet. Wyatt, a 6-foot-11 center, developed a rare blood disorder shortly after the draft, and he never made it to Pittsburgh's training camp in the fall of 1971.

Pittsburgh's coach, the late Jack McMahon, and GM Mark Binstein came out of the draft thinking they had collected the final pieces to the puzzle that would make the Condors marketable in a city that had declared its true allegiance to the Steelers and the Pirates. Instead, they were left with O'Brien, a 6-foot-1 guard, who had marginal shooting skills, but terrific court savvy. Even in the ABA, it was difficult to win without big men. There was now a huge hole in the frontcourt, with Porter and Wyatt both gone.

The Condors weren't an intimidating team. But they had at least one player, John Brisker, who made nearly everyone in the locker room shiver. "Brisker had a dominating personality," O'Brien said. "He just put the fear of God into everybody—opponents and teammates. He was just a tough guy. But when we lost Porter and Wyatt, there was no one to mix it up in the paint with him."

McMahon had seen better days. When he coached the Cincinnati Royals in the mid-1960s, he had guard Oscar Robinson and forward Jerry Lucas. He had also coached the Atlanta Hawks, a team that had three all-stars: center Walt Bellamy and guards Pete Maravich and Lou Hudson. McMahon was a well-respected coach, but he had a tough time selling tickets to Condor games, especially with the Pirates beating the Baltimore Orioles in the World Series and the Pittsburgh Steelers finally putting years of mediocrity behind them. The chances weren't good for McMahon taking the Condors to the ABA playoffs—or keeping his job.

"I ended up going into training camp as Pittsburgh's highest draft pick," O'Brien said. "McMahon really liked the way I played. Things really progressed for me as a rookie, and then they fired McMahon. Binstein took over, and his mentality was totally different than McMahon's. He wanted to play with bigger guards."

O'Brien wasn't a true banger, but he would mix it up occasionally. With Binstein essentially redesigning the offense and reshaping the structure of the Condors, it didn't look good for O'Brien. Predictably, with McMahon gone, Binstein swung a deal with Kentucky—a swap that sent O'Brien to the Colonels for forward Goose Ligin.

O'Brien had been in Pittsburgh for only three months, when he had to pack his bags. At 21, he began his long, three-stop journey through the ABA.

"I'm thinking I just turned 21, and now I'm bouncing around. I've got to drive to Louisville. I was so naïve, I couldn't tell you how far south I was. I thought I was in the deep part of the south. Then I realized I was only 90 miles from Ohio. You never think of Cincinnati as being a southern city. I didn't know where the hell I was."

It wasn't long after O'Brien was traded that the Condors folded. He could have easily been out of work.

"I was lucky when I was traded from a team that was dissolving to a team that was maybe the best in the ABA," O'Brien said. "I would have had to figure out where I was going. In two years in Louisville, we won the divisional championship both times. One year we were 60-14. We had just a great year."

O'Brien roomed with Rick Mount, who, while at Purdue, tormented Ohio State in the early 1970s. O'Brien, though, was closest to assistant coach Bud Olson, whose brother Bill was the former athletic director at the University of Louisville.

O'Brien's days in the ABA were much like his days at Boston College. He played for a number of coaches. With the exception of Kentucky, his basketball teams were usually in disarray. He encountered a series of adjustment periods. That, of course, was a result of his having played for numerous coaches in the ABA. If nothing else, O'Brien's ABA experience helped familiarize him with just how quickly things can deteriorate. "You make the adjustments," O'Brien said. "You just move on to the next thing."

In the days after his final game with the San Diego Conquistadors, O'Brien sensed, if only intuitively, that playing basketball would no longer be a means to support his family. The Conquistadors were no longer providing a paycheck, and the rest of the troubled league left him straddling the waiver wire. He waited patiently in hopes that someone would call.

The phone never rang.

5

MOVING ON

Aften four years of playing before mostly sparse crowds in the ABA, Jim O'Brien had to cope with life without basketball. Surely, the winters would become colder after spending the past 12 years running around indoors, wearing a pair of high-cut shorts. When the Conquistadors snatched the red, white, and blue basketball from his hands, O'Brien pulled his college diploma from a drawer and hurriedly pieced together a resume. The real world beckoned, calling upon him to lean on his marketing degree rather than his ballhandling skills.

Still, in the back of his mind, but mostly in his heart, O'Brien was confident he could continue playing this game. He thought about trying to fulfill his longtime dream of playing in the NBA. It wasn't easy walking away from a game that had afforded him so much—a college degree, an opportunity to travel, and the means to mature. It is why he hung around the phone longer than he wanted.

Now, it was time to move on.

"My wife never asked me about getting a real job," O'Brien said. "She would always say, 'All right, we're going wherever.' I had to evaluate my next move when San Diego put me on waivers. Chris and I discussed staying in San Diego. I figured even if I didn't play, it's not bad out here."

O'Brien wouldn't have minded jogging on the pristine beaches of San Diego, greeting the early-morning sun. He remembered how cold it could get in New England, so life on the west coast seemed an enticing option. He had to decide whether this was a good place to raise his kids. He could always find a job in this growing metropolis. The country was going through a mild recession, so the necessity of survival tipped the delicate balance between choosing his pursuit of a basketball career or finding a nine-to-five job that would pay his bills.

"San Diego was too far away from home," O'Brien said. "I was from New York. My wife was from Boston. What were we going to be doing in California? I was always tempted to stay, but I kept telling myself, 'It's too far away from home and we really don't know that many people out here.' That's what made us decide we had to go back. Pack up the truck, and let's go."

The long coast-to-coast drive through America's heartland gave O'Brien plenty of time to contemplate the future. As he cruised through the Midwest, he wondered if going back home was the right choice. Maybe he could have made the most of life in San Diego. It wasn't until he reached the Pennsylvania border that he accepted the inevitable reality—that his professional basketball career was over. Unlike the case of many of today's young basketball players, there were no other alternatives for O'Brien to make any money playing basketball. There was no Continental Basketball Association, and it wasn't hip for Americans to play abroad. Besides, the professional game hadn't caught on in Europe.

The months had passed slowly for O'Brien since returning to Boston. He was making a fair living, but more important, he was paying his bills and feeding his family. He put that marketing degree to use, finding a job selling computer forms. He was a salesman, really. And he was good at it, too. He had the right personality for the job, convincing his clients that they could not make it without his product.

O'Brien kept pushing himself to be the best. This wasn't a game, but his attitude hadn't changed. No matter how high Jim's sales numbers, Christine O'Brien knew her husband would rather be doing something else. He didn't always smile, even when the news was good. Something was missing in his life. He needed to find that something to excite his soul and challenge his innovative mind.

O'Brien needed basketball. It was that plain and simple.

For nearly two years, he was a coat-and-tie, white-collar employee obsessed with quotas and commissions. There had to be a better way of making a living. Would Elvis do opera when rock 'n' roll was his bag? Would Galileo waste his time looking for fossil remains when he could search the stars? So why was O'Brien carrying a briefcase when a basketball was what he wanted most in his hands?

In 1977, O'Brien found himself back in the game. This time, he was on the sideline, only he was wearing dress shoes and a sports coat. Instead of a ball, he was carrying a clipboard. He could no longer force the action. He could only watch, hoping the Connecticut Huskies would execute perfectly a game plan devised by head coach Dom Perno, who hired O'Brien as an assistant coach.

O'Brien had played the role of coach with San Diego when Wilt Chamberlain could not find the arena. However, he had never officially coached anywhere—not a grade school team, a high school team or for the YMCA.

Perno, though, was impressed with O'Brien's knowledge of the game. He figured O'Brien possessed the intensity and ambition to work the long hours needed to make Connecticut a perennial NCAA Tournament contender. In O'Brien's five years in Storrs, the Huskies made three tournament appearances.

Perno was tutoring O'Brien, teaching him everything he needed to know about coaching college basketball. After his third season at Connecticut, O'Brien had thrust himself into the spotlight. Perno's young and energetic assistant was being courted by other colleges in the East, particularly smaller Division I schools. O'Brien had too much fire in his gut, and his ambitions were too great, to remain an assistant coach.

O'Brien, confident and self-assured, knew he would soon be moving up the coaching ladder, but he enjoyed Storrs. The only thing greater than his ambition was his loyalty.

"I truly admired Dom Perno," O'Brien said. "He believed in me and he trusted that I would get the job done. When I was selling computers, I needed someone to give me a chance. I didn't think a whole lot about coaching, but I kind of knew in my mind that's what I wanted to do, eventually. I think maybe I had prepared myself to do this when I was playing in the ABA."

As spring neared in 1982, O'Brien was merely an interested observer as North Carolina practically stole the national championship from top-ranked Georgetown when Tar Heels forward James Worthy stole an errant pass in the waning seconds to preserve North Carolina's victory. The euphoria surrounding the North Carolina–Georgetown final was an awe-inspiring experience for O'Brien. This is where he envisioned himself, if he was fortunate enough to get a head-coaching job. Even during his playing days at Boston College, O'Brien could always picture himself playing in the Final Four. After four years in the ABA and five years as an assistant at Connecticut, O'Brien was beginning to believe that dreams do come true.

It wasn't his dream come true, but it was good enough. O'Brien was offered the head-coaching job at St. Bonaventure, where he replaced long-time coach Jim Satalin. After 13 years at St. Bonaventure—four as a player and nine as head coach—Satalin had become a beloved and well-respected figure on campus.

The Bonnies weren't on a par with the likes of North Carolina and Kentucky, but this small Division I college with an enrollment of 2,500 had put itself in the spotlight in 1970 when Hall of Fame center Bob Lanier led it to the Final Four in 1970. With the changing landscape of college basketball, this wasn't going to be an easy task for O'Brien. The Bonnies were no longer attracting the likes of Lanier. With the Big East blossoming, any success in recruiting blue-chippers to make this upstate New York town their home for four years would require O'Brien to exercise his splendid salesmanship.

O'Brien inherited a good but unspectacular basketball team. The Bonnies went 20-10 in his first season, which included a trip to the NIT. The Bonnies then went 18-13 during the 1983-84 season. It was hardly a satisfying campaign for O'Brien. His expectations were greater. O'Brien may not have looked at it that way, but there was an understated self-assurance about what he was attempting to achieve at St. Bonaventure. He didn't yell and scream at the Bonnies, so some fans concluded he was too laid back for the job. But they never realized how his stomach churned during the games. The St. Bonaventure fans had always wanted more since the 1970 Final Four. The Bonnies gave them 28-consecutive winning seasons, and O'Brien piqued their enthusiasm with promises that his teams would put forth their best effort. That, of course, didn't always translate into victories.

St. Bonaventure, some figured, was just another training ground for O'Brien, a place where he could hone and polish his coaching skills. As the Bonnies struggled through a 14-15 season, which was their first losing campaign since O'Brien was a first grader in South Brooklyn, O'Brien ignored the criticism. "The losing made me work harder," O'Brien said. "We were always confident that as a coaching staff, we could take the St. Bonaventure program to the next level."

Despite his charisma and people skills, O'Brien wasn't always considered a perfect fit at St. Bonaventure. It hardly mattered that he was a native New Yorker; the fact remained that for some he was an outsider. The square peg certainly wasn't going to fit in with the St. Bonaventure circle of supporters, particularly now that a streak of 28 winning seasons had been snapped. O'Brien, though, was determined to make it right. However, the mountain he was climbing was steeper than he imagined.

O'Brien's critics couldn't dampen his enthusiasm. He was as competitive on the sidelines as he was when he played at Boston College and in the ABA. He didn't like losing. For the most part, he controlled his temper. But he didn't always hold his tongue. In 1983, when Iona was awarded a home NIT game over the more-deserving Bonnies—partly because the selection committee figured Iona would attract a larger crowd—O'Brien protested vehemently before conceding the committee may have had a valid point.

O'Brien enjoyed life in St. Bonaventure. He played summer league softball and also tennis when his recruiting schedule would permit. He would go to the gym before practices to play pickup games with his assistant coaches. O'Brien wanted to be as physically and mentally sharp as his players for the 1985-86 season. The Bonnies, in O'Brien's fourth season, overcame a slow start to complete a comeback season that saw them compile a 15-13 record.

The school's administrators new, clearly more than the Bonnies' fans, that O'Brien was coaching over his head at St. Bonaventure. He was winning games without highly touted recruits and he was doing it in a league that was losing the recruiting battles on every front against the increasingly powerful Big East Conference.

With March Madness reaching its climax in 1986, O'Brien sat inside his St. Bonaventure office thumbing through piles of paperwork. After a long basketball season, he had time to tidy things up because his St. Bonaventure Bonnies weren't extended an invitation to participate in either the 1986 NCAA or the NIT postseason tournament. It was the third year in a row the Bonnies had failed to get a tournament bid. The frustrations, O'Brien said, began to mount.

For an instant, O'Brien pondered his future at St. Bonaventure, a program that was among the best during his playing days at Boston College during the late 1960s. He had accomplished as much as anyone could at a school that no longer attracted the high school blue-chippers. With the advent of the Big East, which a year earlier had accounted for three-fourths of the Final Four, O'Brien was often left to recruit prep players who weren't recruited by familiar Eastern powers such as Georgetown and Syracuse.

O'Brien, though, enjoyed the challenge. Nothing satisfied him more than his Bonnies beating a tournament-bound team. Only in his first season at St. Bonaventure did the Bonnies advance to the postseason, getting an NIT bid after finishing the regular season with a 19-12 record. O'Brien had a good feeling about the program's future. He was beginning to work his recruiting magic, luring some talented high school players to St. Bonaventure in hopes of competing for the Atlantic 10 championship. At the same time, however, O'Brien's stock was on the rise, as his name kept appearing on the short list of athletic directors across the country.

O'Brien had proved he could coach under adverse conditions and that the disappointments of one season could not discourage him from dreaming of better days. He had also proven himself a master strategist, winning games with marginal talent. All the lessons learned from Perno were paying dividends. Now, O'Brien, like many other up-and-coming young coaches, was ready to make the jump to an even more competitive coaching environment.

After his last season as an assistant at UConn in 1982, Boston College's athletic director, the late Bill Flynn, contacted O'Brien and suggested he interview for the head-coaching job at his alma mater when and if Tom Davis stepped aside. Tom Davis left for Stanford after the 1981-82 season. O'Brien had just taken the job at St. Bonaventure, so he did not interview for the Boston College job. Instead, Gary Williams was offered the job at Boston College. Then, four years later, Flynn again called O'Brien to offer him an opportunity to interview for the Boston College job that was vacated by Williams, who accepted an offer from Ohio State, which had fired oft-maligned coach Eldon Miller after the 1986-87 season. In reality, Flynn never seriously looked elsewhere, O'Brien said. There were other coaches, some more highly visible than O'Brien, who were being considered as possible replacements for Williams. In reality, the search committee didn't look far beyond St. Bonaventure, New York.

Admittedly, a joyous O'Brien leaped at the chance to return to Chestnut Hill. He said he wanted to play it cool on the phone with Flynn while discussing the possibilities of coaching the Eagles. Inside, he was bubbling with unbridled enthusiasm. O'Brien and Flynn went through the formalities, but the two practically cemented a deal before hanging up the phone.

Again, the O'Briens packed their kids, Amy and Erin, in the car, and headed back home—back to Chestnut Hill, where the O'Briens first met, back where they began a long, winding journey that included stops in Pittsburgh, Louisville, and San Diego.

Finally, the O'Briens were living the life they had always imagined. They were back at their alma mater. It's where they belonged. They were happy together. Chestnut Hill was their Camelot.

O'Brien's assistant coaches—Paul Biancardi, Rick Boyages, and Dave Spiller—decided to beat the bushes in the east to find student-athletes who could help make Boston College competitive. They knew it wouldn't be easy. They were aware that their hands were tied some by the school's tough admissions guidelines.

"When you fight it out and stumble your way through, it takes awhile to get it going," O'Brien said. "Our first couple of years were very difficult. Then, we got some good classes of recruits and it got to the point we were good. So we accepted that. We would play our way through it."

The Eagles finished the 1986-87 season with an 11-18 record. Boston College followed with an 18-15 record, and earned the right to participate in the National Invitation Tournament in 1988. Then, three consecutive losing seasons followed before the Eagles strung together back-to-back NIT appearances in 1992 and 1993.

"It was remarkable what Jim had done," Biancardi said. "He kept working and working. He never stopped trying to make Boston College a power. He didn't stop even though his wife was sick. His loyalties were with his family, but he didn't want to feel as if he was abandoning the kids at Boston College."

"I felt we could get it done at Boston College," O'Brien said. "I had to prove it to myself, but it was just going to take awhile. It's not the kind of program that could be turned around with any instant quick fixes. It's hard to take junior college kids, and there were no Prop 48 kids or any of that at Boston College. It was always the next group of young, immature freshmen that you had to go through. Once we got it going and turned the corner, we felt we were going to be one of the better teams in the conference for a long time. We felt we had the formula and credibility. We could sense the thing was about to take off."

O'Brien's focus, he admitted, was on recruiting. In essence, the recruiting became therapy as he dealt with the grief brought on by the loss of his wife. In the process, he discovered that he wasn't nearly as thick-skinned as he thought. He was appalled to think that some Boston College supporters thought he wasn't emotionally or mentally stable enough to keep working at rejuvenating his alma mater's struggling program. The disgruntled factions among the Boston College crowd could have waited until the summer to question his mental capacity. "I felt as if I didn't get the respect I deserved," said O'Brien, somewhat shaken. "I felt underappreciated [by some Boston College administrators] until the very end, mostly because there was a barrier between us. It was something that was going to be hard to overcome. It was a real awkward time."

O'Brien, said his assistant coaches, possesses a secretive personality. If he was hurt by the attacks, it was barely visible. "Jimmy is a guy who keeps a lot inside," said Randy Shrout, the Buckeyes' director of basketball operations. "He's trying to keep it quiet."

O'Brien was trying to move on.

When it appeared that O'Brien might be down in the dumps, his circle of reliable friends, mostly his assistant coaches, were there to lift his spirits. In fact, he said, his assistant coaches were big reasons why he never walked away from his job at Boston College. They had become a team. They were willing to stick it out through the hard times, so he had to buckle down. This was their job, too.

O'Brien's assistants had been with him for 10 years. Other schools had approached them all, hoping they had learned as O'Brien had learned under his mentor, Dom Perno. Admittedly, O'Brien leaned on his friends. It would be hard to watch them go.

"If I had my druthers, the best-case scenario for me is that these guys stay with me forever," O'Brien said. "I would like nothing more. They have been so loyal to me. So what I have to do is try like crazy to help them get the jobs they want, but that are good career moves for them. We've had a couple of guys that had other opportunities, but I discouraged them because I felt they could do better. I thought those schools might be dead-end jobs. It's part of my responsibility to get them prepared for the eventuality that they are going to coach their own teams. It's going to happen because all these guys are very good at what they do. I would deal with that with very mixed emotions.

"They know about the ups and downs of this business. I consider these guys to be my best friends. They are like brothers. They were with me through my wife's death. They've heard it all. They've seen it all. They've been at the bottom when we came in last in the Big East. They've been at the top when we won the Big East championship. We have shared many different emotions. I've been through the births of their children. We've gone through a load of things through the years. I'm very fortunate these guys have been with me. I have so much respect for them.

"I think you have to take each guy and break down his strengths and know what they are capable of doing. Early in my career, there were some guys I had to make sure they were doing the things they had to get done. They liked the fact that there is no time clock to be punched, no restrictions. I don't hold them back. I don't look over their shoulders. All I ask of them is to do what I expect of them and in their way. They're in the office a lot, and if they don't show up for a couple of days, that's fine, too. I give them a lot of freedom and space because that's how they function. I know in some situations guys have to be in the office all the time. I know they will get the job done."

For O'Brien, it has always been about loyalty. For his assistant coaches, loyalty has become a two-way street. Yet, as O'Brien began to build Boston College into a national contender, his assistants were torn between the loyalty toward their head coach and their own personal aspirations to be head coaches.

"It would be difficult for me in a personal sense to leave Jim," Biancardi said. "I've tried to think of myself of being a head coach, and not be able to lean on him as a coach as I do so often. It would be strange. When you're with someone for so long, and you've been through the high of the highs and the low of the lows on a personal level, it could be strange not to be working with him on a day-to-day basis. I've learned most of all how to handle the downs because we've experienced it together.

"He never lost his head during the downs. He never took it out on anybody on his staff. He never blamed anybody. He never went off the deep end. With those downs in his professional life, he had a tragedy in his life at the same time. He kept things in perspective and he was mentally tough. He trusted the people who were with him and he could trust our loyalty to him. He trusted us, and it has all parlayed into success.

"In the ups, he keeps a low profile," Biancardi added. "He never lets it get to him in terms of him always in the spotlight. In this profession, it's very easy to get a big ego. There are a number of coaches with tremendous egos. The way he handles it is, he is the exact, same person when times are bad and when times are good, in terms of how he treats people. I've been with him enough to know he just takes the time to be nice to people. It showed me a lot, because I've seen success change people."

O'Brien's success has indeed been tempered by a series of ups and downs. His playing and coaching careers have endured three tragedies—the loss of his mother, his father, and his wife. While his friends marvel at his ability to coach amid adversity, O'Brien carried on, said Spiller, "because he had to if the program was going to thrive—and if he and his daughters were going to make it."

"There's nothing extraordinary about what I do," said O'Brien, who usually comes to work these days in a pair of casual slacks and a short-sleeve Ohio State shirt. "I try to be myself, and hopefully that works. If it works for some, they will be with you. If it doesn't work for others, they won't be with you. If it doesn't work in recruiting, then those guys won't come with you. But if you try to be somebody that you're not, there's always going to be some flaws in what you're trying to do.

"I'm just another guy who has been fortunate and now has a high-profile job. The things I say to my players—and I believe this—the highest compliment someone can give a player is to say, 'That guy was a good team-mate.' And if someone can say I was a good teammate, it would be a good thing. That would be a nice thing. It's important to be a good teammate."

O'Brien considers his assistant coaches his teammates. They are the ones, like his old Boston College teammates, with whom he shares his inner-most thoughts. When he is seeking peace of mind, O'Brien wanders out to a golf course. Basketball remains his passion, but golf is what lights his competitive fire. Even on the links, with several mulligans at his disposal, O'Brien would rather play it straight—by the book.

Even as he was clinging precariously to his job at Boston College, he eluded the turmoil by swinging his clubs whenever he could get a tee time. With the unrelenting pressures to win in the Big East, his golf game suffered some while he jetted around the country or drove around the New England area in search of the best high school basketball recruits who would help the Eagles shake their losing ways.

"I love to play golf," O'Brien said. "I would play every day if I could. It's not just about the sport; it's about whom you play with, too. I've played on some of the nicest courses, but just being with good guys and being some-where where no one can get to you is satisfying. The game allows me to escape from what I'm doing and appreciate the beauty of where you are, but all the time you're trying to beat the game and shoot par. We never do that, but you like to hit good shots. It's like being comfortable with whom you're playing with. It's therapy for me. I've never thrown a club. I'm never going to throw a club. I'm never going to get that pissed.

"I laugh because I'm always telling my kids you can't get any better if you don't practice. And here I am, I never practice my golf game. I don't ever work on putting or getting out of sand traps. I never took a lesson. I don't have the time. I want to just enjoy it. Why do I think I'm going to get a whole lot better?"

O'Brien once had a respectable 11 handicap while he was at Boston College. But since leaving Chestnut Hill for Columbus, he has slipped to a

13 handicap. A few weeks after accepting the job with the Buckeyes, O'Brien and Ohio State's athletics director Andy Geiger, were out at Muirfield Country Club in Dublin, Ohio, which is the site of The Memorial Tournament. He had an up-and-down round of 88 one day, and then followed with a round of 89. "That place just tears me up," he said. "I shoot well on the front, and I say I've got it going on. Then, I turn around and shoot 48 on the back. The next day I'm 47 on the front. I'm struggling through it. But the next thing I know I'm shooting 41 on the back. I always have holes I have major blowups on."

For O'Brien, life has sometimes been like his golf game. There have been a series of good swings and bad swings during a career that has a pendulum-like swing of emotional ups and downs. Yet, he has never asked for a mulligan.

"Just tee it up, and let's go," O'Brien said. "Let's move on."

6

NOT EXACTLY A TEA PARTY

The Ups and Downs at Boston College

On the golf course, Jim O'Brien will take a few chances when surrounded by trees. He might take the ball over an 80-foot maple or draw it around a row of towering pines. In the tug of war that is college recruiting, O'Brien took few risks at Boston College. Typically, he was conservative in his approach, looking for players who would fit perfectly with his team and in Boston College's classrooms. While praised for his recruiting successes, the Eagles—save for a few exceptional seasons—were always looking up at the Big East heavyweights.

For the better part of his 10 previous years at his alma mater, O'Brien had few run-ins with the school's chief administrators. There were some restrictions, but he was never criticized for the type of student-athletes he recruited. Yet O'Brien and his staff were forced to accept the changing dynamics of college basketball. They had to adapt accordingly if they were to contend with their Big East rivals in trying to sign impact players who would make Boston College a perennial conference contender.

"There's a sense of satisfaction when you take guys who weren't as highly recruited, then take them to win some games," O'Brien said. "There's a lot more involved than coaching the best players in the league. Howard Eisley averaged only nine points a game in high school. Who was recruiting him? I challenge anybody to think about how many teams in the Big Ten or

Big East or the SEC or ACC have recruited somebody who didn't score double figures his senior year in high school. I don't think very many. He wasn't great, but I liked him. I liked his demeanor and his game."

"I remember Voshon Leonard [Minnesota] and Jalen Rose [Michigan] got most everyone's attention at an AAU tournament we scouted," said O'Brien, whose desk has a neatly stacked pile of recruiting files of potential Ohio State recruits. "Those guys were juniors on the same team. There were only so many points to be scored. Maybe, one of them could have been good for us. Now, they might be in the NBA for 12 years. Everybody thought Danya Abrams was too fat. He played football in high school. We got in on him early, and he turned out to be a great player for us."

In the fall of 1996, O'Brien went shopping for the kind of players who could exchange blows evenly with the likes of Connecticut, Syracuse, Georgetown, and St. John's. With point guard Scoonie Penn already on the roster, O'Brien sought to surround his star player with an array of young talent—players who possessed immeasurable athleticism.

The recruiting wars were fought on all fronts. O'Brien scoured high schools from rural Massachusetts to the urban boroughs in New York City in search of talent. No matter where he traveled, he would likely cross paths with Connecticut's Jim Calhoun or Syracuse's Jim Boeheim. Indeed, the competition to lure the best basketball players to Chestnut Hill had intensified.

"We had six terrific kids committed to us," O'Brien said. "Four of them were going into their senior years [in high school]. Two were juniors. Out of the six, none of them made a visit to any other school. We really had our recruiting going.

"There's no question in my mind there was a real chance to get those kids to the Final Four. They were some of the best recruits we ever had at Boston College. We would have had a very good team. It was the best opportunity for me to take my alma mater to a championship game."

The six-member recruiting class included two highly recruited high school juniors—6-10 forward Elton Tyler and 6-1 guard Jonathan DePina. The others were 7-foot center Adam Allenspach, 6-10 power forward Michael Bradley, 6-5 guard Sean Connolly, and 6-5 guard Billy Collins.

"[O'Brien] had it all lined up in 1996," said *Boston Globe* columnist Bob Ryan. "He had a great recruiting class. They would have been in that reloading position. It would have been a Syracuse-like situation. It took him 10 years to get to that point. He did it at a school that does not remotely understand what basketball is all about. He was about to cash in. It was all going to be idealistic. He was going to get to the Final Four, and prove what he can do—as if we needed to know."

However, O'Brien's dream of taking his alma mater to its first Final Four, began to fade amid a controversial admissions debacle that the Globe dubbed the "Great Admissions Caper."

While the admissions office began to take a long look at O'Brien's six recruits, the Eagles brushed aside the distraction. They soared above the infighting, staging an unexpected challenge for the Big East championship. There were, however, bumps in the road. The season began with Abrams suffering an orbital fractures. In addition, Penn missed five games for academic reasons, and Abrams was suspended one game for fighting. Ironically, O'Brien did perhaps his best coaching job at Boston College that stormy yet satisfying season. He patched up all the broken pieces, practically squeezing blood out of a turnip.

The Eagles won the 1997 Big East Tournament, beating Georgetown and Villanova at Madison Square Garden in New York. They finished with a surprising 22-9 record and earned an NCAA Tournament bid for the third time in four years.

It was a time to rejoice. It was a time to celebrate.

With a Big East title secured, it seemed inevitable that Boston College's immensely popular basketball coach would soon be rewarded with a lucrative contract that would keep him in Chestnut Hill. It was a move, some thought, that would defuse rumors that he might go elsewhere.

Whenever firings or resignations created vacancies at other schools, O'Brien was routinely mentioned as a possible candidate. O'Brien, though, rarely discussed changing his address. He could have taken any number of coaching jobs, but none were as attractive as the job he had at Chestnut Hill. O'Brien and the Boston College administrators seldom had their contract negotiations bogged down by a failure to reach an amicable financial settlement. It didn't take much to persuade O'Brien to stay put at his alma mater. This was, after all, the job he coveted above all others. Furthermore, he was inspired to pursue a national championship at Boston College after his team's Herculean effort during the 1996-97 season.

"I will never forget how the kids hung in there with all the controversies they had to deal with in my final year," O'Brien said. "To come back from all of that and win the [Big East] tournament, I can't say enough how the kids handled themselves through all of it. We felt good about our future at Boston College.

Then, unexpectedly, O'Brien's future at Boston College became somewhat cloudy when the admissions office decided to reject two of Boston College's blue-chip recruits—Elton Tyler and Jonathan DePina—despite the fact that both had been approved by the NCAA Clearinghouse, which determines the eligibility of incoming first-year players. Those rejections created a backlash that would cause irreparable differences between O'Brien and Boston College's administrators, particularly those in the admissions office.

"They [Tyler and DePina] were NCAA qualifiers and two really good kids from Boston," O'Brien said. "When they were rejected, there were all kinds of controversy. Then, we figured the other four kids might decide they weren't coming to Boston College, either.

"When it got to the point where we were rejecting qualifiers, that's when I thought this was going to be next to impossible. It was one thing not to take partial qualifiers, but once we began to reject kids who qualified by NCAA standards, it was an academic posture that was very difficult to deal with."

O'Brien and his assistants were furious. Even more troublesome for the coaching staff was that the so-called Great Admissions Caper would create fear and doubt among other possible recruits. They were right. It wasn't long before prized recruit Michael Bradley, the 6-10 center from Worcester Burncoat High School, withdrew his letter of intent. Bradley rescinded in protest, then signed with Kentucky.

Suddenly, O'Brien was left without one of the six prep stars he recruited. It was a recruiting class that was considered by many to be among the best in the nation – even better than Big East rivals Syracuse, Villanova, and St. John's. It was O'Brien's best recruiting class in his 15 years as a head coach.

"Michael Bradley committed to Boston College as a 15-year-old sophomore," O'Brien said. "We made a commitment to him and his family real early. They thought it was a great opportunity, and he committed to us. Then, at the end of his junior year, it all fell apart at Boston College."

The once-promising recruiting class disintegrated soon after the Eagles' improbable Big East title chase.

Adam Allenspach, a 7-foot center from Parkland, Florida, hadn't yet submitted a signed letter of intent. Despite O'Brien's assurances that the admissions problem would go away, Allenspach didn't want any part of the controversy. He withdrew his verbal agreement and decided to visit Notre Dame, then later accepted a scholarship offer from Clemson, where he averaged 11.6 points and 7.2 rebounds per game as a role player during his junior season.

Bradley, though playing sparingly, helped Kentucky win the national championship in 1998. He later transferred to Villanova following the 1998-99 season after considering a move to Ohio State. Bradley realized his potential during the 2000-01 season, earning All-Big East first team honors.

Tyler helped lead Miami into the Sweet 16 in 1999. Then he came back to haunt O'Brien when the Hurricanes ousted Ohio State from the 2000 NCAA Tournament. Tyler scored 20 points on 7-for-13 shooting and grabbed nine rebounds in leading Miami to a surprisingly easy 75-62 victory. "There was so much irony and emotion in watching Elton Tyler play so well against us," O'Brien said. "We had no answer for him. He played the way we thought he would when we recruited him at Boston College."

DePina, a 6-1 guard from Boston stayed closer to home. He enrolled at the University of Massachusetts. He averaged 3.4 points and 2.4 assists per game as a backup.

Sean Connolly, a 6-5 forward from Boston, chose to play in the Big East at Providence. He became an all-conference player for the Friars, then transferred to Ohio State prior to the 1999-2000 season. In his first game as a Buckeye, Connolly scored 18 points off the bench in Ohio State's 2000-01 season opener against Yale.

Billy Collins, a 6-5 guard who was Mr. Basketball in New Hampshire, enrolled at Rutgers before transferring to Boston University, where he was selected as a team captain before playing his first game of the 2000-01 season.

O'Brien felt that some student-athletes should have the opportunity to enroll at the university, even though their entrance tests and grade-point averages were slightly below the prerequisite minimum allowed at Boston College. The college experience, he said, was sometimes as valuable as the classroom lessons.

Moreover, said assistant coach Dave Spiller, "Coach O'Brien has always believed that young men deserve a second chance to prove themselves both on and off the basketball court, but mostly in the classroom."

O'Brien figured Tyler and DePina could handle the academic load. He had hoped that Boston College's admissions office would trust his instincts. "I was basically looking for kids who I thought could do the work," O'Brien said. "It wasn't as if I was trying to get anybody just because they were good basketball players who were incapable of succeeding academically. What I was looking for from the university was a little bit of flexibility. With my track record, combined with the academic support offered by the university, these kids could do the academic work.

"There were some hard feelings. Some of the things said to me to explain why our recruits weren't admitted, I didn't like it at all. I challenged them on it. It became a real driving force between Boston College and me. We had a first-year president [the Rev. William P. Leahy] who clearly sided with the academic side. It wasn't as if I wanted something abnormal, something that would not fit into the mission of Boston College. They did not want to hear it."

O'Brien, who had all 30 of his previous recruits graduate from Boston College, wanted to keep in step with the constantly changing college basketball environment—one that influenced some major basketball powers with selective admissions reputations to counter the migration of freshmen and sophomores to the NBA. Boston College was losing some of the recruiting wars, and the number of prospective blue-chip recruits diminished as high school *Parade* All-Americans such as Kobe Bryant (Los Angeles Lakers) and Kevin Garnett (Minnesota Timberwolves) were bypassing college life for the high life that is the NBA.

"I see a school [Boston College] that has Notre Dame envy," said the *Globe's* Bob Ryan. "It has Harvard envy. It thinks it can have a Notre Dame-level football program and a Harvard-level academic program, and win in the Big East conference.

"You don't ask a coach to beat Syracuse, Georgetown and Connecticut, then don't give him the resources to do it. Until they learn that lesson, no coach will be successful for any length of time. O'Brien got caught in the middle of that."

In reality, O'Brien was trying to establish a major-college basketball power in a college community that is absorbed itself in college hockey. Chestnut Hill is the end-of-the-destination job for hockey coach Jerry York, who in 1994 led Mid-American Conference power Bowling Green to the national championship.

"It's a hockey culture," Ryan said. "If the Celtics had been anything less than the greatest team in the world, they probably would have gone out of business in the 1960s. The people here couldn't grasp that there were infinitely more people who care if Boston College goes to the NCAA regional tournament in basketball than the Frozen Four in hockey."

The way O'Brien figured, the least Boston College's administrators could have done was to compromise. After all, he felt his track record (a 100 percent graduation rate) should have been given some serious consideration. "I was looking for the university to have some confidence in what I was doing," he said.

Still, it seemed that O'Brien and Father Leahy were ready to agree on a compromise shortly after the 1996-97 campaign. They were to meet at Father Leahy's office with the hope of resolving the most difficult problem that had faced O'Brien during his 11-year tenure at Boston College.

The drive up Beacon Street was never this long for O'Brien. It kept winding around a seemingly endless row of ivy-covered brick buildings that lined the picturesque landscape of Chestnut Hill. As O'Brien passed by the Conte Forum on a blisteringly cold winter morning in March, he took a long, sentimental look at an arena in which his Boston College teams had enjoyed some of their finest moments.

"I love the school," O'Brien said. "I love the city. I enjoyed some of the best times of my life there. I couldn't imagine leaving."

When the *Globe* reported that Father Leahy and O'Brien had tentatively agreed to a provision that would allow O'Brien more leeway in recruiting NCAA qualifiers, the contract talks broke down almost immediately. Father Leahy put the extension on hold because he questioned O'Brien's loyalty to the university.

"I couldn't deal with them if they didn't feel I was trustworthy," O'Brien said. "I needed time to think about the extension myself."

That, said O'Brien, is when he began to look elsewhere. This was bad news for the Eagles. It was difficult for them to comprehend the scene that was playing out before them. They couldn't believe that O'Brien was considered leaving Chestnut Hill—that he would walk away from his dream job.

As O'Brien pulled into the parking lot adjacent to the school's administrative building that March morning in 1997, he began to reflect on some of his most cherished moments at Boston College. He could sense, if only intuitively, that in his team's moment of triumph, there would be a dose of reality to swallow. This is big-time, big-money college basketball; it is a sport with thin, yet distinctive lines drawn between loyalty, friendship, and business. It is hard for all three to coexist in the current atmosphere of college athletics.

The differences between O'Brien and Leahy were soon to be exposed publicly by the New England media like a poorly rehearsed melodrama. Almost everyone stumbled over his or her lines in an effort to shield the impending bad press. However, the *Boston Globe* and the *Boston Herald* had already processed the leaks, publishing the facts of the feud between O'Brien and Boston College's administrators. There was supposed to have been a veil of secrecy among the antagonists.

"I made mistakes in believing that certain information given by me in confidence to associates would be kept confidential," O'Brien said. "This is not the same thing as feeding information to the press with the intent to damage Boston College. Why would I want to damage Boston College? I was their coach and had every intention of staying indefinitely."

In May 1997, O'Brien reached a financial settlement in a suit he filed against the university in an effort to receive money he felt was owed to him. At that time, Father Leahy acknowledged publicly that O'Brien hadn't been disloyal.

Some within the Boston media covering Boston College steadfastly denied that O'Brien had fed them confidential information.

Globe writer Mark Blaudschun wrote: "Jim O'Brien was honest and open in his dealings with the media. If you asked O'Brien a question, he answered it. If something negative happened, he was available. And no, a thousand times no, he never orchestrated any of this. Never once did O'Brien initiate a call saying, 'You wouldn't believe what's going on.' Never once did he volunteer damaging information. Most of the time, his response would be, 'How'd you hear about that?' And if it were true, he had the integrity to admit it. If it weren't, he would tell you so. And that's it. No hidden agenda.

"If his name weren't mentioned in any other context than comments about how his basketball team performed, O'Brien would have been just as happy. But that's not the way it worked out. Stuff happened, and people found out about it and reported it, and Jim O'Brien got blamed."

Father Leahy was pointing an accusing finger at a coach who had pumped life back into a basketball program that had finished among the top 20 teams in the country only once (a No. 11 ranking in the Associated Press poll in 1983) since O'Brien's junior season in 1970. O'Brien rebuilt the Boston College program by masterfully recruiting some unheralded high school players who were often overlooked by rival Big East schools. The Eagles finished 11th in the final USA Today/CNN poll in 1994 and were 23rd in the AP poll in 1997.

O'Brien was only two games over the break-even mark at Boston College, having compiled a 168-166 record. Boston College had endured a stretch where it lost 32 of 33 conference games under O'Brien. Generally, however, his teams were overachievers.

In 1994, O'Brien guided the underdog Eagles to an improbable victory over No. 1 North Carolina in the second round of the NCAA Tournament in Landover, Maryland. The Eagles had already defeated Washington State in their first-round game and then ousted Indiana in the third round in Miami, Florida, to advance to the Elite Eight. The Eagles came within a victory of playing in the Final Four for the first time. They lost to Florida in the East Regional championship game in Miami.

Yet, despite all of his success, O'Brien remained a relative unknown among college coaches. It never appeared to bother him. He wanted everyone to notice his teams, the quality of men who represented the university, and how the Eagles competed when they were decisive underdogs. He wanted to win. He wanted to do his job. He wanted to be loyal to the university. He wanted loyalty in return.

"After all O'Brien did for that school—and for them to think [he was being disloyal]—tells you how sick and perverted the situation had gotten," said the *Globe*'s Bob Ryan. "He wanted to be here. He liked the school. He didn't have any great ambitions about going to some other major place and he didn't want to go into the pros."

At the time, O'Brien wasn't particularly interested in coaching in the NBA. He shied away from network television. There is big money in television for college coaches who are either exhausted by the pressures of recruiting or stressed from chasing gold at the end of a Final Four rainbow or unable to secure the jobs of their dreams—coaches like O'Brien. He still enjoyed teaching basketball to unpolished athletes—even those highly touted high school All-Americans, some of whom are convinced they already know everything about the game. He couldn't rid himself of his insatiable appetite for victory or his thirst to compete for a national championship.

For O'Brien, a cheap shot to the gut would have been easier to absorb than a stab in the back. He believes loyalty is the essence of one's character. He professes it to his players, demanding nothing less. To him, it is what transforms a collection of strangers into friends who, despite varying ideologies, share similar aspirations.

Blaudschun wrote that O'Brien's departure from Boston College wouldn't have happened if school officials had decided to make public what the media would eventually discover: "The sad part about all this was that it was completely avoidable. Jim O'Brien could have met with Father Leahy to discuss a contract extension and the school could have put out a three-paragraph statement acknowledging the meeting, adding innocuous quotes from Father Leahy and O'Brien, and no one would have paid much attention. It wouldn't have been a story, or much of one. O'Brien could have signed his five-year extension and life would have moved on. But it didn't work out that way."

O'Brien was left rocking on his heels. All he could do was deny the rumors and allegations that he had betrayed someone's trust.

O'Brien, Father Leahy reasoned, had aired Boston College's problems despite the two having agreed, in principle, to honor a secrecy pledge. When the *Globe* published a story detailing the discussions between O'Brien and Leahy, that, in effect, ended the relationship between O'Brien and Boston College.

O'Brien began to feel like a fighter with his back against the ropes. He doubted if he had one last burst of energy to counter his critics' flurry of verbal blows.

"After a while it was an uphill struggle," O'Brien said. "Sometimes, we asked ourselves 'Why are we doing this?' But the nature is, you have to fight your way out of it. There were some very low points. It never gets to the point where you say I'm going to walk away. It's a case of moving on and doing the right things.

"If you found yourself in and out of the NCAA Tournament [at Boston College], you would have been having a pretty good season. In that regard, we could keep working to achieve that goal."

O'Brien's goal was to win a national championship. He could have settled for being competitive in the Big East, the *Globe*'s Bob Ryan said, but it would have been out of character for him to lower his expectations. Even when a seemingly talented Eagles team struggled, O'Brien wasn't hammered too hard by the Boston-area media. And when matters got worse, many reporters sided with him on most issues.

"They [the Boston College administrators] had a perception that I wasn't being loyal to them because I had relationships with guys in the media who had become friends of mine. In fact, one comment mentioned to me was that I had masterfully manipulated the media. When I looked at the guy who said that, I said you have to be kidding me about this. That, to me, suggested I had spent time trying to figure out ways to get people in the media to say or write things I wanted them to. How was I going to be so calculating that I could control the guys in the media? It was so far from the truth. They misinterpreted my relationships with the media. Frankly, I admit I have a problem as to when to turn the faucet off or flip the switch when I'm talking to a working member of the media whom I consider a friend. Must I say every time, 'This is off the record'? Can I not have a simple conversation without always worrying about what I say being reported by the media? Unfortunately, the answer is yes and no. I struggled with that sometimes.

"It was about mutual respect. It was about those guys doing their job. It was about me knowing they had a job to do. All we talk about in this business is exposure and promoting your program. How are you going to do that? You give guys access. I got to be very friendly with guys in the media in Boston. So you say things and maybe somebody has information that the school thinks they shouldn't have. I didn't run to the media and say, 'Hey, let's manipulate Boston College.' I didn't say, 'Here, write about this.' That was the furthest thing from reality.

"It prevents you from establishing deeper relationships with people in the media. You just worry all the time. I find myself being a little bit standoffish. It's really not my nature, but I find myself being guarded. I find myself thinking did I say too much. I can't say how many times I've had conversations with guys and I've thought, 'Oh, my God, I hope he doesn't write that.' I don't like having to be so careful about what I say. I don't like that aspect of what and how I've become."

O'Brien wasn't Andy Geiger's first choice to fill the Buckeyes' vacancy. Geiger had already contacted several other coaches—including Mike Jarvis of George Washington (now at St. John's), Steve Alford of Southwest Missouri State (now at Iowa), Eddie Fogler of South Carolina (who resigned after the 2000-01 season), Rick Barnes of Clemson (now at Texas), Mike Montgomery of Stanford, and Tubby Smith of Georgia (now at Kentucky). Ohio State made an enticing offer to O'Brien—a package estimated at $700,000 a year.

Leaving Boston College was a dream-shattering experience for O'Brien. He had meticulously and methodically prepared himself to become the school's head coach. This wasn't just another bitter pill he had to swallow. It was like choking down a bowling ball. Admittedly, O'Brien couldn't stomach the controversy at Boston College, partly because he had worked diligently in keeping the basketball program clean.

"In the back of my mind, it was always Boston College," O'Brien said. "When I first got to Columbus, there were times when I might think BC, instead of Ohio State. But that's behind me now. It's yesterday's news."

FORMULA
FOR SUCCESS

7

In the perfectly aligned seats at Value City Arena, Ohio State fans raised their voices above the rafters while the Buckeyes went through a short pregame shoot-around minutes before their Big Ten clash with Minnesota on January 23, 1999. The crowd had grown louder with every home game. The fans' cheers and applause resonated throughout the arena and bounced off the walls, intensifying with every Ohio State victory.

The Buckeyes' new home had never rocked as it did on this Saturday afternoon. The atmosphere wasn't quite this magnetic even after the Buckeyes manhandled three conference foes—Indiana, Purdue, and Iowa. The Gophers were 12-4 overall and 3-3 in conference play, but it wasn't the prospect of a shootout that pumped up the fans. Instead, it was Ohio State's unexpected drive toward a Big Ten title.

As game time neared, the Buckeyes jogged back to their locker room for a final strategy session. The Gophers exited, too, and were showered with a chorus of boos. They were not a popular team in Columbus, considering they laid the wood to the Buckeyes, 76-53, in the teams' previous meeting on February 11, 1998. The fans reminded Minnesota only briefly that it was not welcome, and then they resumed their wild pregame chants.

The Buckeyes raced back into the arena with their scarlet sweat suits buttoned and zipped from top to bottom. As Scoonie Penn started the pregame warm-up drills with a layup, the fans suddenly erupted in a thunderous, three-minute ovation. At press row, reporters and photographers looked left and right to see what they were missing. The crowd stood in unison, clapping madly as O'Brien entered the arena, escorted by the team's managers.

O'Brien, who had positioned himself for a run at Coach of the Year honors, had become the toast of Columbus.

The fans wrapped their collective arms around him as he walked into the arena. Whether sitting courtside in the VIP boxes or perched in the balcony, the fans shouted, "OB, OB, OB!" in a remarkable display of affection for a coach who negotiated his way through a basketball mine field to will something of a miracle by turning perennial losers into winners. O'Brien, hesitantly waving to an adoring crowd, seemed overcome by the attention. He stopped to shake hands with Minnesota coach Clem Haskins, who appeared oblivious to the ovation. By the time O'Brien reached the Ohio State bench, his cheeks were red from perpetual blushing.

This was a spontaneous act of appreciation and affection from the Ohio State fans. Many of them remembered how deep the ship had sunk before O'Brien cast his oars into the water to save the Buckeyes from the sharks—a sea of critics, media, and alumni who were ready to strike if the program even inched in the wrong direction.

"I was embarrassed," O'Brien said of the standing ovation. "I tend to get so appreciative that I get a little emotional when things like that happen. I remember when we walked out, I couldn't wait to get to the bench to sit down. I wanted out of the spotlight. I was a little choked up about how the crowd responded to me. It was amazing. It had never happened to me. Maybe, at that point, I felt as if I had found a home here."

Years back, O'Brien had given his heart to Boston College, but when things got bad in the Heights, his alma mater's love for him, a Boston writer suggested, wasn't reciprocal. In Columbus, the Buckeye faithful gave their love unconditionally. O'Brien had won them over with his bulldog tenacity, irrepressible optimism, and desire to make Ohio State's 100th year of college basketball something to remember and cherish.

Although the Ohio State fans expressed great admiration and respect, O'Brien knew few of them understood completely how hard he and his staff had to work at rebuilding the Ohio State program. It wasn't as simple, said assistant coach Dave Spiller, as finding a can't-miss, blue-chip recruit. It was much more complicated. "OB rebuilt and reshaped the [Ohio State] program by maintaining a recruiting philosophy that has been the cornerstone of his success as a coach," Spiller said.

"There are college basketball coaches all across America talking about doing things the right way," said assistant Rick Boyages. "Jim does it right. He knows it takes talent to win, but character earns a program respect."

When Andy Geiger handed Jim O'Brien his office key in the spring of 1997, he walked out the door and never looked back. He trusted that O'Brien would carefully walk the fine line that sometimes transforms college coaches into zealots whose misguided devotion creates a win-at-all-cost mentality.

"What you promise recruits is the opportunity of getting an education and a chance at competing at the highest level," O'Brien said. "There is pressure to win in college basketball, but you have to stay within the rules. We want to stay in this business as long as we can. If we make promises we can't keep, we can't go back to those schools or communities in which we recruit. It's more important to me to keep my credibility and my good name. You want to be in this for the long run. It's why I feel comfortable doing what I do and the way I do it."

O'Brien had been asked many times why he didn't sign a *Parade* or McDonald's All-American during his 11 years at Boston College. There are recruiting experts who wonder why O'Brien hasn't lured a supposedly all-world high school player to Ohio State after taking the Buckeyes to the Final Four. Typically, he answers them politely—or with a raspy, sarcastic quip. Then, he goes back on the recruiting trail and looks for some high school kid whose desires and convictions are similar, if not greater, than his own.

"The NCAA gives you a lot of rules and stipulations about how you go about your business," assistant coach Paul Biancardi said. "You have to have an eye for talent and a feel for people. You have to observe what a recruit does that makes you believe he is a good person and he is capable of doing the work academically."

When O'Brien began assembling his first recruiting class, the character issue played a significant role in his search for talent. There was no room to err, no narrow window afforded for miscalculation of a recruit's personality. The program could not afford to harbor another undisciplined teenager. O'Brien had to make the right calls. He had to weigh talent and character almost evenly. It wasn't necessary to recruit within the restrictive walls of a monastery or offer scholarships only to the well-groomed, clean-cut recruits. O'Brien, though, had to choose his recruits carefully. The simple fact remained that Ohio State, in its willingness to chip away its tarnished image, couldn't strike out.

"You can sense during the recruiting when you can say this is not going to happen," O'Brien said. "It doesn't happen that often, but it does. We tried to recruit John Wallace [Syracuse] and Marcus Camby [Massachusetts] at Boston College. I was in the house for five minutes with Wallace, and I am saying to myself, 'This isn't happening.' He doesn't even know who we are. He had no interest. He doesn't want to attend Boston College. It was a short meeting.

Admittedly, O'Brien and his assistant coaches have to trust their instincts. When it came to Wallace, in particular, O'Brien could tell by Wallace's body language and fidgety mannerisms that O'Brien's recruiting pitch was falling on deaf ears. It was apparent, too, that Wallace wouldn't be comfortable playing O'Brien's style of basketball. More important, O'Brien had to follow his gut feeling. Even though Wallace was among the most highly recruited blue-chippers in the country, O'Brien would hold onto his scholarship offer, preferring to offer it to a recruit who wanted to play with the Golden Eagles.

"You try to be the same with all of the recruits. Sometimes we get a call a week later and a kid is not interested in us. It's rare that I leave a kid's house thinking we didn't have a good meeting. You have to be realistic and understand that other coaches do a good job in their houses, too."

The key to Ohio State's remarkable 19-win turnaround was a combination of things. Mostly, it was the result of recruiting.

It's not, said Biancardi, that O'Brien cannot recruit blue-chippers. In fact, he has had a few, including Scoonie Penn and Bill Curley, an All-Big East center at Boston College. They didn't knock your socks off with their shooting or leaping ability. They were, however, fundamentally sound, genuinely good people and winners – all of which Ohio State was lacking when O'Brien showed up for work on that mid-October morning in 1997.

"You always have to get the best guys you can get or those who fit best in your system," O'Brien said. "When you have an opportunity to get a very good player, you got to try to get him. However, you don't go crazy looking at those guys all across the country. You look at local guys who you know you have something to offer. We go after those guys hard."

Even though the Buckeyes were enjoying their best season in six years, O'Brien couldn't help but think what might have been if Ohio State could have convinced Ohio's best high school players to choose Columbus. They were scattered about the Big Ten, including two blue-chippers, Andre Hutson and A.J. Granger, at Michigan State.

O'Brien hadn't been on the job long when he heard criticism of his first recruiting class. Some Ohio State alumni questioned why he recruited Brown and Dudley out of New York and Savovic from New Jersey. For the most part, those three recruits didn't have any preconceived notions about Ohio State. They were aware of some of the problems, but when O'Brien promised to straighten things out, Columbus became an attractive choice.

"Those kids going to Michigan State are sore spots with us," O'Brien said. "The program wasn't in good-enough shape for those kids to want to come to Ohio State. Michigan State did a good job of recruiting those kids. We lucked out that Michael Redd still wanted to come here. Our goal is to keep these kids at home. We like to think it's going to be a little more difficult for other Big Ten schools to come into Ohio and take those kids away."

Admittedly, O'Brien took some heat when he dismissed several players, mostly Ohio natives, before his first season. If he was going to restore order within the program, O'Brien reasoned, he had to act swiftly, yet judiciously. It would be difficult to recruit Ohio's top high school players with a cloud still hovering over the program.

"The single biggest thing became the personalities and what we thought would be the right thing to do," O'Brien said. "It didn't matter where the kids came from. It just turned out that they were from Ohio. It wasn't about getting rid of the Ohio kids so we could bring in the New England and New York kids. We were happy to get Jon Sanderson, and we attempted to recruit some of the better kids from the state. Eugene Land went to Cincinnati; Sam Clancy Jr. went to Southern Cal. The next year we tried to get Adam Wolfe from Westerville, but he goes to Michigan State. We couldn't get the best guys interested in the program. We had to be realistic.

"We didn't know how people would receive us or what their perceptions of us would be. We just knew there had to be some changes. That was the most uncomfortable thing to go through because it happened so quickly. When I looked at it from a parent's perspective, I'm asking, 'What if that was my child and what if that happened to my kid?' We knew this wasn't going to be a real nice or pleasant situation for these young men and their families, but sometimes you've got to make some tough calls.

"The people here didn't know me from a hole in the wall," said O'Brien, who faced a similar predicament at St. Bonaventure. "They didn't know the first thing about me. It was almost like starting from scratch. Now, you develop friendships and relationships all over again and it's a long process. I'm sure there were some eyebrows being raised. When I got the job, they may have asked, 'Who is this guy?' After eight wins, I'm sure they were asking themselves, 'Is this who we got to coach Ohio State? Is this who [Athletics Director] Andy Geiger spent all his time searching for? We could have had Tubby Smith. We could have had Rick Barnes. We could have had Bob Huggins. We could have had Rick Majerus. This guy comes in here and wins eight games.' I'm sure there was some of that."

Ohio State had acquired a coach who was considered among the best recruiters in the Big East. The Eagles didn't always get the five-star recruits, but O'Brien beat every corner of New England and the east coast to find players who could compete in the Big East. Ohio State, which had scaled back its enrollment numbers since 1995, has a more selective admissions policy than it did when O'Brien took over in 1997.

"There's going to be more kids available to us at Ohio State just by sheer numbers," O'Brien said. "It's pressure on our shoulders not to have carte blanche or an open-door policy, which isn't the case here. However, a middle ground exists at Ohio State that did not at Boston College. We just can't admit anyone. We don't want guys coming here who are just interested in playing basketball. It's not worth it for me to recruit a McDonald's All-American who might be here for only a year. I say that, yet if I knew one of those kids wanted to come to Ohio State, we would probably recruit him. You have to take your chances. I guess you need to get a good player whenever you can, but you can still be selective.

"I think we have kids who are going to be good in time. The good sign is, if you have guys leaving early, you must be getting some good players. I think you can survive and have a competitive program with guys who are going to be with your program for the long haul. We have not recruited a Top 10 player in the country yet. Of course, we haven't been here that long. Unfortunately, there haven't been many great high school players in Ohio the last few years. But we think there is a good group of kids coming up. If we're going to compete for those kids, we have to give them a reason to want to enroll here."

O'Brien does not have a complex recruiting philosophy. Admittedly, he doesn't engage in many recruiting battles for highly touted high school players, such as Darius Miles (a 2000 *Parade* All-American) and Jamal Crawford (who played one year at Michigan in 1999-2000), who are likely to spend a year or two in school before turning professional. It's a recruiting philosophy, O'Brien believes, that will become fashionable in the not-so-distant future.

"I do think about recruiting kids who are going to be in the program for four years," O'Brien said. "Right now, more than ever. It is incredible how many of these kids are coming out right now. When I think about the success we had at Boston College, it was never with All-Americans. Bill Curly was the only high school All-America player we had in 11 years. He wasn't a McDonald's All-American, but neither was Scoonie or Danya Abrams, a native of Greenburg, New York. We always found guys who got better and would be guys you want to have on your team. They were never so good that you had to worry about them leaving. I really think there is something to that now. When guys leave, it disrupts everything."

Ohio State's athletics, like some other Division I football and basketball programs across the country, have had to deal with that unpleasant reality. The Buckeyes lost All-American Jimmy Jackson after his junior year.

"With Michael [Redd] leaving early, it hurt us some because we were counting on him," O'Brien said. "We didn't recruit him. I didn't know him from a hole in the wall. I had no idea how good he was going to be. We were saying we have this guy for a couple of years. I don't know why we were so naïve to be shocked by Michael leaving. Nevertheless, you still make plans for him being around because you know Scoonie, George [Reese] and Ken [Johnson] are going to leave. We will still be able to score points, but it disrupts your program when kids leave early for the NBA.

"I'm thinking Billy Donovan is excited about the future of his program at Florida after he gets them to the Final Four [in 2000]. Then he loses a couple of young players to the NBA. Florida goes from playing for the national championship game to having questions about its future. Everyone is saying what a dynasty they might have with all those freshmen and sophomores, who were just unbelievable. Suddenly, it's over. Just like that. It's over in one year."

That, however, is an alarming trend for college basketball coaches. O'Brien wanted Redd to stay for his senior season. At least Redd stuck around for three years. There was a mass exodus of underclassmen after the 1999-2000 season. Even a few high school players chose to bypass college. One by one, some of the more promising underclassmen entered the NBA draft.

In reality, some left out of necessity. Others left after dueling with the NCAA about their eligibility status. Jamal Crawford, Erick Barkley of St. John's, and DeMar Johnson of Cincinnati were all first-round NBA picks. An even more disturbing, but increasingly troubling, reality is that high school All-Americans such as Darius Miles skipped college altogether, perhaps unaware that the NBA promises nothing. Kevin Garnett of the Minnesota Timberwolves, Kobe Bryant of the Los Angeles Lakers, and Tracy McGrady of Orlando are among the few exceptions enjoying success in the NBA.

"I'm sure [St. John's coach] Mike Jarvis prepared his team thinking he would have Darius Miles and Erick Barkley," O'Brien said. "Miles doesn't even show up at St. John's. Then, I'm thinking, 'Hey, we don't have to face those guys next year.' It was crazy. St. John's lost two very good players, which could set their program back a little. I don't know how you go about recruiting other guys. Do you recruit another guy at his position by telling him that he is leaving, but you're not sure? Therefore, you don't recruit a guy. That's what happened at Georgia Tech. Stephon Marbury comes out after his first year after they beat us [Boston College] in the tournament. They were very good, and Cremins talks about he can't get another guard to play there because he had the best point guard in America. Then Marbury leaves, and they hadn't recruited anybody.

"I would rather have a guy who is a little bit lower rated, but who I'm confident will be with us for four years. I think there is lot more stability within your program if you think in those terms. You have that year or two to get it done. Nowadays, there's such a short window to get it done.

"I remember when kids never left Duke. If it happens to Duke, it can happen to anybody. If there's anyone who doesn't think so, he is dreaming. Duke was everybody's model because those guys graduated. They enhanced the quality of their program by promoting the fact that their guys earn degrees. The Grant Hills are the cover boys for all that is good about college basketball. It's not about kids being bad kids; it's the lure of the money. Duke loses Corey Maggette and Elton Brand, but they get Jason Williams and Carlos Boozer."

In his first three seasons at Ohio State, O'Brien has gotten pretty much what he wanted during the recruiting season—except for 7-3 center Aleksander

Radojovic and Ohio's Mr. Basketball, guard Julius Johnson, a Cleveland product who was denied admission for academic reasons. O'Brien still has not recruited a *Parade* or McDonald's All-American, but he hasn't changed his philosophy. He continues to look for players with immense skills, and he remains unrelenting in his search for players who are solid citizens.

"I don't want good players who are going to be bad guys," O'Brien said. "I will sacrifice the level of ability to get guys who would rather be a part of a good group of kids. We try to be selective with whom we take. We don't have the best players, but we have a good group. Maybe, we'll get somebody in here that everyone has talked about."

O'Brien may not have a reputation for recruiting future NBA superstars, but his players tend to graduate. Of all the accomplishments on his resume, he treasures that fact most of all when he considers that only 40 percent of Division I college basketball players graduated during the 1990s. Only 44 percent of the student-athletes who played for the championships in the 1990s—including Kentucky, Michigan State, Connecticut, and Arkansas—went on to graduate.

While at Boston College, O'Brien had a perfect graduation rate among the players who used all four years of their eligibility, but it didn't make him irreplaceable. Dean Smith and John Wooden seemingly lasted forever, but their job security was strengthened by the fact that North Carolina and UCLA were of championship caliber most every year. While most university presidents voice concerns about the declining graduation numbers, the advent of multimillion-dollar network television deals leaves many school presidents and athletic directors searching for coaching candidates who can win instead of improving their graduation rates.

"Schools are falling all over themselves to find coaches who can relate to the changing personalities and dynamics in college sports," O'Brien said. "It's more about winning basketball games. Unfortunately, you can stand on your pedestal, and say, 'I've been here for 10 years, and my kids are graduating.' What happens to a guy like that if he doesn't win? He is fired, of course. All of those other things are nice, but if guys want to keep their jobs, it's about how many games they win.

"I don't want to hear about the small Catholic schools or the big universities; it's all the same. You had better win some games. It's about being successful. It's about getting into the NCAA Tournament. It's about getting to a bowl game or making some money. You're not getting any of that stuff by just having great citizens who everyone loves. If it happens in addition to winning games, now you have something to hang your hat on. If a coach goes to an athletic director and talks about his kids' citizenship or how the graduation rates are impeccable, the athletic director looks at you and says, 'Yeah, but you only got to the NIT this year.' The winning is important. When do we decide that for the sake of the kids, it should be more than about just winning?"

In the last three years of Ayers's tenure at Ohio State, attendance dropped steadily. The losing had a peripheral effect as well, because, as a result, it was much harder for Ohio State to recruit some of the nation's top players. The Buckeyes tumbled to the bottom of the Big Ten because they lacked the talent to keep up. There isn't a major Division I college program in the country enjoying much success with walk-ons and recruits who can best be described as marginal or serviceable players.

Randy Ayers was unsuccessful in recruiting top out-of-state players, in part, because Ohio State had played itself off national television. It's clear, said O'Brien, that exposure makes recruiting considerably easier.

Admittedly, Geiger hired O'Brien for the same reasons other athletic directors hire coaches. He wanted Ohio State's winning tradition restored. There also was the reality of filling the seats at Value City Arena, and it would be difficult to accomplish that without a good men's basketball team. When the Buckeyes' fortunes changed, it was good for business. The advertising revenue increased and sponsors lined up to etch their products and corporate signatures somewhere in the arena.

"I don't like the way it is, but it's big business," O'Brien said. "I say to Andy Geiger all the time that he is a CEO and that he doesn't make enough money. He is definitely underpaid. It's all about the dollars now. I marvel at the fact that there are no corporate sponsors at Indiana. There is just a simple "IU" on press row at Assembly Hall. There are no scrolling advertisements. Now that Bobby Knight is gone, watch and see what happens. Indiana has been forfeiting so much money, but Bobby is old school. He was adamant about them not doing that at Indiana.

"Even Indiana's uniforms are simple and consistent as the days are long. Our uniforms are much like Indiana. Theirs are quiet, simple and classy —except those ugly candy-striped warm-up suits they wear. But it's Indiana. There is no junk."

O'Brien isn't a protégé of Knight's, but the two have similar visions of college athletics. They may not always agree, but their styles are reflective of their tight-fisted personalities. In this age of basketball expressiveness and defiance among college athletes, O'Brien talks about sportsmanship and respecting authority.

"You don't see Indiana guys high-fiving like crazy or chest-bumping," O'Brien said. "You don't see all the gesturing. You don't see it at Ohio State. I guess from that perspective, Bobby Knight has influenced me.

"In our very first game here—an exhibition game—we talked to our guys about keeping their humility and not drawing attention to themselves. We go out and guys are jumping around and banging into each other. My assistant coaches and I are all looking at each other, so after the game we address it. I told them that's not what we are about. We need to tone it down. It's not that it's good or bad, it's just that we're uncomfortable with it.

"I don't think I want my guys wearing the headbands guys are wearing now. Is it old school? Is it too much? Maybe, but you will not see Indiana's guys wearing them. Those guys are respectable and they handle themselves in a nice way. I would like to think that our guys do that. I had to tell Scoonie to turn his hat around. This is why I like what Bobby's program represented. You didn't see all that junk. They are classy guys. You don't see them acting up."

Of course, Ohio State fans are hardly fans of Bobby Knight. It doesn't matter that he is a former Buckeye. Or that he grew up two hours from the campus in Orrville, a rural city known more as the home of Smuckers preserves than the birthplace of Bobby Knight.

O'Brien, though, has learned to go with the flow. He has stayed in step with the ever-changing methods of coaching. He has even created some of his own, adding variations of schemes used by coaches he respects. While he has adjusted to the changing landscape of college basketball, O'Brien continues to try to adapt to the inevitable evolution of student-athletes.

O'Brien sees Ohio State as a microcosm of what college basketball will be in the coming years. The Buckeyes are a collection of varied personalities, cultures, religions, and ethnicities. At the start of the 2000-01 season, Ohio State was the only team in the Big Ten with three Serbian student-athletes on the roster. What all the players have in common, said assistant coach Dave Spiller, is an undeniable trust of and allegiance to O'Brien.

"I hope they think I'm someone they can trust or someone they know who cares for them," O'Brien said. "I'm a little bit old school. They kid me about my music, but I kid them about some of the awful stuff I have to listen to when I'm in the locker room. It's horrible music. They think I'm an old fart because I'm always criticizing their taste in music. I'm not anything more than a guy they can depend on. We have been consistent about how we were then and how we are now.

"We lose sight sometimes of what this is all about. It always has been about the players. As somebody who has played a little bit, I never thought the coach had any impact on the game. As players, we thought, 'This is how we play and this is what we do.' But I know if I didn't trust that Bob Cousy had my best interests at heart, I probably wouldn't have gone to Boston College."

While O'Brien scans the country for good kids, there's the added pressure of recruiting good basketball players. O'Brien's formula for success hasn't changed much since his days as an assistant coach at Connecticut. He wants that raw, indisputable blue-chipper, but his bread has always been buttered with good big men and a well-disciplined, well-schooled point guard. So many times, he has had to carve a diamond out of the rough, finding a gem that hardly anyone else noticed. Now, with advanced technology and other recruiting services and devices, it's nearly impossible to overlook a good high school player.

"When we recruited Aleksander Radojevic, an eye-popping 7-foot-3 kid, people didn't know how to pronounce his name," O'Brien said. "Nowadays, everyone knows about high school players. Forget that he is foreign; a 7-3 kid is going to get some attention.

"The model hasn't changed very much at all. I want big frontcourt players. The bigger they are, the smaller you can be on the perimeter. At 6-6, Redd was our leading rebounder the last couple of years (1998-2000).

"They tease me here because I don't like gimmicks. There are no shortcuts. The thing that I do know, is you have to be yourself, especially in the recruiting. If it's good enough, kids will be attracted to your program.

"I'm a little more conservative than most of my players. I thought about how the kids at Boston College complained that the Big East championship rings I ordered were too simple. I decided this time I would let Scoonie design the rings because he helped us win a Big East and Big Ten championships. I never wear rings. I have the rings on my shelf someplace. These guys wear the rings, and they want big rings. I bring Scoonie in and told him and George Reese to design the ring. He and George fought it out about what they wanted. I knew it would not be remotely close to what I would have done.

"When I go recruiting, I'm looking for a simple ring. I'm not looking for anyone special. I want him to be a solid kid. They all want to be pampered to some degree, but I want a kid who isn't looking for anything. My hope is he just wants to be a part of something that is good. That's what we want. We don't want guys who think they have to be our savior or expect to get special treatment. You have to develop relationships with the kids, because so many kids are offered scholarships. You have to be around and you got to get to know them. We try to keep it simple. I have a tendency to recruit the kid and his family."

O'Brien tries to be a realist, too. He knows the task of trying to recruit some of the nation's best players gets tougher each year. It gets even tougher when he has to bump heads on the recruiting path with the likes of Duke, Kentucky, and North Carolina. As he and his coaches canvass the country, looking for recruits in summer leagues and AAU tournaments, Ohio State is often scouting the same player who is coveted by the more dominant programs.

"We hear all the time that a kid really likes our school, but Duke called," O'Brien said. "We've been recruiting this kid for two years, but Duke just called yesterday. They have not seen him play, but they have to listen to Duke. That's fine and I understand that, but I have to recruit other guys. If you look at other schools, we have to look at other players. The ones that come are the ones we want. Are you always getting the best kid? Probably not. But I'm getting the kid who wants to be here. We are never waiting for the one great player. There is value in having a kid wanting to play for us. It's not always about getting the best players.

"When you're successful like Duke, you can be a little more selective. We are a little selective now, but it would be easier when you get to the level that Duke, Kentucky, and North Carolina are right now. The way people respond when those programs get in late bums you out. It gets you pissed a little. But they aren't getting everybody. It's what you have to deal with."

O'Brien dealt himself a pretty good hand when he signed Reese, Brian Brown, Boban Savovic, and Penn in his first year. Penn, of course, was the only recognizable face in that recruiting class. The others were essentially role players, but all of them would play significant roles in helping to rebuild the Ohio State program.

8

NEW HOME, NEW ATTITUDE

On a splendid autumn morning in mid-October 1998, the sun peaked over Value City Arena as the Buckeyes gathered at their plush, new practice facility inside the Schottenstein Center. They may not have looked like winners the previous five seasons, but at least the Buckeyes would have the classiest arena in the Big Ten. Maybe, just maybe, their new home would bring out the best in them.

"I've heard people say that when you look good, you play good," guard Neshaun Coleman said. "I wouldn't say the arena is why we turned things around, but Schottenstein had a good feel about it. We felt closer to the fans. We certainly played with much more confidence at home, and that is the way it's supposed to be. We hadn't felt that way in years."

Long before the Buckeyes opened their exhibition season with a 107-75 win over the Worldwide All-Stars, most of the talk during the off-season was about their new arena. It would have a seating capacity of 19,100, making it the largest in the Big Ten. It would be among the most versatile on-campus facilities in the country. It would be a venue for most everything—including country music concerts, the World Wresting Federation tour, the Ringling Brothers and Barnum & Bailey's Circus, and hockey. It would be a revenue-producing bonanza, putting Ohio State in the forefront of revolutionizing free enterprise on America's college campuses. Andy Geiger, the school's athletics director, had become, in effect, the school's chief operations officer. Geiger's fiscal ingenuity helped put high-priced personal seat licenses in upscale, VIP loges. With Ohio State's loyal alumni, the PSLs sold like hot dogs on game night.

Ohio State was moving smartly into the new millennium. All across the country, new stadiums and arenas were being built. In Cincinnati, taxpayers were paying for a new ballpark for the Reds and the Bengals. In Cleveland, the city aided the construction of a new stadium as part of a deal to bring back the Cleveland Browns after the team moved to Baltimore in 1995. Even with a declining enrollment, Ohio State found a way to finance its new arena with an array of private funds and donations.

Some NBA teams would envy the Buckeyes' new playhouse. It has everything imaginable. The locker rooms are spacious, and the players' lounge has the look of some country club cabin at Augusta. Even the Nebraska Cornhuskers' football team would be impressed with the Buckeyes' weight training and fitness rooms.

This is the major-college life. The Buckeyes are blessed with all the amenities. In its first year at Value City Arena, Ohio State led the Big Ten in attendance, averaging 17,223 per game, an increase of 7,253 during its final year at St. John Arena. It ranked seventh nationally behind Kentucky (23,367), Syracuse, North Carolina, Louisville, Arkansas, and New Mexico.

St. John Arena—named after former AD L. W. St. John—may have been old, but it didn't lack character. Every seat wasn't a good one, especially those brushing the rafters. It wasn't the noisiest arena in the country, nor was it the coziest, but often it was the coldest. The fans sometimes seemed too far removed from the action. Yet, it had 41 years of tradition stored within its decaying red brick walls. The Buckeyes enjoyed some good days there. They would leave behind a wealth of history, so the school administrators didn't have the heart to ram a wrecking ball through it.

It had been center stage for great players such as All-Americans Jerry Lucas, John Havlicek, Frank Howard, Jimmy Jackson, and Kelvin Ransey. Still, it had become obsolete compared to more modernistic, multimillion dollar-facilities such as the Kohl Center at Wisconsin and the Breslin Center at Michigan State. This wasn't about keeping up with the Joneses. Rather, it was about accepting the reality of a new era. No other school in the Big Ten, except Indiana, was determined to cling tightly to tradition. The Hoosiers, winners of five NCAA titles, weren't making any plans to abandon Assembly Hall.

The Buckeyes had put their history behind them as they prepared to move across the Olentangy River to Value City Arena at the Schottenstein Center. But could they put their recent history behind them? Could a new home really make a difference?

The Buckeyes had tumbled so far down the Big Ten ladder that some of the school's major contributors and donors were beginning to wonder aloud if this was money well spent. It surely seemed as if the timing was bad to move from an arena that had opened in 1956—four years before Ohio State's run of three consecutive appearances in the Final Four. Perhaps the move would have been more widely accepted if the Buckeyes had been winning. Instead, their last season at St. John Arena didn't conjure an emotional charge that would rally them into the NCAA Tournament or the NIT. The Buckeyes lost their last home game to Penn State at the old gymnasium.

This was a new year, a new season. Things would be different. The Buckeyes, wiser and more experienced, would defy the odds. They would become winners after half a decade of losing.

Penn promised.

No one—coaches or media—expected Ohio State to finish higher than eighth place in the Big Ten. When Penn walked onto the practice floor for the first time, Ohio State took on a different look almost immediately. The Buckeyes had found someone who could distribute the basketball. In his first official practice, with his teammates curious about his talents, Penn bounced a perfect pass to freshman Boban Savovic. The pass went through Savovic's hands, and Penn, his smile lost in anger, demanded that Savovic catch it next time. If his promise was going to be fulfilled, the Buckeyes had to be efficient at the little things—passing, catching, and making layups.

And they had to win their first six games of the season—all at Value City Arena.

The Buckeyes' first practice lasted two long hours on this football Saturday. O'Brien skipped Midnight Madness, choosing instead to let his players get a good night's sleep. There were no distractions because most everyone on campus was gearing up for No. 1-ranked Ohio State's football game at Illinois. Ohio State was in the midst of challenging for the national championship, so preseason basketball wasn't on the minds of most Ohio State fans. When the Buckeyes' title hopes were dashed four weeks later with a home loss to Michigan State, attention shifted some to the men's basketball team—much of it out of resentment for the football team losing a game they were expected to win.

The Buckeyes didn't have such lofty expectations, but they certainly wanted to make a good impression in their first game at Value City Arena. Of course, the task was less demanding, with their opponent being the World-wide All-Stars. The Buckeyes looked like Big Ten contenders. They got into the open floor. They ran their half-court offense with remarkable efficiency. This was nothing like the season before. The crowd was digging the new-look Buckeyes. Yet, in their hearts they knew the Buckeyes weren't playing a worthy opponent.

Most observers did not take the Buckeyes seriously at the start of the season. How could they? The Buckeyes were young. They were still trying to pick themselves up after being knocked to the ground, with the Indiana Hoosiers delivering the final blow at the Big Ten Tournament at the United Center in Chicago on March 5, 1998.

O'Brien was talking about giving significant playing time to three freshmen—Savovic, center Will Dudley, and guard Brian Brown. He would have to find a way, of course, to turn over the leadership role to Penn while curtailing the team's dependency on Redd. He would have to demand more of Ayers's class of 1995 survivors, Coleman and Singleton. Center Ken Johnson could dazzle you at the piano, but he wasn't nearly as rhythmic in the paint with the ball in his hard hands. George Reese, a junior college transfer, showed signs of promise while at John A. Logan Community College in Carterville, Illinois. The task of completing the turnaround didn't lessen any when one of his prize recruits, guard Doylan Robinson, had to sit out his first year to ensure he could cut it academically.

O'Brien wasn't sure exactly what he had. No one else knew, either. He closed his practices, not because he feared his secrets would be revealed to opposing coaches, but because he felt his players would respond better without the eye of a camera focusing on their every move. This team, in part because of its past ineptitude, could do without media scrutiny.

Even with four returning starters—Redd, Johnson, Singleton, and forward Jon Sanderson—the Buckeyes weren't thick-skinned enough to take criticism of any kind. Even with Penn, one of the top five point guards in the country, running the point, the Buckeyes were still haunted by their past failures. They needed something good to happen early in the season that would enhance their growth.

In their last exhibition game, an 88-67 win over Marathon, the Buckeyes didn't look nearly as invincible as they had in their first game. Redd, still pressing some while familiarizing himself with Penn's game, didn't shoot well. Yet, he scored 16 points and snatched 12 rebounds. Penn scored seven points and dished out seven assists. It didn't seem to matter at the time, but Ohio State's 21-point win came against a Marathon team that had lost by only three points to second-ranked Connecticut.

Afterward, O'Brien spent much of his postgame talk trying to convince his team that that kind of effort would win them games against even the good teams. Penn had no reason not to believe O'Brien. Even before Ohio State began preparing for its season opener against Oakland [Michigan] University, the former Boston College point guard boldly predicted that the Buckeyes had made enough strides to challenge for a berth in the NCAA Tournament. Never mind the NIT. It was all right to boast of having a winning season during preseason practices, but this was raising the bar of expectations out of sight for a team that had struggled to win eight games the season before. "When I heard him say that, I didn't know what to say," O'Brien said. "We were just trying to figure out a way to win our next game—not get into the tournament. The other kids looked at him like he was crazy. The problem is, he had been in college basketball two years, and he went to the tournament two times. He thinks that's what you do in March."

O'Brien may have flinched when Penn made his prediction, but he had to admit it was a positive sign that Ohio State was gaining some confidence. "Scoonie knew what we wanted," O'Brien said. "Even though he hadn't played the year before, he was able to tell everyone this is what I mean and what I want. He told guys what we were about. It wasn't easy bringing them all together. We wanted them to appreciate what we were trying to do. The guys who didn't want to buy into it, well, those were the ones who ended up leaving."

During the previous five seasons, the Buckeyes sometimes settled for being merely competitive. That wasn't good enough for Penn, and he spent the entire preseason trying to change his teammates' attitudes. He understood, however, that his teammates had every reason to feel shy, even if they were convinced the team was better. At times, Redd would suggest the Buckeyes could be the surprise of the Big Ten. However, he was hesitant to commit himself. It was better, Redd suggested, that Penn do the talking, because, if nothing else, he was the only player on the roster who had experienced winning.

"I felt some responsibility as far as making the team believe it could win if we played our best basketball," Penn said unblinkingly. "I don't think the guys realized how good we could be. The atmosphere had changed, and with every win, we were beginning to think that we could win the next game. I remember there were games last year when we would go in thinking we didn't have a chance. We had to change that. We had to do something—or say something—to shake things up."

The Buckeyes gained a little more confidence during their 78-70 win over Alabama before a still-curious Ohio State crowd of 16,763. The Crimson Tide was Ohio State's first real challenge. The victory wasn't nearly as important to O'Brien as the manner in which his team played. Redd was always considered a finesse player, but he drew hard fouls when he dared to challenge Alabama's frontcourt on a baseline drive. He cut his hand, but developed a sense of toughness. Savovic, a backup guard, came in diving for loose balls. It didn't matter to O'Brien that the Buckeyes committed 21 turnovers, only because his team didn't back down when Alabama challenged it late in the game.

The Buckeyes got what they expected out of Redd and Penn—a combined 40 points. They got far more than anyone could have imagined from Singleton. "Jason does a lot of little things that go unnoticed," Penn said. "He didn't have big numbers, but he always played big when we needed a spark." Singleton put up some impressive numbers against the Crimson Tide, scoring 19 points and snaring eight rebounds. He got into the open floor on fastbreaks, making 6 of 7 shots from the floor and 7 of 8 free throws.

Singleton, who earned a degree in communications, isn't the vociferous type. He is quiet and unassuming and secure enough with himself and his abilities that he never appeared bothered that he spent much of his high school and college career playing in the shadows of more dominating personalities. He was a three-time All-Michigan selection at Southgate Aquinas High School, yet two of his teammates, Jon Garvaglia and Mark Montgomery, got most of the attention. Garvaglia and Montgomery decided on Michigan State, while Singleton chose to go south, to Columbus.

Singleton grew up imagining himself a Wolverine or a Spartan. It didn't matter where he ended up, but surely it would be Ann Arbor or East Lansing. If he couldn't make it to one or the other as a basketball player, there was always baseball. He twice lettered in baseball, getting a few looks from smaller Division I and Division II schools that thought he could develop into a serviceable outfielder. Singleton knew he could shoot the ball better than he could hit one with a Louisville Slugger. He averaged 18.9 points and 12.5 rebounds for Southgate and was named MVP in the Detroit Catholic League.

Singleton, like most of his Ohio State teammates, had won plenty while in high school. In his sophomore season, Aquinas won the Class C state championship with a 28-0 record. He is the school's No. 2 all-time leading scorer, yet with the exception of Ohio State and several Mid-American Conference schools, Singleton wasn't among one of the most sought-after recruits in 1995. Ayers wanted him because of his athleticism and his ability to score off the dribble.

With Redd and Penn doing most of the scoring, Singleton wasn't going to be a primary option in the half-court offense. Johnson began to develop a reliable half hook, giving the Buckeyes another scoring option. Then, there was Reese, whose medium-range jump shooting would often pull defenses out of their packed-in zones. Singleton wanted the ball more, but he accepted his new role—that of defensive specialist.

Admittedly, O'Brien could not foresee just how important Singleton's role would be as the Buckeyes began their irrevocable charge toward March Madness. O'Brien had counted on Singleton's unselfishness. He needed someone to take one for the team. Singleton had been hit by a baseball often enough that taking a charge under the basket or getting steamrolled in the open floor was mild in comparison. Singleton personified a renewed toughness that had been missing. In his first three seasons, Singleton averaged 8.5 points in 83 games. He wasn't going to be a scorer, and if the Buckeyes were going to make inroads, points would be gravy; defense would be his meat and potatoes.

"Sometimes, coaching is about getting kids to buy into what it is you're selling," O'Brien said. "What's lacking in college basketball is our ability to bring everyone together for one common goal for our university. I really think we've been lucky that we've had some guys who have made some sacrifices for this team. We have guys who recognize that they were not stars and that they had to be role players. One of those guys who did that more than anybody was Jason Singleton."

Singleton had become disillusioned after his first two years at Ohio State. Things changed drastically for him while Ohio State made the transition from Ayers to O'Brien. He watched his friends—Tate, Stonerook, and Stringer—all leave under difficult circumstances. He didn't know what to make of O'Brien. He knew only one thing: that he was tired of losing.

In the summer of 1998, Singleton reshaped his game. In August, he traveled to Europe with a Big Ten All-Star team coached by Michigan's Brian Ellerbe. They played tournaments in Belgium, Germany, and the Netherlands. It was a different kind of experience for Singleton, who had spent much of his time playing summer-league basketball in Michigan and Columbus. For the first time since graduating from high school, he was having fun playing the game.

"We all wanted to win," Singleton said. "It's easy to lose your confidence and desire when you lose as much as we did. It was a hard time for all of us. Coach Ayers is a good man, but he had a lot of bad luck, and it affected the team in a way that I thought wasn't possible."

The losing had left Singleton doubting whether he could play at the Division I level. He doubted, too, if he could fit into O'Brien's system. The clock had already run out on his friends. He wondered if the clock was still ticking, and if that ticking was the sound of inevitability—time for his exit. Singleton, though, believed even stronger than Penn that the Buckeyes weren't that far from being good or good enough to get everyone's attention on campus and in the Big Ten.

"Jason had endured three consecutive losing seasons, so he was willing to do whatever it took for us to be successful," O'Brien said. "We're telling everybody the stars on our team are Redd and Penn. The toughest thing about that is Jason is a senior, while Michael is a sophomore and Scoonie hadn't played a game for us. A lot of kids in Jason's situation would have asked, 'Hey, what about me? I stayed. I've been a good guy.' But he understood that Michael and Scoonie were going to be the stars.

"I said to Jason, 'This is your role,' and unless he buys into it, maybe we don't have the same success. It was about having good guys who became coachable; and no one was as willing to learn as Jason. Once he decided he was going to focus on being our defensive stopper, he became a more complete player. Scoonie has a great knowledge of the game, but you could see Jason soaking it all in.

The Buckeyes' hope for a turnaround rested primarily on the shoulders of their role players. Penn and Redd would get their points, but Ohio State would have stretches in games or stretches throughout the season when Penn and Redd weren't enough. And that's when Singleton would step up to the plate and deliver a big shot or get a big steal or snatch down a key rebound.

For the Buckeyes to have any chance of getting into the NCAA Tournament—or as outrageous as it seemed at the time, the Final Four—O'Brien and his assistants had to find the right mixture of role players. Singleton and Johnson were the consummate role players.

"Ken Johnson was a kid who was just ready to be molded by anyone who wanted to mold him," O'Brien said. "He didn't know any better. He was going to go along with it. George Reese, once a third-team junior college All-American, was in his first year. He was just happy to be here. I think about his success story. There were people asking did he ever play high school basketball in Columbus. They had never heard of him. He goes on along with the program. Neshaun Coleman was a little antsy, but he was not destructive. We just kind of molded all those personalities together.

"But we knew we weren't going to win without good players. We had some freshmen we felt could play a little bit. We were happy winning those games early, but we weren't satisfied. These guys had been losing so much, it was important for them to find some kind of inspiration."

Singleton had provided much of the spark with his aggressive defensive play. In the earliest Big Ten opener in school history, Ohio State found inspiration against Penn State in one of the school's legends—John Havlicek. Havlicek, who won nine NBA title rings with the Boston Celtics, sat courtside at Value City Arena, urging on the Buckeyes against the Nittany Lions. The Buckeyes won 70-62, and they did it with a suffocating perimeter defense that held Penn State to 34 percent shooting.

Singleton worked over Penn State guard Joe Crispin, who had almost single-handedly beaten the Buckeyes in both of their previous meetings. Crispin couldn't find enough room to take an uncontested shot. He missed all 10 of his field-goal attempts, including all seven from three-point range. Singleton's defensive effort on Crispin and Titus Ivory overshadowed an off night by Penn, who was only 1-for-7 from the field. Havlicek wasn't impressed with the Buckeyes' half-court offense, but the Buckeyes thrilled him with the kind of defense with which he was familiar—a hustling defense that challenges every shot, both on the perimeter and in the paint.

As bad as the Nittany Lions were shooting, they were still in the game. The Buckeyes allowed them to hang around because, as O'Brien had feared in the preseason, Penn and Redd weren't shooting well. The Buckeyes had to lean on someone else. Johnson, who struggled to contain Penn State center Calvin Booth, did just enough to make a difference. He scored five points and added eight rebounds. Singleton chipped in with eight points before fouling out late in the second half.

The Buckeyes had lost games like these in the past. With Ohio State's role players outscoring Penn State's bench 25-5, the Buckeyes were off to a 4-0 start. "Our offense struggled," O'Brien said afterwards. "But our defense came through and won the game." The win enabled Ohio State to move into first place in the Big Ten for the first time since 1992.

O'Brien was happy with the wins, but what thrilled him most of all was that his players were getting used to winning. Suddenly, victory seemed more of a reality than a dream. The Buckeyes handled Army with ease, winning 86-45. It was their most lopsided win in 33 games (a 67-49 win over Robert Morris on November 22, 1997). They followed that with a 78-51 beating of Tennessee Tech to improve their record to 6-0. Ohio State hadn't won that many games consecutively since a nine-game string of victories during the 1991-92 season, when they finished 26-6.

Although the Buckeyes were undefeated, not everyone was convinced that they had turned the proverbial corner. They were criticized for playing a cupcake schedule. Their first six opponents had combined for only a 74-100 record during the 1997-98 season. Only Penn State had finished with a winning record the season before—19-13, with two of those victories over the Buckeyes. "Do we have to upgrade our home schedule in the future?" O'Brien asked. "Yes, but we have to be ready to play that kind of schedule. We can't lose sight of the fact that we won eight games last season."

For a team that was coming off a last-place finish in the Big Ten with a 1-15 record, its early-season success transcended mere victory. The Buckeyes, Neshaun Coleman argued, needed their egos stroked. They had tasted defeat so often that victory of any sort was sweet. However, each victory attracted more poll voters who were hesitant to pencil in Ohio State on their ballot only because of its easy schedule. With many of the preseason top 25 teams falling early, the poll was turned upside down, elevating fringe teams— which Ohio State had become—into the mix.

There remained, however, hard-core holdouts. They looked over the numbers with a microscope. Thus far, the 8-2 Buckeyes had beaten five of their 10 opponents by at least 27 points, causing some to ask the inevitable, "How could a team that had lost 22 games the year before make such an abrupt about-face?" Again, doubters pointed toward a strength-of-schedule rating that was 11th among the 11 teams in the Big Ten.

Yet there was a method to O'Brien's madness. He wanted to work on his players' psyche before throwing them into the pit with bulldogs that bite. "Everyone made a big deal of our schedule," O'Brien said. "We knew what we were doing."

O'Brien was readying his team for an upcoming holiday tournament in Puerto Rico. First, the Buckeyes would make a road trip to Nashville,

where they would meet the Vanderbilt Commodores. On Nov. 28, the Buckeyes' team bus arrived at Memorial Gym at Vanderbilt early in the afternoon.
The Buckeyes went through an extended shoot-around in preparation for
their game with the Commodores. Penn worked on the jump shot that sometimes deserted him. Johnson, with freshman center Will Dudley throwing
his 220 pounds into his thin, 6-foot-11 frame, worked on his inside moves.
The Buckeyes would need Penn's outside shot, and Johnson had to get something done inside against the Commodores' bigger frontcourt.

This was one of those games, O'Brien warned, in which the Buckeyes
couldn't lean too heavily on Penn and Redd. He was prophetic. Redd was
held to 2-for-6 shooting and 10 points. Penn, though, tormented the Commodores, pouring in 23 points and grabbing seven rebounds. Johnson fash-
ioned his best game of the season, totaling 15 points, seven rebounds, and
seven blocked shots.

It took six games, but at last, Johnson looked as if he was maturing. He
wasn't trying to block every shot within his reach, and he didn't force up any
bad shot attempts, as he was tempted to do in his first year as a starter. He was
more disciplined now, and his progression would be greater when, and if, he
committed to crashing the boards with more enthusiasm. The Commodores
took advantage of Johnson's tentativeness under the basket to get several
second-chance points that left Ohio State trailing 88-86 in the final minute
of overtime.

The game wasn't lost until Penn was called for traveling with 22 seconds remaining in overtime. Penn followed that miscue with an errant jumper.
In the pregame warm-ups, he had hit that shot almost effortlessly, but this
time it ricocheted off the front of the rim. Dan Langhi knocked down two
free throws with four seconds to go, giving the Commodores a narrow 92-86
victory.

The Buckeyes didn't hang their heads. They had been competitive
against a Vanderbilt team that some thought good enough to compete for the
Southeastern Conference title. That said a lot for Ohio State, considering an
SEC team had played in the national championship game in each of the
previous five years. Kentucky won the title in both 1996 and 1998, while
Arkansas mounted a successful title run in 1994. The Buckeyes knew they
were facing their first true test of the season; the Commodores had handed
O'Brien his first loss at Ohio State, the year before, a 64-54 setback that
ended a 3-0 start for the Buckeyes.

Again, Vanderbilt had spoiled the Buckeyes' perfect beginning. The
Commodores hadn't lost a nonconference game at home since 1995. That
loss, ironically, was to a Boston College team coached by O'Brien, with Penn
as his point man. "We learned a great deal about ourselves against Vanderbilt,"
O'Brien said. "We took the game into overtime when it looked as though we

were out of it. People could question our schedule, they could question our recruiting class, but no one could question those guys' hearts."

On the ride back to Columbus, the Buckeyes didn't dwell on their first defeat of the season. After all, they were expected to stumble occasionally. So they kicked up their Nikes and listened to their music and talked basketball. Mostly, Penn and Coleman did the talking. They were true basketball junkies who thumbed through newspapers, storing away scores, statistics, and standings. They knew most everything about the Buckeyes' next opponent. It wasn't lost on them that Redd had put together one of his best performances during his freshman season against that opponent, the Toledo Rockets. Redd, along with Sanderson, had played all 40 minutes. He had made nine of his 10 field-goal attempts and scored a game-high 26 points.

The numbers that mattered most to Penn and Coleman were on the scoreboard. With Coleman still sidelined with an injured knee, the Buckeyes lost back-to-back games on the road, the second a 64-63 setback against the Rockets. That loss—to one of the Mid-American Conference's best teams—again had the Buckeyes' critics claiming their 6-0 start was a façade. O'Brien managed to smile through the criticism. The Buckeyes returned home to hammer Tennessee-Martin 92-56 and Florida Atlantic 99-70.

The Buckeyes were now 8-2. They were about to embark on a Caribbean trip that would be anything but a vacation cruise. Value City Arena was the Buckeyes' comfort zone, but they would find themselves in Bayamon, Puerto Rico. No one expected them to compete with North Carolina State, Alabama-Birmingham, and Mississippi. If they could get away with a win, maybe two, the trip would have been a valuable learning experience. Instead, the Buckeyes grew up in a hurry. They surprised everyone—including their coaches—with how well they handled three more experienced teams.

The Buckeyes played like a team starved for success. They beat Alabama-Birmingham 71-64 and routed North Carolina State 81-64. Then, in the title game, Ohio State came from behind to beat Mississippi 67-62 to claim its first three-game, regular-season tourney title since Lucas and Havlicek led the Buckeyes to wins over UCLA, USC, and Washington in the Los Angeles Classic in 1961. If the Buckeyes had doubted their own abilities, their conquest in Puerto Rico now made them believers.

"I think that Puerto Rico Tournament changed the whole team's attitude," assistant coach Paul Biancardi said. "We won three games in three nights. It was even more impressive considering we beat two NCAA Tournament teams (Alabama-Birmingham and Mississippi) from the year before. It was the first time we had won anything. Or accomplished anything as a team. We proved we could be a good team. We didn't have any hostile fans. We didn't play before any fans. At that point, we knew we could beat people."

Again, Penn and Redd led the way against the Rebels in the title game. They combined to score 39 points, including 12 of 17 free throws. For the tournament, Redd averaged 23.3 points per game and was named the tourney's MVP. Penn scored 16.7 points and dished out 4.3 assists to earn all-tournament team honors, along with Redd and Singleton. Again, Singleton quietly compiled some impressive numbers. He scored 11 points and took down nine rebounds, including six offensive boards, in the victory over Mississippi.

"The thing that got all of our attention was how we played in Puerto Rico," O'Brien said. "It's one of the places where some of the best teams want to go because there are some really good teams. We ended up beating three teams that went to the NCAA Tournament. We talked to our guys about their goals, and to a man, they talked about getting to the NCAA Tournament. Our mantra was, we were going to push you. When we got to Puerto Rico, we started talking about quality wins. We reminded our players about their goal of making it to the NCAA Tournament, so part of the equation is quality wins over quality opponents from quality conferences. In this case, we were talking about three teams ranked in the Top 20. Everybody talks about the SEC and ACC, and beating their top teams helps you.

"When we returned to the hotel, our players were walking around the hotel with a little hop in their step," O'Brien added. "We felt good about what we were able to do and that was a part of us coming together. We tried to keep it loose on the road. You have to give them some freedom, but you have to tighten the reins when it's time. To be able to walk out of there with a championship was a huge step for our program.

"In the tournament in Hawaii the year before, we lost to New Mexico State by 30 points, then lost by 20 to BYU, and came back stateside 6-6. Our confidence was shattered. We go to a tropical setting and come back with three losses. A year later, we go to a tropical setting and come back with three wins. When we came back from Puerto Rico, we were like floating a little bit."

The win over Mississippi was special, said O'Brien, because the Buckeyes had to hang on after the Rebels backed them against the ropes in the waning minutes. The Buckeyes didn't get much point production from their bench, mostly because Coleman and freshman center Will Dudley were out of action. Freshman guard Brian Brown scored only two points, but he played a solid 25 minutes, spelling sophomore forward Jon Sanderson, giving Ohio State a better defensive matchup against the Rebels' quick guards. The Buckeyes led 41-34 at halftime, only to have Mississippi come from behind to take the lead. But it was Ohio State's unheralded role player, Singleton, who put the game on ice with a steal and a three-point play that gave Ohio State enough of a cushion to withstand a rally in the last minute by the Rebels.

In his hotel room in Puerto Rico, assistant coach Dave Spiller didn't take time to savor the victory. His mind was on recruiting. He wondered if he would have time to see two or three blue-chip prospects who would fit perfectly into O'Brien's system. Spiller and Biancardi spent as much time on the phone as they did drawing up game plans. The Buckeyes were showing signs of coming out of their five-year funk. Now, the task before them was to turn over every rock in search of the student-athletes who would make Ohio State a perennial title contender in the Big Ten, which is consistently rated among the top three conferences in the country.

Spiller, a 1978 graduate of Canisius College, Biancardi, and Boyages were selected by *Sport* magazine as three of the best assistant coaches in America. Spiller considered other coaching jobs while an assistant at Boston College, but his loyalty to O'Brien had led him to Columbus. In Puerto Rico, he could sense that Ohio State's fortunes were about to turn. "We had recruited some outstanding young men to help us rebuild the program at Ohio State," Spiller said. "After we won the Puerto Rico tournament, I was beginning to feel confident that something good was about to happen."

As the Big Ten season approached, the Buckeyes were wrapping up a 10-day road trip—six days in Puerto Rico and four days in Miami. While most everyone in Columbus envied them, the Buckeyes longed to be home. They had consumed too much sunshine, and this extended road trip was beginning to feel more like a vacation. In reality, they were emotionally spent after surprising everyone in Puerto Rico. O'Brien could see it in his players' body language that the long trip had taken its toll, at least mentally. This, however, was not a time to take a step backward. The white, sandy beaches and the pristine golf courses in South Florida were tempting attractions for O'Brien, so he had to remind himself—and his team—that this wasn't a pleasure trip.

The Buckeyes could gather a lot of momentum if they could go into Sunrise, Florida, and win back-to-back holiday tournaments. The Orange Bowl Classic featured three other ambitious teams—the Miami Hurricanes, the Michigan Wolverines, and the Florida Gators. The Hurricanes' forwards, Tim James and Johnny Hemsley, were among the top-rated players in the Big East. They would pose a tough matchup for Singleton and Sanderson.

The Buckeyes were fighting uphill from the start, falling behind by as many as 14 points to the Hurricanes. Ohio State would put together a familiar rally in the second half, but come up short, 72-64. O'Brien told reporters afterwards, "We had no answer for Tim James. He demonstrated why he was one of the premier players in America. He was a real tough matchup for us, because we were small at his position and he jumps over guys. I believe being on the road for 10 days kind of took its toll on us because we were lethargic."

The Buckeyes played as if their feet were stuck in potholes on a Ft. Lauderdale beach. They shot only 28 percent from the floor, missing shots from around the basket. Their legs were as rubbery as a winded heavyweight's. Only the Hurricanes didn't pack a big-enough punch to deliver the knockout. The Buckeyes made one last flurry to close to within four points twice in the last five minutes.

"We were disappointed with the loss, but we were impressed with how our team kept fighting back," O'Brien said. "We were tired and we were on the road. We had just had enough of each other. We had played four games away from home against four good teams, and we won three of them. We figured if we could get a split, we would have done pretty good for ourselves."

The Buckeyes were headed home to play in their new arena, where they had won their first six games. They closed their nonconference schedule with an 11-3 record, but they still hadn't beaten a ranked team since upsetting No. 17 Indiana 73-67 at St. John Arena on January 30, 1997. It didn't matter to O'Brien, because he saw something in his team that he hoped would bring the Buckeyes back to the Sunshine State to participate in the Final Four at Tropicana Field in St. Petersburg.

BIG PAYBACK IN THE BIG TEN

9

After winning the preseason tourney in Puerto Rico and losing in the Orange Bowl Classic, the Buckeyes prepared to resume play in the Big Ten, having gathered a great deal of momentum and confidence. Even though they scored a seemingly mild 70-62 upset of Penn State in an unusually early Big Ten opener on December 20, 1998, the Buckeyes—despite an 11-3 record—impressed few college basketball analysts, most of whom predicted the Buckeyes would finish far behind conference favorites Michigan State, Indiana, Purdue, and Minnesota.

Besides, the Buckeyes had lost 22 of their last 23 games against Big Ten opponents—including a school-record 20 consecutive conference setbacks. In fact, they had won only five of 35 Big Ten games during the previous two seasons, including a 1-15 record in O'Brien's first season in Columbus. The Buckeyes didn't bust a grape in the Big Ten for six consecutive seasons, as they compiled a 25-81 record.

Indeed, it was easy for the experts to write off the Buckeyes. No one, even in his or her wildest dreams, could have imagined a scenario in which Ohio State would contend in one of the most competitive conferences in America. The Buckeyes were overlooked in part because their conference brethren beat them sometimes unmercifully during the 1997-98 season, which included a 107-75 loss to Purdue and an 84-58 whipping at the hands of Michigan State.

The Buckeyes had many scores to settle in the conference during the 1998-99 season. It was time for a big payback in the Big Ten.

The Buckeyes marched into the Kohl Center in Madison, Wisconsin, on January 2, 1999, with a huge chip on their collective shoulders. This was a good place to start, considering the Buckeyes had won their only conference game there the season before.

Even though the Buckeyes had positioned themselves at the doorstep of the AP Top 25 poll, the Badgers and their fans weren't yet convinced that the Buckeyes' 11-3 start was a sign of a turnaround at Ohio State. The Buckeyes had already heard such cynicism on radio talk shows in Columbus. There were a few who believed, but for the most part, the Buckeyes hadn't attracted a caravan of supporters.

The Buckeyes had something to prove to everyone. They Badgers' only worry, it seemed, was taking Ohio State lightly. The 19th-ranked Badgers, despite losing their conference opener to Michigan, were 12-2. They had knocked off No. 16 Temple and Texas, leaving the oddsmakers to believe that Ohio State couldn't stay within 15 points.

If nothing else, the Buckeyes possessed a more positive attitude. They believed they could win in Madison. They wanted to do more than compete and just push the favored Badgers. The Buckeyes wanted a rare Big Ten victory.

An hour before tip-off, guard Brian Brown stayed on the court to take a few more jumpers. He didn't particularly like the rims. It seemed every shot bounced hard off the rim. So he had to zero in on the bottom of the net. He couldn't depend on a friendly bounce, because many of his shots were lacking the loft that would give him that second-chance bounce off the backboard or the rim. It could happen, he figured, that he might need that shot later in the game if the Buckeyes were close.

When O'Brien recruited Brown, he wasn't looking for a shooter. In fact, he wasn't looking for Brown at all. He had been out trying to recruit center Will Dudley, who was forced to miss the entire 1998-99 season after a knee injury sidelined him in November. Brown was going to be the consummate role player. More important, O'Brien wanted another solid citizen on the bench. He envisioned Brown someday assuming the leadership role along with Penn. Brown relished his role, and he fit perfectly within O'Brien's system.

Brown, a 6-3, 190-pound guard, had averaged 17.6 points and 5.4 assists during his senior season at Brooklyn Bishop Loughlin High School in New York. He had earned many honors, including selection as the eighth-best guard prospect in the country by basketball analyst and former University of Detroit coach Dick Vitale. But O'Brien had focused his recruiting efforts on Brown's teammate, 6-foot-9 center Will Dudley. The Buckeyes had other guards in mind, and had already gotten a commitment from one of the top Serbian junior national players, Slobodan "Boban" Savovic, who was scoring 23 points per game at Eastside High School in New Jersey.

"I remember talking with Dudley's high school coach [Bob Leckie] and his mother at Will's house, and everyone understood that I was looking for good guys," O'Brien said. "But you also need talent to compete at this level. Then, Dudley's mother turned to me and said, 'You should be talking to Brian Brown, because he is a super-nice young man who is also a very talented basketball player.'"

Brown's recruitment with Providence College didn't work out, and all of sudden, he became available. O'Brien went fishing for Dudley, but left New York with an unexpected catch. And it was Dudley's mother who turned O'Brien on to Brown. Leckie said, "Will Dudley is the second-best guy I've coached."

O'Brien asked, "Who is the first?"

Then, Dudley's mother said, "...Brian Brown."

"Will Dudley says Brian Brown is the best guy he's ever met," O'Brien said. "But when Will Dudley's mother names Brian Brown instead of her own son, I'm saying to myself, 'Something is up here.' I knew Dudley a little bit. We were already trying to recruit him. We talked to everybody in New York. They said, not great players, but unbelievable kids who have the potential to be good players. So we got two high-caliber kids."

O'Brien took their advice and offered Brown a scholarship. At the time, O'Brien figured he could mold Brown into the type of player he thought he could become. He would give the Buckeyes some solid minutes off the bench and play the aggressive style of defense necessary to compete in the rugged Big Ten. Brown, though, didn't see himself being thrust into the spotlight as a freshman, especially during this game at Madison.

In a game of shifting momentum, Wisconsin seemingly had regained control as the teams finished regulation tied at 68. The Buckeyes had relied almost exclusively on Penn and Redd, as they combined to score 48 points. The other three starters—Singleton, Sanderson and Johnson—had one field goal apiece. O'Brien had to go to his bench, which finally had oft-injured senior guard Neshaun Coleman back on it. Coleman, a usually reliable outside shooter, played only six minutes. That meant Brown and Savovic had to step up to lend a hand to Penn and Redd, who were drawing double teams every time they came close to the ball.

The Badgers took a 74-71 lead on a pair of free throws by forward Sean Mason with 2:27 left in overtime. Redd countered with two free throws to narrow the gap to a single point with 1:58 to play. To the amazement of the partisan Wisconsin crowd of about 5,000, the Big Ten's whipping boys were fighting back. The Badgers had also lost their usual home advantage—as nearly 11,000 seats were empty because a blizzard kept the majority of

Wisconsin fans home. Still other Wisconsin fans were partying in Pasadena following the football team's win in the Rose Bowl.

Penn made only seven of his 17 shots, but he kept encouraging Brown and Savovic to shoot whenever the Badgers would leave them unattended on the perimeter. Savovic didn't have to be told twice to put the ball up. He made the most of his 15 minutes, scoring nine points—all on three-point field goals.

Brown had always been unselfish, sometimes too unselfish. He always looked to pass before shooting. He had done much of his scoring inside, getting the garbage baskets off loose balls and offensive rebounds. The Badgers stepped away from him at the perimeter because they didn't fear his jumper. As the clock moved inside the one-minute mark, again Brown was left alone. He couldn't get the ball inside to Johnson, and the Badgers denied Penn and Redd the ball.

Then, with 58 seconds left on the clock, Brown pulled up from 21 feet, just a step or two from the three-point arc, and let go a jumper from nearly the same spot he had taken shot after shot during the pregame warm-ups. O'Brien stared down the shot. He knew the odds of Brown making that shot weren't good. Brown had taken 26 three-point attempts during the season and had made only nine. The numbers weren't as bad as they looked, really. Brown had canned one of every three of his three-point shots. O'Brien was thinking, too, that this isn't why he recruited Brown. But he knew way back during the exhibition season that someone other than Redd or Penn would have to make a meaningful, game-winning shot if the Buckeyes were going to challenge for the Big Ten crown.

As the wide bodies filled the paint in anticipation of a missed shot, Brown's 21-footer landed gently in the net to give Ohio State a 75-74 lead. The Buckeyes increased their lead to 77-74 on a pair of Redd free throws with 11 seconds to go. Ohio State, a team that had lost 16 of its previous 17 conference games, had convinced the Badgers' fans its 11-3 start wasn't a fluke, as the Buckeyes earned a hard-fought 78-74 win over Wisconsin.

"We played as hard as we could," said Brown, who finished with five points. "We weren't as interested in proving anything to Wisconsin and the rest of the conference as we were in proving to ourselves that we could win these kind of games. You always dream of making that shot in that situation, but it doesn't happen too often. I felt I could make the shot. Actually, the shot felt good the moment it left my hands. I think at that moment, I started to believe in myself. I believe in this team."

The Buckeyes were still searching for converts, those lost souls whose enthusiasm had waned after six consecutive nonwinning seasons in the Big Ten. The Buckeyes would need their support when they returned home to Columbus on Jan. 9 to face No. 13 Indiana. The Buckeyes had convinced a few coaches that their 12-3 start was legitimate. For the first time in six years, the Buckeyes were ranked in the Top 25. They received enough points to nail down the No. 25 spot in the *USA Today*/ESPN coaches poll.

Even with all their early-season success, the Buckeyes were still trying to get a second look from the Ohio State fans. On New Year's Day, most of Ohio State's student body and alumni spent the day watching college football bowl games. They were mostly interested in the Ohio State–Texas A&M battle in the Sugar Bowl. It wouldn't have been the slightest exaggeration to assume that a great number of Ohio State's followers were totally unaware that the basketball team had an outstanding 11-3 record that would move to 12-3 the next day. The Buckeyes had sneaked up on most everyone.

The Buckeyes' turnaround didn't get much attention because six other Big Ten teams were ranked in both of the major polls. The Buckeyes weren't the feel-good team of the year because unheralded Gonzaga had become the media darling. The Buckeyes weren't always the lead story on local television, even when nothing else was happening in Columbus. The focus, instead, was on the football team and the imminent impeachment of President Bill Clinton.

The White House scandal dominated the news during the entire college basketball season. While all eyes were on Monica Lewinsky, the former White House intern whose affair with the president left the country with an ethical dilemma, Ohio State made its move without much fanfare. The Buckeyes hadn't been on national television, so they were strangers to most everyone outside the Columbus city limits.

"I'm thinking it's a good thing no one knows anything about us," Redd said. "We didn't have to worry about any distractions. We didn't have any pressure on us because no one was watching."

The nation had been gripped not only by the impeachment hearings, but also by the escalating conflict in Kosovo. There were a number of great performances and great teams—such as Connecticut and Duke—that were overshadowed by life's reality and the fragility of world peace, particularly in Kosovo and the Middle East. The uneasiness in Kosovo was felt in Columbus. Savovic and his brother Predrag, who transferred from the University of Alabama–Birmingham to Hawaii, were sometimes distracted by the civil war that threatened to tear apart their country. Savovic sometimes regretted leaving, thinking perhaps he should have accepted the numerous offers he had to play professional basketball in Europe.

"It's hard to play with all that's happening in my country," said Savovic, who had survived at Eastside High despite being the only Serbian on campus. "My family is happy that I am playing basketball in America. When I first came to school here, I didn't understand anybody. Nobody spoke my language, but I had to learn. I had to learn to deal with the fact that, right now, there is nothing I can do about what's going on back home."

Savovic had come to Columbus after turning down scholarship offers from several Division I programs, including St. John's, Miami of Florida, and

Nevada-Las Vegas: "I came to Ohio State because Coach O'Brien was awesome. I felt comfortable with the coaches and all the guys on the team. I had a feeling we were going to play in a lot of big games."

In Columbus, no game is as big as Ohio State–Indiana. The Hoosiers are to Ohio State basketball what Michigan is to Ohio State football—the Buckeyes' most hated rival. "The television and radio talk shows talked about it all week like it was Ohio State–Michigan in football," assistant coach Paul Biancardi said. There was little love lost between the Ohio State fans and Indiana coach Bobby Knight, who had been a member of the Buckeyes' Big Ten championship teams in the early 1960s.

Penn was now familiar enough with the Big Ten that he knew how much the Buckeyes' fans wanted this game. This wasn't about the Buckeyes proving themselves as legitimate Big Ten contenders. It was about pride. Nothing else. If the Buckeyes could beat Indiana, then everyone—including the hold-out converts—would gleefully jump on the Ohio State bandwagon and sing the Ohio State fight song long into the night. "Bob Knight is such an icon in this area, a win would really get the people in Columbus behind us," said Penn, who hoped to celebrate his 22nd birthday with the Buckeyes' biggest victory in nearly six years.

O'Brien and Knight talked briefly before tip-off, and Knight appeared as confident as ever despite the Hoosiers' 1-2 start in Big Ten play. The Hoosiers entered Value City Arena having lost five straight Big Ten road games and seven of their previous eight over the past two seasons. The Buckeyes were perfect in their new home. Their win at Wisconsin had the Buckeyes talking about holding serve in the first of two games against Indiana. They were no longer talking about holding on at the end and hoping something good might happen. The Buckeyes wouldn't say it, but O'Brien could sense that his team felt it belonged on the same floor with Indiana.

The game hadn't reached halftime before the Buckeyes established themselves as the dominant team and went on to win easily. Singleton told reporters afterwards, "The difference was desire. We really wanted this one. We had guys diving for loose balls. We had guys coming in and off the bench and contributing. Whenever Indiana made a charge, we refused to back down—not like we did in the past."

The Buckeyes blitzed the Hoosiers, beating them by 17 points, 73-56. Ohio State's win was so thorough that Knight couldn't even throw a tirade late in the first half to ignite his Hoosiers into action. Knight sat on the Indiana bench with a solemn expression on his face. He had to have counted this as an Indiana sure-thing victory during the preseason. His Hoosiers hadn't lost but 15 times to Ohio State in his 27 years, which is the primary reason why the Orrville, Ohio, native isn't considered a favorite son in the state capital. Knight tried every combination possible to ruin Penn's birthday, but in the end, Penn had his cake and ate it, too.

"It was the best birthday present I could have had," Penn said. "I didn't get a chance to do much celebrating. I was too exhausted both mentally and physically. There was so much hype surrounding this game that all I wanted to do afterwards was relax. At Boston College, we beat Indiana in a tournament game, and I don't think that game had the same kind of excitement we experienced in this game."

The Buckeyes had just scored their most decisive win over an Indiana team since 1970, a 100-83 beating they put on the Hoosiers at St. John Arena in 1970. The Buckeyes hadn't beaten a Knight-coached Indiana team this badly in 55 meetings. In fact, Knight hadn't lost to Ohio State by more than nine points in 28 seasons. Knight could do nothing to change those ominous numbers. "The one thing we could not do was get knocked out at the start of the second half and we did," Knight said. "That was absolutely the key."

The Buckeyes, who hadn't won back-to-back games against ranked opponents since beating Indiana and Iowa at the start of the Big Ten season in 1990, broke open the game with two 9-0 runs in the second half. The Buckeyes wouldn't let the Hoosiers get within nine points over the final 10:07. The Buckeyes scored nine unanswered points to take a 59-42 lead. At that point, the crowd erupted, sensing imminent victory over an Indiana team whose superiority had failed as it dropped to 1-3 in the conference. The crowd grew louder and louder as the final seconds ticked away, assuring Ohio State of only its second win over Indiana in eight meetings.

Said O'Brien, "I don't hear a whole lot during the course of a game. But there were a couple of stretches where it was very hard not to hear the people. This could be a terrific place to play."

"There were moments in the game when it got really loud, and it was like old St. John Arena," said Singleton, who led the Buckeyes with 17 points. "We could barely hear the coaches in the huddle. I just hope the crowd keeps coming out to support us."

The Ohio State fans didn't want to leave the arena this night. They wanted to savor this victory like a sacred, aged wine. This was a sweet victory, one you inhale with all your senses. It was one, too, that helped the Buckeyes' fans get over the bitterness of a 93-76 loss to the Hoosiers at Assembly Hall in 1997, a game that personified the Buckeyes' six long years of frustration in the Big Ten.

The Buckeyes weren't winning with smoke and mirrors. They beat Indiana as they had their previous 12 victims, with true grit and determination. The Buckeyes had four players score in double figures, and they outrebounded Indiana 40-27. And if they kept floor burns as an official statistic, Ohio State would have enjoyed a 2-to-1 advantage. "There were no special schemes or different tactics," Penn said. "It was all about who wanted it most. We just didn't let up. Whenever you play Indiana, they can come back and bite you. We didn't want to let that happen."

If there were doubters still lingering among the sellout crowd, they couldn't be found anywhere near Value City Arena. You probably couldn't find them in Bloomington, Indiana, or Madison, Wisconsin, either.

"As we started to win, we were going down to the end of games, saying something good is going to happen," O'Brien said. "Somebody is going to make a play. It became a real confidence thing. Instead of going into games like we did a year ago, hoping to keep it close and maybe get lucky at the end, we went into games thinking we were going to win. The whole mind-set was different. It all kind of started early with two home games against Alabama and Penn State, two teams that had aspirations of getting into the NCAA Tournament. Penn State had beaten us twice the year before, and they were picked fifth in the conference. It got me feeling we could play good teams. Then, we go lose two in a row. I remember thinking the Toledo loss was a hard one for us. We knew going on the road was never going to be easy, regardless of where you are.

"We didn't play particularly well in Nashville [in a 92-86 overtime loss to Vanderbilt], but we focused on the positives. We were stressing we could have gotten beaten badly, and the fact that we got the game into overtime was a credit to our guys. We showed we were the kind of team that was not going to go away. We were not just going to bag it.

"It was important that we gave ourselves a chance to win. We wanted our guys to be upset when they lost. A year ago [during the 1997-98 season], they would sit around in the locker room, and it would look as if it was easy for the guys to accept some of the losses. We didn't want anyone to accept the losing. It was our whole mentality. All we wanted them to do was to keep playing, and it became a positive trait of our team."

O'Brien is sometimes hard to impress. He and his coaching staff celebrated only briefly the Buckeyes' win over Indiana. They weren't giving congratulatory high-fives in the coaching lounge. They almost immediately turned their attention to the 12th-ranked Iowa Hawkeyes, who were coming to town in three days for another show-me game in the Big Ten. O'Brien knew that every game would be big for the Buckeyes, considering the Big Ten was ranked first in the RPI rankings.

Ohio State's wins over Wisconsin and Indiana were greeted with mixed reviews from O'Brien. The Buckeyes had finally impressed the Associated Press voters, moving into the Top 25 at No. 21. It was the first time the AP had recognized Ohio State's efforts since January 24, 1993. (Ironically, shortly thereafter, the Buckeyes were bumped from the AP poll after back-to-back losses to none other than Wisconsin and Indiana). Despite losing to Ohio State, both Wisconsin and Indiana remained in the poll to help the Big Ten tie the record of seven conference schools in the rankings at the same time. With only four Big Ten teams—Penn State, Northwestern, Michigan, and

Illinois—out of the rankings mix, O'Brien knew the Buckeyes had to bring their A game to the show every time out:

"It's nice [to be ranked] because, for no other reason, it shows that we've gotten a little bit of respect, and it shows we're making a little bit of progress. But that's all. We can't read much more into it right now."

O'Brien had preached consistency and constantly reminded his players that they couldn't afford to lose at home. "The key in the Big Ten is to win your home games," Penn said. "As big as the win over Indiana is, it isn't going to sustain us for the rest of the season. If we can win some games on the road, that'll be great, but we have to take care of business at home. We have no choice."

The Buckeyes played like a million bucks at Value City Arena. To all the big spenders and high rollers who spent $45,000 to $65,000 a year for the 45 luxury suites, the Buckeyes were well worth the investment. The Ohio State brass could toast themselves with their gold-trimmed champagne glasses. There weren't enough seats in the house to accommodate the Ohio State fans, many of whom became believers following the Buckeyes' merciless spanking of Indiana.

On the eve of the Ohio State–Iowa showdown, the fans swamped the phones in an effort to win whatever tickets remained in a radio giveaway contest. Many of the Buckeye faithful, showing their rekindled loyalty by wearing their scarlet-and-gray clothing, gathered outside the Schottenstein Center hours before tip-off in hopes of obtaining scalped tickets. No way could Geiger or O'Brien have imagined such an unlikely scenario. The Buckeyes, just 10 months after finishing the 1997-98 season at 8-22, were now the hottest ticket in town. Ohio State was even hotter than a Dixie Chicks concert or a World Wrestling Federation brawl-a-rama. The fans stood outside in the cold, searching until they found someone who would ante up a $9 ticket for $75 or a $20 seat for $100.

The Buckeyes were back. They were playing well and generating the kind of excitement most everyone thought they would after the 1991-92 season, when they advanced to the Elite Eight and lost 75-71 in overtime to Michigan in the Midwest Regional final at Rupp Arena in Lexington, Kentucky, on March 29, 1992.

In just his second season in Columbus, O'Brien had turned things around. The Buckeyes were making noise in the Big Ten. They were delivering the promising performances that had been expected seven years earlier.

"I think we were all stunned in a very positive way by the way things happened," Geiger said. "The team was exciting, it was charismatic, it was a class act in every way. It was characterized by an incredible work ethic by players like Jason Singleton and the success of a virtual unknown like George Reese.

"I was pretty sure we were on the right track in terms of the program. I had tons of faith in Jim in terms of what he was going to do here. The fans were excited about all we were doing.

"I had almost an instant feeling when I met him. When we had a chance to spend time together, he was absolutely the right person for the job. The other key factor for me was the recommendation I got from Dave Gavitt, former Big East commissioner. I think he has a peace about him. He has confidence and he knows what to do. He has an uncanny way of expressing himself. He says exactly what you hoped you would say in that situation. He has a strong sense of value. We were in very good hands. His personality grew in his players. They believed in him."

O'Brien cautioned his players during a light workout the day before the Iowa game not to pat one another on the back too soon. He wanted them to be confident, but not cocky. After 22 years of coaching at the Division I level, O'Brien was well aware that you can be slapped off your high horse while in perfect stride. He ignored the rankings and didn't notice all the commotion outside the arena as he pulled up late in the afternoon to ready his team for the Hawkeyes. "I know we have two games ahead of us in Iowa and Michigan," O'Brien said. "Those teams are going to be ready to play us, because now we're starting to get a little attention."

The Hawkeyes had noticed. They walked into Value City Arena and were greeted by a vociferous sellout crowd. The Hawkeyes and Buckeyes couldn't hear themselves think. There was no guarded optimism among the fans, who three days earlier had witnessed the Buckeyes' blowout of Indiana. This was not the same Ohio State team that Iowa had crushed 61-46 at St. John Arena and slammed 82-70 in Iowa City the previous season. The Buckeyes were finally playing the Hawkeyes with something at stake—first place in the Big Ten.

Again, Penn played well, scoring 21 points and handing out eight assists. The Buckeyes, though, were handcuffed some, as an ailing Redd, who was slowed by a flu virus, struggled to find an open shot. Still, he finished with a flurry down the stretch to wind up with eight points. It was a grueling 40 minutes, and neither team trailed by more than a field goal over the last four minutes. It was the kind of game, said Penn, that Ohio State had to win at home. But the Hawkeyes weren't accommodating, and they silenced the crowd by handing Ohio State its first loss at Value City Arena.

The Buckeyes hadn't been this error prone since their loss to Miami of Florida in the Orange Bowl Classic on December 27, 1998. They committed back-to-back turnovers after Iowa guard Dean Oliver hit a three-pointer over the outstretched hands of Penn with 22.5 seconds remaining. Oliver then sank both ends of a one-and-one to seal Iowa's victory and leave Ohio State in second place in the conference standings.

O'Brien consoled his players afterwards. But he chastised them, too. He reminded them of the mountain they must climb to conquer responsibility. Now wasn't the time to rest on their laurels. If Ohio State was going to continue to rebuild, there were still a lot of nails to hammer and doors to hang. Surely, Penn and Redd were the foundation, but there remained far too much touch-up work to do.

O'Brien had earned a reputation at Boston College as a masterful motivator. He knew he would be tested this time, because the Buckeyes were down on themselves after falling short in an emotional game. "It's obviously very disappointing to not have won this game, because I thought that we played very hard," said O'Brien, his raspy voice strained from yelling out instructions in the final exasperating minutes. "I thought it was a terrific college basketball game. We put ourselves in position to win, and unfortunately we just didn't make some plays at the end when we needed to."

Four days later, the Buckeyes failed to make enough plays in Ann Arbor in an 84-74 loss to Michigan that showcased a career-high 22-point, 10-rebound effort from center Josh Asselin. Asselin had his way in the paint because Johnson was saddled with foul trouble and played only 18 ineffective minutes. The Buckeyes trailed only 31-30 at halftime; but with Penn and Redd forced to beat the Wolverines from the perimeter, Ohio State lost two straight for the first time.

The loss to Michigan turned O'Brien's guts inside out. He didn't want to lose to Michigan. These were the same Wolverines who a year earlier had taken salt and rubbed it into Ohio State's wounded pride on January 17, 1998, during a 79-61 thrashing at St. John Arena.

"We were always looking for things we could use to help motivate our guys and to make some point," O'Brien said. "We were playing zone, and the game was over and we were getting drubbed. Michigan rubbed it in by scoring dunks on two ally-oop plays. I said to our kids, 'You need to remember this, and you can't accept this kind of stuff.' You can't accept the fact that you're down right now, and you're getting your nose rubbed into it a little bit. You can't allow that to happen.' I asked them, 'Doesn't anyone have any pride in what's going on here?' I remember saying if you're going to get beat, go down swinging. It's not meant to go down fighting, but go down competing and don't allow this to ever happen again. Just remember it. Just remember it."

After the two straight losses, the doubting Thomases resurfaced. Had the Buckeyes hit the wall? Had the rest of the Big Ten figured out their act? Could anyone except Penn and Redd turn defeat into victory? Had Cinderella's slippers gotten a bit tight?

O'Brien and his assistants scratched their heads, but according to him, they didn't, "reach for the panic button."

The Buckeyes were about to begin a critical stretch in the season. They would play No. 16 Purdue and No. 17 Minnesota at home before taking to the road to play No. 8 Michigan State in East Lansing. Redd emphasized to his teammates that a split at home would be unacceptable. The Buckeyes had to win both games to improve their chances of earning an NCAA Tournament bid. "We got together as a team and talked about how close we are to achieving our goals," Redd said. "It was obvious that we hadn't lost our hunger. We had only lost our momentum."

Ohio State regained its momentum with convincing wins over Purdue and Minnesota, two teams that had embarrassed it over the last five years. The Boilermakers had beaten the Buckeyes nine straight times. The Golden Gophers had won seven of the last eight meetings, including five in a row. This time, however, the Buckeyes took both teams to the woodshed and lashed out at them, beating them both by 29 points—72-43 over Purdue and 89-60 over Minnesota—in a span of four days.

In their win over Purdue, Redd scored 30 points to help hand Purdue coach Gene Keady his most lopsided defeat at Ohio State in his 18 years with the Boilermakers. In hitting 14 of his 21 shots from the floor, Redd became the second fastest in Ohio State history to reach the 1,000-point plateau. Redd accomplished that feat in 49 games, while former two-time national Player of the Year, Jerry Lucas, did it in only 38 games. The Buckeyes got only six points from Penn, but the bench chipped in with 18, including seven by forward George Reese.

Penn's point production was down, but his leadership stock soared after the Buckeyes' lackluster outing against Michigan. He summoned the Buckeyes the day after and demanded a more gutsy effort against Purdue. Even though Penn's relationship with Redd was sometimes lukewarm, he approached Redd, candidly imploring the sophomore swingman to get his groove on. It was bad enough that Redd was in a shooting slump, but he also began to play head games with himself by taking ill-advised, off-balance shots that wouldn't have found the net even if they had been blessed.

"Some of our guys' heads were hanging," Penn said. "Some of us were right on the edge and could have gone either way. We had to turn this thing around. We had done it before, so it wasn't impossible for us to believe we could get it done." Admittedly, O'Brien doesn't put much stock in players' meetings. His old-fashioned values reasoned that a good work ethic would point the Buckeyes in the right direction. "I was just happy to see it was Scoonie organizing the meeting, because I knew something good would come out of it," O'Brien said. "I trust him. His teammates trust him, too."

Keady and Minnesota coach Clem Haskins were convinced that Ohio State was no longer a fluke. "They're vastly improved, and they've got more talent on that bench than people realize," Keady said. "Their guards are hard to match up with, and they have good quickness and excellent athletes up front."

Seven-year-old Jimmy O'Brien's first love was baseball. (Jim O'Brien's personal collection)

One of the stars of Toomey's Indians stands in the back row, third from left. (Jim O'Brien's personal collection)

Fifteen-year-old Jim (front, second from left) and his dad (back, left) teamed together on an adult CYO squad. (Jim O'Brien's personal collection)

Jim (14) earned All-New York City honors for St. Francis High in Brooklyn. (Jim O'Brien's personal collection)

Jim O'Brien scores two of the 1,273 points he tallied for the Boston College Eagles from 1968 to 1971. (Courtesy of Boston College)

Chuck Daly (left) was Jim's coach at Boston College during his junior and senior years. (Courtesy of Boston College)

Basketball Hall of Famer Bob Cousy, shown celebrating his 100th victory at Boston College, taught Jim O'Brien the fine points of guard play. (Courtesy of Jet Commercial Photographers)

Jim O'Brien played for the ABA's Pittsburgh Condors in 1971. (Jim O'Brien's personal collection)

Guarded here by Indiana's Billy Keller, O'Brien was a member of the talented Kentucky Colonels from 1971 to 1973. (Jim O'Brien's personal collection)

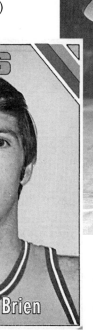

The 6-1 guard was a regular on the ABA's San Diego Sails from 1974 to 1975. (Jim O'Brien's personal collection)

Jim O'Brien and Art Perry (top, left) served as assistant coaches at UConn for head coach Dom Perno (top, right). (Courtesy of University of Connecticut)

O'Brien became head coach at St. Bonaventure University in 1982 and won Atlantic 10 Coach of the Year laurels in his first season. (Courtesy of St. Bonaventure University)

In 11 seasons as head coach at Boston College, Jim O'Brien directed the Eagles to postseason play six times. (Courtesy of Boston College)

Led by all-star center Bill Curley, O'Brien's Boston College squad made big news in 1994 when it upset top-ranked North Carolina in the NCAA Tournament. (Jim O'Brien's personal collection)

Scoonie Penn (12) followed Jim O'Brien to Ohio State from Boston College and helped lead the Buckeyes to a Big Ten title and an appearance in the Final Four. (Courtesy of The Ohio State University)

Jim O'Brien celebrates the fruits of success by cutting down the nets after his Buckeyes won the South Regional championship in Knoxville, Tennessee. This win sent the Buckeyes to the Final Four. (Courtesy of The Ohio State University)

Every coach dreams about taking his team to the Final Four, and that dream came true for Jim O'Brien in 1999. (Courtesy of The Ohio State University)

Jim O'Brien and his two daughters, Amy (left) and Erin. (Courtesy of The Ohio State University)

The Buckeyes had spent almost the entire season trying to gain some respect. Their wins over Minnesota and Purdue weren't simply about drawing even with their Big Ten brethren. They were about getting even, too. They were payback for years of embarrassing losses to conference teams that not only kicked them while they were falling, but also stomped the Buckeyes into submission.

"It was the same thing with Purdue," O'Brien said. "They beat us bad at home. I remember at Minnesota, they beat us bad. We weren't going to accept it. It became a pride thing. It was nice to get a little something back. We used the year before to bring back some memories. I asked them, 'Do you remember what happened to us at Minnesota last year?' It was the same thing with Purdue. We wanted them to remember what it was like. I think we had a big chip on our shoulder. Our guys had to decide if they were going to keep letting people in the Big Ten embarrass us.

"All the losing those kids had to experience for their three years, then all of sudden, wins at Purdue and Minnesota—and big games, convincingly, at home. It was about having some pride about being a Big Ten member. It was about getting some respect. We talked about that a lot. Nobody respected anything we did last year. I said to them, 'If you want to get some respect, beat Indiana in Indiana.' That would get somebody's attention in a heartbeat."

"The Minnesota game was important because we had to convince ourselves that we could win on a consistent basis," Penn said. The Buckeyes won, making 33 of 61 field-goal tries and 8 of 21 three-point attempts. Ohio State was winning impressively, but there were kinks in the Buckeyes' armor.

At 15-5 overall and 5-2 in the Big Ten, the Buckeyes heard the shouts all around Columbus that they were nearing a tournament bid. There was reason for optimism, considering that Ohio State was only three wins shy of its combined victory total over the previous two seasons and that its five conference wins were only two short of equaling their conference win total during the same stretch.

According to Redd, the Buckeyes had exceeded their own expectations. With Michigan State on the horizon, Biancardi summoned the Buckeyes together to share with them some invaluable advice, some wisdom that O'Brien had offered years ago at Boston College. "Jim would always say, 'You're never as bad as other people think you are, and you're never as good as you think you are,'" Biancardi said. "When you buy into all the hype, that's when the newspapers can shoot you down. All the Boston College teams I coached with [O'Brien] had a great sense of chemistry and unselfishness, and that was one of the reasons why we were successful in the Big East. We couldn't compete in the Big Ten without chemistry and a bunch of unselfish guys working together.

"If you have good talent with good character, you should have a good team. Now, good coaching can help mold that team. To find those kids to do the work is the hard job. It's clear that one of the things Jim does well is manage people. He keeps everybody in check. He relies on people in different ways. And that's the way he builds his team—through honor and hard work."

For more than 10 years, O'Brien had trusted no one the way he does his coaching staff. He relinquished much of the game-day scouting responsibilities to Boyages. He relies greatly on Biancardi and Dave Spiller to find the type of players he believes best fit his system. The burden is on Randy Shrout, director of basketball operations, to make sure that the basketball program runs smoothly and that Ohio State avoids the recruiting mishaps that helped to undo Ayers. O'Brien's bottom line, of course, is finding talent that will keep the Buckeyes in stride with Michigan State, Purdue, Minnesota, Iowa, Indiana, and Wisconsin—all perennial postseason tournament participants.

Even as the Buckeyes chased after their first Big Ten title since 1992, Spiller and Biancardi were spending as much time on the phone and watching game films of possible recruits as they did on the practice court. "You can't take a break from recruiting," Biancardi said. "I am either on my phone in the office or on my cell phone, the Internet or my home phone. There is so much competition for the best players, the only way to get the best players is to outwork everyone else."

The recruiting trail is where O'Brien's assistants earn their money. It's where they have to be at their absolute best if they have any hopes of luring some of the nation's top players to Columbus. The recruiting wars are always hotly contested. If Ohio State is looking at a prize recruit, then the odds are good that a Big Ten foe is trying to work his way into the home of the same blue-chipper with hopes of delivering an even more persuasive sales pitch.

In the final four years of Ayers's tenure, the Buckeyes lost one recruiting battle after another. They came firing blanks, while their conference rivals zeroed in on Ohio's best talent. Two of Ohio's premier high school players, Calvin Booth of Columbus and Jason Collier of Springfield, ended up at Penn State and Indiana, respectively. Michigan State coach Tom Izzo came across the northern border to secure signatures on letters of intent from Toledo's Andre Hutson, Findley's A.J. Granger, Akron's Quinton Brooks, Lexington's Jamie Feick, and Westerville's Adam Wolfe.

"We think the best way to win the recruiting battles is to start recruiting kids as sophomores and continue until they commit," Spiller said. "It doesn't stop there, because you keep in contact with them once they are on the team, and you keep up on what is important in their lives. We need to develop that kind of relationship with everyone we recruit, and that's especially important in Ohio because we would like to have the state's best high school athletes playing basketball in Columbus. Michigan State has built its program around Ohio kids, and they have become very productive players."

On January 27, 1999, the Buckeyes traveled to East Lansing, where they would face Hutson and Granger at the Breslin Center. The Buckeyes, riding high after impressive wins over Purdue and Minnesota, were hoping to get even with Michigan State, a team that had beaten them nine times in a row since 1994. The Buckeyes had their egos boosted some by a big jump to No. 15 in the AP poll. Every game had something riding on it now. The Buckeyes seemed assured of at least an NIT bid. A victory over No. 4 Michigan State would not only bring them closer to securing an NCAA Tournament bid, but it would also serve as proof that Ohio State had finally left its checkered past behind.

O'Brien didn't do anything out of the ordinary in preparing the Buckeyes for the Michigan State tilt. The Buckeyes, amid a cascade of boos, looked comfortable playing in this big-game atmosphere, as they smartly went through their pregame drills. They didn't look nervous or awed by the green-and-white-clad Spartan fans filling every row of the Breslin Center. They were used to noise. The decibel level would have to increase a bit to be as deafening as it gets sometimes at Value City Arena.

Although the Ohio State–Michigan State game would give the winner the upper hand in the Big Ten race, there was also an intriguing personal battle worth watching. The hype surrounding the backcourt matchup involving Penn and Mateen Cleaves had taken on a life of its own. O'Brien and Izzo tried downplaying this duel of point guards, but both teams' destiny rested most often in the hands of Penn and Cleaves. Penn delivered the early blows, staking the Buckeyes to a 37-33 lead at the half. The Spartan fans grew silent as Ohio State stepped out to an eight-point lead, 42-34, when Redd hit a three-pointer early in the second half.

Izzo motioned to Cleaves to call time out to stem the tide. It seemed this couldn't be happening to the Spartans, who had won five straight Big Ten games after losing their conference opener by 15 points to Wisconsin. The Buckeyes were good, but Izzo didn't doubt for a second that the defending conference champions were the better team. Somehow, the Buckeyes were hanging tough. They wouldn't crack.

Finally, the Buckeyes' knees buckled. The Spartans, buoyed by three Jason Klein treys, staged a 9-1 scoring spurt to take a 51-47 lead with 8:36 left in the game. O'Brien, hoisting up his britches as the Spartans mounted their charge, walked calmly along the sideline, grimacing as Ohio State missed jumpers and layups in a scoreless five-minute stretch that would have them fighting from behind in the closing minutes. The Buckeyes' rally fell short, and Cleaves hit 10 of his 16 points in the final 2:09 as Michigan State ground its way to a 76-71 victory.

O'Brien had told his players long ago that actual wins are what count in the standings—not moral victories. They had left their guts on the floor, but they had also left victory behind because Michigan State had executed its half-court offense better at crunch time than Ohio State had. The Buckeyes had also committed nine more turnovers, 14 to 5. The Spartans had only four more rebounds [33-29], but they put back two key offensive rebounds to keep Ohio State at bay.

The Spartans had survived. Izzo, however, was convinced that the huge gap that had separated Ohio State from the Big Ten powers had shrunk to almost nothing. In his postgame interview, Izzo said, "Jim has done an incredible job in a year with that team. They play hard and they're very athletic. I've got a lot of praise for that team." Inside the Ohio State locker room, O'Brien and the Buckeyes didn't take Izzo's well-intended remarks as much of a consolation prize. "We truly believed we should have won the game," said Redd, who finished with a game-high 20 points. "You can't feel good about what happened. We have to move on."

In defeat, the Buckeyes had matured in East Lansing. It was easily their most valuable and fruitful loss.

"Andy Geiger was at the game, and he was in the locker room afterwards," O'Brien said. "I was as upset after losing that game than any other game we had lost. Andy told me not to lose sight of the fact that Michigan State was fourth in the country and don't lose sight of the fact that we played a helluva game. I said to Andy, 'I'm not upset we lost the game, but what I'm upset about is that we forfeited a chance to have a great win.' We didn't win a game we had a chance to win. At this point, all we were trying to do was get into the NCAA Tournament. The more games you win, it meant we were getting closer to the tournament. I said to the kids before the game that if you want to get into the tournament, beat the No. 4-ranked team on their home floor.

"I thought it was two good teams really getting after each other. We got off to a good start, and we were in a position to win. It was clear to me we missed out on a great opportunity. If we go in there and lose by 20, people ask, 'Hey, what did you expect?' They made a couple of big shots, and we had a hard time scoring in some stretches. I was on the guys hard at halftime, but I embraced them all when the game was over because of the way they hung in there.

"If you come into this environment in East Lansing, you can win in any environment. It was a confident scenario. Even though we lost, there was a lot to be taken from that game. We weren't bad. We had convinced ourselves we could do this."

Now, the Buckeyes were poised to embark on one of their most impressive runs since galloping into Lexington, Kentucky, to challenge for a Final Four berth in 1992. As unlikely as it may have seemed at the start of the Big Ten season, Ohio State's trip to Illinois would prove to be a character builder, a game that would challenge the Buckeyes' fortitude and mental toughness.

"The Illinois game was a gut check," O'Brien said. "Even though Illinois was not having the best of seasons, we didn't play well. It was very hard for us. It was not a gimme game, even though they were struggling. To be able to win the game on the road, and one in which we didn't play well, was a good sign. It was a game in which we persevered. I remember thinking I shouldn't get on the players too much. We had to be patient and keep encouraging. I kept thinking something good would happen. I don't know if I thought the same thing in East Lansing."

The Buckeyes weren't supposed to be in this position as the oddsmakers' choice to win this game. The Fighting Illini were young, but Illinois coach Lon Kruger had one of the top recruiting classes in the country. These teams were headed in opposite directions, and Illinois pointed to this game as an opportunity to begin its own turnaround. Freshman guard Corey Bradford turned heads with a 29-point performance that left O'Brien throwing his hands up in frustration.

Every time Bradford gunned down a long-range jumper, O'Brien would stare down the defender who backed off, allowing Bradford to pull the trigger. And with every dropped shot, the 13,756 fans would leap from their seats in wild celebration. At game's end, even the crowd appeared exhausted. The Buckeyes, their legs still weary from the dogfight in East Lansing, didn't have much spring in their step. Penn and Redd made only nine of their combined 25 shots. And neither could keep up with the elusive Bradford, who despite playing 39 minutes, was not breathing hard as Ohio State tried to rally from a 28-22 halftime deficit.

Amid this hostile environment, the Buckeyes needed someone to give them a spark. Neshaun Coleman was still trying to find his legs after missing nearly half the season. Coleman discovered his rhythm, as he made three treys, including a 20-footer that gave Ohio State a 56-54 lead with 3:09 remaining. Then, with 1:12 to go, the senior shooting guard swooshed another three-pointer to leave Ohio State with a 60-58 lead in the last 1:12. Coleman had fallen victim to a series of ailments all season, and he practically dragged his gimpy leg onto the court to inspire his teammates as they exchanged blows with the unrelenting Illini. The Buckeyes held a 62-61 advantage with 13.8 seconds to go, but their backs were against the wall, and Illinois had them set up for the knockout punch.

O'Brien got in his players' faces as they pulled up their stools during the final timeout. His instructions were simple. Check Bradford. Deny Bradford. Keep a hand on Bradford. And Bradford couldn't shake himself free, leaving Victor Chukwudebe as the last option. Time, from O'Brien's perspective, slipped away as if the scoreboard clock was an hour glass. Two nights earlier, Chukwudebe had beaten Michigan with a baseline jumper to give Illinois its first Big Ten win in nine games. He squared himself toward the basket and fired what Kruger hoped would be another game-winner. Only this time, Ohio State center Ken Johnson swatted the shot away. Guard Sergio McClain's put-back missed, and Brian Brown clinched the 64-61 win with two free throws.

The Buckeyes won more than a game. At last, Coleman told reporters, the Buckeyes were now serious contenders—not pretenders—for Michigan State's Big Ten throne. "So many times we've been in this position since I've been here, and so many times we've let it slip away," Coleman said. "This is one of the first times that we actually got it. And I'm just glad I was a part of it." O'Brien couldn't figure out how his team won this game. The Buckeyes won it with balance. Penn and Redd both scored 15, while three players— Coleman, Singleton, and Johnson—all tallied 10 points.

The win over Illinois proved that the Buckeyes were resilient and could bounce back from disappointment. The Spartans had taken something out of them, but they were reenergized in Champaign. With the bench playing a more significant role, the Buckeyes marched methodically through the Big Ten, beating Purdue 80-69 in West Lafayette, Michigan 74-49 at home, and Iowa 73-69 in Iowa City. The Buckeyes were riding a four-game winning streak, but were about to embark on a trip that would take them to their house of horrors—Assembly Hall in Bloomington, Indiana, where they were to face the Indiana Hoosiers.

10

COMING OF AGE
IN HOOSIER LAND

The Buckeyes arrived in Bloomington riding a four-game winning streak, yet little fanfare accompanied them. Despite their unlikely success, the Buckeyes were playing in the shadows of Michigan State, which had torn through its Big Ten rivals like a mad tornado through a cornfield. Even though OSU was peaking while Indiana was spinning its wheels, the oddsmakers didn't like the Buckeyes' chances at Assembly Hall—usually a harbinger of inevitable defeat for Ohio State.

Guard Neshaun Coleman, who had been slowed by a series of bumps and bruises, seemed to find strength during the pregame shoot-around. He was feeling good about his stroke, which had deserted him midway through the season. He was motivated, too, by having one last chance at beating Indiana in Assembly Hall, where the Buckeyes had managed to win only twice since 1972. The Buckeyes had last won in Bloomington when they were the third-ranked team in the nation. The score was 93-85. The date was January 21, 1991.

An hour before the game, Redd and Penn talked in the locker room of the importance of playing their best games of the season. They weren't consumed with their final numbers. They were hoping to get the rest of the Buckeyes involved, particularly on defense and on the boards. The Buckeyes' cocaptains emphasized to their teammates a need to play with confidence and exchange blows with an Indiana team that had counted this game as a certain victory. It had been an automatic Hoosier win in the past.

Even though the Buckeyes had whipped Indiana 73-56 in Columbus earlier in the season, the Hoosiers entered the arena with a swagger. This was a more comfortable setting for the Hoosiers, who were struggling mightily to earn a postseason tournament invitation. The Buckeyes appeared vulnerable, considering they had barely survived both Iowa (73-69) and Michigan (74-69). The pressure was immense; a win would likely assure Ohio State of its first NCAA Tournament bid since 1992, when it won the second of back-to-back Big Ten titles.

The Hoosiers enjoyed a psychological advantage, though. The Buckeyes, it seemed, had always cracked like a soft nut whenever Indiana pressured them in the waning moments of games they were almost certain to win. For 27 years, the Hoosiers had bullied the Buckeyes. Indiana coach Bobby Knight sat on the bench, waiting for Ohio State's inevitable collapse.

O'Brien, though, had made Ohio State mentally tough. Plus, the Buckeyes had exorcised some demons along the way—winning on the road at Illinois, Purdue, Iowa, and Wisconsin. The Buckeyes hadn't beaten Purdue in West Lafayette, Indiana, since 1993. They hadn't won at Illinois since 1992. In fact, the Buckeyes had lost 11 straight games to the Fighting Illini. The Hawkeyes had taken nine in a row from Ohio State and hadn't surrendered a game in Iowa City since 1990.

Yet the Buckeyes never flinched as tip-off neared. It was as if they were oblivious to their checkered history at Assembly Hall. There was a feeling, guard Michael Redd said two days before game day, "that this game meant something greater than victory."

If the Buckeyes could sneak out of Bloomington with a victory, it would give them their first 20-win season since 1992. It would also give the Buckeyes their first regular-season sweep of Indiana since the 1990-91 season. More important, it would show that OSU had narrowed the talent gap between itself and Indiana—and everyone else in the Big Ten.

"I don't sense this game being all that big," O'Brien said during a pregame press conference the day before his team traveled to Bloomington. "It isn't one of those games that will make or break our season. The thing that stands out in my mind is that we beat them soundly the first time we played them."

As it turned out, the Buckeyes got a game-high 17 points from forward Jason Singleton and trounced the Hoosiers 73-56 in Game 16 at Value City Arena before a packed house of 18,068 on January 9. The margin of victory was the largest by the Buckeyes since a 100-83 thumping of Indiana on February 14, 1970, at Bloomington. It was also the most lopsided home win over the Hoosiers since a 108-86 victory on March 4, 1969. The Buckeyes got only a combined 26 points from their top guns, Redd and Penn, but exploited Indiana's inability to challenge the Buckeyes in the open floor.

The challenge facing Ohio State at Assembly Hall was to prove that its win in Columbus wasn't a fluke or an aberration. So the Buckeyes came out running, pressing, and dictating the game's tempo. Still, in the back of O'Brien's mind, he wondered if the Buckeyes would pull it off.

"I was thinking in terms that they would get something out of it, no matter what happened," said O'Brien, whose Buckeyes lost to Indiana in his first visit to Assembly Hall in 1998. "You couldn't escape the history of Ohio State in Bloomington. Every time you play your next game, someone would write about how well you've done there or how poorly you've done there.

"I don't know the exact numbers, but it was something like, in 27 years, Ohio State had won only twice [at Indiana]. So that whole thing played into it. We were thinking, obviously, this is going to be hard. I thought we were playing well the way our season was going and we were hanging in there the year before."

The Buckeyes took the pressure off early, as they sprinted to a 14-point lead, 27-13, with 7:14 remaining in the first half. The Hoosiers, particularly their big men, couldn't keep up with Ohio State's versatile big men— center Ken Johnson and power forward George Reese.

Ohio State didn't do nearly as much damage in the open court as it did in the post. Johnson (10 rebounds, seven points and four blocked shots) and Reese (10 points and seven rebounds) took it to Indiana's frontcourt, muscling inside for easy layups and short jumpers. Johnson scored six of Ohio State's first eight points. He ripped down two offensive rebounds, turning both into points. Reese was too quick for Indiana's defenders. He was 3-for-5 from the floor and hit two free throws in his 12 minutes of action to help silence Indiana's fans.

"I think for the first time, we weren't afraid to play our game," Johnson said. "We were tired of being pushed around or worrying how the officials would call the game. We knew in our hearts that we were a better team. We weren't going to give this game away—not without a fight.

"Coach kept telling us to keep working hard and keep playing our game. I think the biggest difference for us was our confidence. I thought we had as much talent as they did, but we would always find a way to lose."

In that roller-coaster first half, when it appeared that the Buckeyes were poised to turn out the lights, Knight flipped a switch that ignited the Hoosiers in the final 6:30. Knight was assessed a technical at one point, but he didn't stage one of his familiar tirades. Instead, he calmly orchestrated his team back into contention by masterfully deploying a strategy that enabled Richardson and center Kirk Haston to get easy shots in the paint.

Indiana put together an 8-0 run to cut the Ohio State lead to 29-21. Luke Recker hit a three-pointer; Guyton made three free throws; Lewis converted both ends of a one-and-one at the foul line.

Johnson slowed the Hoosiers some with a baseline jumper to give Ohio State a 31-21 advantage. But Indiana went on a 9-0 run to close to within a point, 31-30, before Ohio State took a 33-30 lead at halftime.

As the teams jogged back to their respective locker rooms, the Hoosiers looked confident. The crowd was back in the game. The Buckeyes appeared to have their backs against the wall at Assembly Hall—again. Of course, this time the ending would be different.

Still, despite the Buckeyes' early lead, O'Brien wasn't fooled that Indiana would be that easy. He expected this road game to be a battle just like the others. And he expected Ohio State to respond as it had at Wisconsin, Iowa, Purdue, and Illinois.

"It was going to be a hard game," O'Brien said. "It was never different than going on the road anywhere else in this league. I think this is a hard league to win games on the road, but we had some success. We played Michigan State close in East Lansing, and that bolstered our confidence.

"We went into Indiana's place knowing we could win. It meant a lot to them emotionally. It took me awhile to understand the rivalry, but it became clear to me that anytime Ohio State plays Indiana, it's like playing Michigan in football."

"The rivalry had a lot to do with the fact that Bobby was an Ohio State graduate," O'Brien said. "It's obvious that because of who he is and his success, beating Indiana means a lot to our fans. It also means a lot to our program.

"We did play there last year; it was hard to put your finger on how much we played into the atmosphere my first year. You had to assume that the atmosphere is like that all the time. When Indiana comes to Columbus, it's a little different. But it doesn't matter whether the game is in Bloomington or Columbus; you can sense the whole thing is a little bit bigger.

"In the Big Ten you play in front of big crowds everywhere you go. I remember telling my kids that if they can't get excited about playing basketball in this league, then something is wrong. One of the things we are stuck with as coaches is motivating your players, getting your guys to play hard all the time, especially on the road. We have to constantly find ways to motivate our guys. It wasn't hard to get our guys excited to play a night game at Indiana."

Penn and Redd talked again at halftime. They could sense that the Buckeyes had lost some of their momentum as Indiana rallied in the final minutes of the first half. They challenged their teammates to stick out their chins and dare the Hoosiers to deliver the knockout punch. It was time to mix it up with the Hoosiers at their place. It was time to ante up like men—desperate men in search of an improbable victory.

Penn and Redd knew that one or both of them would have to deliver in the second half. The Buckeyes hadn't had a floor general with Penn's skills and discipline during O'Brien's first season. In Penn, they had an All-American candidate who wouldn't allow his teammates to be distracted by past failures.

The Buckeyes' two Big Ten All-Americans also figured they both had to go the distance. They each played 37 minutes, but neither left the floor during the last 15 minutes of the second half. Yet the bench contributed some quality minutes. Reese and freshman guards Brian Brown and Boban Savovic played a combined 36 minutes.

No one's minutes appeared more significant than the 15 allotted Coleman. The former Toledo high school star made every minute count. When Coleman was recruited in 1995, he was supposed to be the sharpshooter the Buckeyes hadn't had since Jimmy Jackson. However, on this night, Coleman's role was that of a defensive stopper. He scored only five points, but his block of an A.J. Guyton jumper sparked a defensive stand that denied Indiana a field goal for nearly five minutes in the second half.

"The way we played defense at Indiana made everyone pay attention to what we were doing," Coleman said. "It made us believe in ourselves. If we didn't before, we really began to believe in what Coach O'Brien had been telling us. He would always say that we could be as good as any team in the Big Ten. But we were determined to leave Indiana believing we were as good as any team in the country."

With the 11th-ranked Buckeyes trailing the 19th-ranked Hoosiers 65-61 in the final 3:35, Penn was determined to change the course of history. In doing so, he could help the Buckeyes secure a postseason tournament bid for the first time in seven years.

"I wanted the ball at the end of game. It's what I live for. I don't mind the pressure," said Penn, who finished with a game-high 20 points on 7-for-16 shooting. "With the tough games we had on the road, we were used to the pressure."

The Hoosiers, though, were used to having things their way at home. Knight constantly worked the officials, trying to stem the tide of momentum that Ohio State had gathered early in the game, that had silenced the usually loud Indiana fans. Knight looked like a king in check as he tried a plethora of combinations in an effort to secure the desired results. But Knight wasn't about to retreat or concede defeat.

The Hoosiers overcame their 14-point deficit behind the shooting of reserve forward Larry Richardson, who scored 15 of Indiana's 28 points off the bench. The Hoosiers were familiar with pressure, having played into overtime in four of their previous five games. Indiana forced the Buckeyes into a half-court game and subsequently took the lead midway through the second half.

The biggest lead either team had in the second half was four points, and the lead changed hands 17 times before Penn put Ohio State ahead 68-67 on a pair of free throws with 49 seconds to go.

O'Brien kept pleading with his players to maintain their composure. In the end, the Hoosiers cracked, committing two critical turnovers and taking several ill-advised shots. In the past, it was the Buckeyes who typically came unglued down the stretch with victory within their grasp.

Still, with less than 35 seconds remaining, Indiana guard A.J. Guyton had a chance to put the Hoosiers ahead. But Guyton missed an off-balance 10-footer that Redd gathered in off the glass before giving the ball up to Penn, who was fouled with 29 seconds to go. Penn hit one of the two free throws to increase Ohio State's lead to 69-67.

The Hoosiers had one more shot at forcing overtime or winning with a three-pointer. The Buckeyes collared their usual suspect, Guyton, forcing the Hoosiers to look for guard Michael Lewis. Lewis, one of the few Hoosiers ever to defy Knight publicly, had lost his starting job to Dane Fife. Lewis had scored nine points and dished out six assists in 24 minutes. While Knight wanted Guyton or forward Luke Recker to take the shot with the clock winding down, he felt comfortable with the ball in Lewis's hands.

Lewis, with Redd guarding him closely, looked toward Guyton breaking into the corner. But Singleton stepped out quickly to seal the passing lane. Now, with the clock at six seconds, Redd forced Lewis's hand. Lewis pulled up from 24 feet and fired an awkward three-point shot at the buzzer. As Lewis bumped into Redd in hopes of drawing a foul, his shot bounced harmlessly off the rim.

The horn sounded. The game was over. The Buckeyes had won 69-67 in the house that Bobby Knight built. Penn scored Ohio State's last 10 points, including three game-clinching free throws in the final 49 seconds to lead the Buckeyes to the gut-wrenching win before a stunned Indiana crowd of 17,142.

"I knew they wanted to get the ball to Guyton or Recker," said Redd, who finished with 16 points, including 10 of 12 from the free-throw line. "When I realized he couldn't possibly make that shot, I fell out of the way."

Knight was incensed. He couldn't believe that the officials didn't call a foul. That they didn't make the call at Assembly Hall—and against the Hoosiers' perennial whipping boys, the Buckeyes—was insulting, if not disrespectful. After all, hadn't the Hoosiers always gotten similar calls in the past against Ohio State?

This, however, was an Ohio State team that had earned the officials' respect. And it was clearly better than the Hoosiers. The officials, then, practically swallowed their whistles, refusing to bail out Indiana at home.

The Buckeyes surrendered only two points in the last 3:35—a pair of free throws by Lewis. And they denied Indiana's top scorers, Guyton (14 points) and Recker (7), many good looks at the basket.

The Buckeyes were mentally sharp at the foul line, too. Ohio State, last in free-throw shooting in the Big Ten, made a season-best 22 of 28 foul shots. "It's incredible isn't it?" O'Brien asked.

The Buckeyes had won their 20th game of the season in of all places, their Waterloo–Assembly Hall. The Buckeyes cast out the demons that had haunted them in their house of horror, winning in Bloomington for the first time in eight years. The Indiana faithful had hoped that this Ohio State team was a fluke of basketball nature, a once-inept and disgruntled team that had seemingly always fallen flat on its face in Bloomington.

In this strange, inexplicable Big Ten season, when the decade's perennial cupcakes—Ohio State, Northwestern, and Wisconsin—had risen from the ashes, the Buckeyes had humbled the Hoosiers in their own backyard. The Buckeyes had gotten the monkey off their back.

Neshaun Coleman sat in the center of the Ohio State locker room at Indiana's Assembly Hall, crying uncontrollably. His tears of unabashed joy were indescribable reflections of Ohio State's most satisfying victory of the 1990s—a decade in which the Ohio State men's basketball program suffered through one of the most intolerable bouts of inconsistency in the school's history.

The Buckeyes had come to Bloomington, Indiana, and earned their most important win of the season before a hostile crowd that ultimately booed the Buckeyes afterwards as they huddled at center court amid a haunting hush.

For Coleman, this was the proudest moment of his four years at Ohio State. His previous three seasons had been marked by a multitude of injuries and three consecutive losing campaigns. He savored this victory because he remembered how the Hoosiers had slapped the Buckeyes silly in years past. It was revenge for a humiliating defeat in Bloomington two years earlier—a game in which Indiana attempted 52 free throws (second to most ever against an Ohio State team) during a 93-76 conquest of Ohio State at Assembly Hall on Feb. 8, 1997. Coleman could never shake that loss. It tormented him a like a recurring nightmare. In that loss, Coleman scored a team-high 18 points. It was his best performance of the season. But it was a bittersweet personal high that was overshadowed by a bizarre, ugly sequence of events. Coach Randy Ayers was ejected for the first time in his coaching career after vehemently arguing over a succession of fouls whistled against the Buckeyes before halftime that resulted in Indiana making 25 of 31 free throws in the first half. Then, shortly thereafter, guard Damon Stringer was tossed for arguing over his fourth personal foul.

While the Buckeyes were booed unmercifully for gathering at center court—a move the Hoosiers' fans deemed poor sportsmanship—Coleman latched onto some semblance of redemption. He had promised that the Buckeyes would return to Assembly Hall to avenge the ego-bruising defeat in 1998 that sent the Buckeyes spiraling toward a 21-game-conference losing streak, which was the longest stretch of futility in school history.

Still, even as the Buckeyes sprinted jubilantly toward their locker room, Knight protested vehemently for a foul, but to no avail. O'Brien stood near the scorer's table, staring at the officials. Then he stared at the scoreboard, finally letting go his pent-up enthusiasm. O'Brien and his assistant coaches couldn't resist the temptation to charge their troops and celebrate with them.

"I didn't think there was any way they [officials] could call a foul on a shot like that," O'Brien said. "The last possession was as good a defensive stand as any team I've ever coached.

"I remember Scoonie making a big three-point play off of a timeout, which was huge. I remember Michael making a couple of very big baskets. But the thing that stands out more than anything is the very last possession of the game.

"It will be a possession that's hard for me to forget. I thought that might have been the best defensive stand for one possession the entire season. They [the Hoosiers] had 20 seconds to get a basket and couldn't get anything going.

"We were very aggressive and real quick to switching. They ended up having to make a wild shot. I thought we played exceptionally well in that one possession. We were just on them. They didn't get a good shot to win the game. We had Johnson, Singleton, Brown, Redd, and Penn on the floor, and we thought that was our best defensive team."

During the timeout before Indiana's last possession, O'Brien warned his players not to concern themselves with the officials. He didn't want Recker or Guyton floating unattended on the perimeter.

"It's different when a guy has a legitimate chance at making the basket," O'Brien said. "I feel this way, even it doesn't benefit us. I say to my players all the time, don't be looking for the officials to make a call, you've got to go and put the ball in the basket. You got to make yourself win. I felt that's exactly the way that play should have been officiated. To bail them out when they had nothing going offensively would have been an injustice.

"It was a tough loss for Bob at home. I felt bad at that instant that Bob's team ended up losing that game. He didn't have a pleasant look on his face. It's the kind of look you have when we all have a tough game. I felt bad because I really like Bob."

Knight, though, was clearly disturbed by the officiating and said so during the postgame press conference. He lashed out at the officials, claiming they failed to call several traveling violations against the Buckeyes in the second half that would have given Indiana possession of the ball as Ohio State protected its slim lead. He even promised to buy reporters steak dinners if they could prove that Ohio State didn't travel or palm the ball at least 20 times.

O'Brien and Knight did not exchange pleasantries after the game. They shook hands and then went their separate ways.

"Knight wasn't very happy about the officiating afterwards," O'Brien said. "As a matter of fact, he was disappointed. He made a comment about we got away with a lot of traveling violations. I remember that.

"As much as I like him, when you lose you don't want to talk to anybody. He [Knight] didn't want to hear me talking about how his guys played great. You just don't want to hear it. I don't want to hear it. I know what happened during the game. You just leave. I have a high regard for Bob. He was very complimentary of how our kids played."

The Hoosiers' disappointed fans weren't as cordial. They resented the Buckeyes celebrating afterwards. According to Indiana forward Luke Recker, it was as if Ohio State was rubbing it in. The Buckeyes were simply the much more physical team. They held the Hoosiers to 27 percent shooting from three-point range and outrebounded them 39-36.

"We were just happy to win," Coleman said.

There were tearful eyes among the Hoosiers faithful. They had grown accustomed to the Hoosiers beating the Buckeyes—41 tries in 56 games since 1972.

"They didn't like the way our kids stayed in the middle of the floor after the game," O'Brien recalled. "It was as if we were coming together like never before. Everybody was in the huddle jumping together. I guess some of the people in the arena weren't happy with it.

"They started booing us while we were all out there. It wasn't meant to show up anyone or taunt anybody. It was just a genuine emotional response. Our players came together at a place that they had experienced only bad memories. I can't remember us doing that anywhere else. It didn't happen at Purdue or Illinois or Wisconsin. The atmosphere was different at Indiana."

The media had finally begun to embrace O'Brien and the Buckeyes. They were the rags-to-riches fairy tale that captured most everyone's imagination. The victory at Assembly Hall was anything but anticlimactic.

"There were a lot of media, a lot of television cameras," O'Brien said. "The whole thing was a like a big-time environment."

This was a big step for the Ohio State program. O'Brien and the Buckeyes refused to be cowed by their surroundings—or by the often-intimidating Bobby Knight.

"I guess there is a mystique about playing against Bob," O'Brien said. "That's the thing. If you allow yourself to become paranoid about him intimidating the officials, if you concentrate too hard on that, you lose focus on the game. It becomes a mind thing. It was a mind thing with Jason and Neshaun."

Coleman and Singleton were the only surviving members of the 1995 recruiting class. They had endured all of the losses and humiliation at Assembly Hall. Now, they were reaping the rewards of their dogged determination to help forge a reversal of fortune for the Buckeyes. Finally, Coleman and Singleton had on the Ohio State bench a coach who matched Knight's intensity.

"I think the mystique of Bobby Knight is at times a very difficult thing to overcome," O'Brien said. "We didn't let Bobby Knight factor into this game at all. We never had to talk about him. We talked about what we had to do to beat his team. There were too many other things going on to worry about that.

"I know the general feeling in Columbus is that you're not going to get a break in Bloomington. We had beaten them convincingly at our place, so getting our guys to believe we could beat them was easy. We thought we were better than they were. There was no reason we couldn't win the game."

There were reasons to be intimidated. The Buckeyes couldn't help but notice the three championship banners that hovered above the arena floor. It was hard to ignore the volatile Knight sitting on the bench or the painted faces among the crowd heckling the visiting Buckeyes.

"When you go into Assembly Hall, those three big national championship banners get your attention," O'Brien said. "We didn't have to talk to our kids about Indiana's tradition. They already knew. We didn't do anything special. We approached it like any other game. We were very business-like about it.

"We had a good shoot-around. We watched some game film. We left the dressing room feeling very confident."

Long after the game, Coleman shed his last tear. He embraced Singleton as the two celebrated one of Ohio State's most impressive and meaningful victories since the 1991-92 season.

"Neshaun kept saying he never believed we could win there after the three years of frustration and losing to Indiana the way we had," O'Brien said. "It was a really significant win for Jason and Neshaun. To win a game there was an emotional thing for them. For the coaches, we hadn't experienced all the bad things the players had.

"I think, in retrospect, the game influenced the rest of our season. After winning at Bloomington, we realized that the atmosphere anywhere else couldn't intimidate us. It doesn't get a whole lot harder than playing at Indiana. It was a big confidence thing. We were at a point that it didn't matter where we were going to play. We believed we could win."

11

THE BIG TEN TOURNAMENT

Lessons in Defeat

The soft snowflakes settled on the bronze bust of Michael Jordan outside the United Center in Chicago on the opening day of the 1999 Big Ten Tournament on March 4. Even on this cold Thursday morning, young college basketball fans braved the elements to absorb the magnificence of basketball's larger-than-life icon. Some took off their gloves, ignoring the bone-chilling wind, to stroke it, as if some of Jordan's wizardry and magic would rub off on them.

For many of the young men playing in this conference tournament, these were awe-inspiring surroundings. For them, destiny awaited within the hallowed walls of Jordan's Place.

The 11 teams, even those with unrealistic postseason aspirations, were about to embark on a four-day bash that would shape their immediate future. Michigan State and Ohio State came to the Windy City as the No. 1 and No. 2 seeds, respectively. If everything went according to plan, the Spartans and Buckeyes would meet in Sunday's title game. Often, conference tournaments fail to follow the plot. There always seems to be a long shot waiting to crash the party. The 10th-seeded Wolverines struggled all season, but somewhere in that maize-and-blue confusion was a dangerous team. Illinois, the 11th seed, was a youthful team, one that had no fear of defeat.

As much as they would try to focus on the business of winning the tournament—with an automatic NCAA Tournament berth as the ultimate prize—the players couldn't resist the allure of being captivated by the six NBA title banners hanging from the rafters, trumpeting the Bulls' reign of superiority. The Jordan-led Bulls were the epitome of excellence, of greatness. Everyone wanted to be at his very best on this stage. It's the place where they hoped to save their best for last, just as Jordan often did when victory was a last-second shot away.

When the Buckeyes arrived in the Windy City, they were no longer the Bulls' antithesis. They were no longer the Bad News Boys of the Big Ten. Though still in search of excellence, the Buckeyes were playing at a higher level than they were when O'Brien brought them to the United Center in 1998. As assistant coach Rick Boyages scouted Michigan's win over Purdue in a first-round elimination game, the Buckeyes were in transit from Columbus, preparing themselves mentally for their rubber match with the Wolverines. The Buckeyes had split a pair of regular-season games with Michigan, with each team winning on its own home floor.

Even though Michigan was only 12-18, the Buckeyes were considered vulnerable because their playmaker, Penn, had injured his hip in a nasty fall in the regular-season finale at Penn State, a game the Buckeyes lost in overtime. The Buckeyes had come to rely almost exclusively on Penn's leadership and his ability to inspire his teammates with a simple pass, a poignant word of advice, or a three-pointer that often shifted momentum toward Ohio State. The Buckeyes, it was thought, couldn't win without Penn—or with a hobbled Penn.

Penn had gained a reputation as a big-game player. He also was tournament tested. His resume was scattered with superlatives, but none more impressive than his MVP performance during the 1997 Big East Tournament, in which he led Boston College to a surprising championship-game victory. If he was less than 100 percent, the Buckeyes would have to rely too heavily on Redd or turn to Johnson and Reese, particularly on the offensive end. Penn never considered sitting out this tournament. He and O'Brien knew that a conference championship would likely earn Ohio State a first or second seed in the NCAA Tournament. There was too much at stake not to answer the bell when the Buckeyes and Michigan convened at the United Center on March 5.

Predictably, the unexpected happened in the first round. The favorites failed to escape unscathed—except No. 8-seed Northwestern, which defeated No. 9 Penn State. Michigan upended the seventh-seeded Purdue Boilermakers. The determined Fighting Illini, who started three freshmen, defeated sixth-seeded Minnesota. The opening round was either an aberration or a foreshadowing of things to come.

O'Brien had spent much of the season trying to convince the Buckeyes that they could hang with most any team in the nation. Yet, he was smart enough to check their egos, assuring they took no opponent lightly. As is the nature of sport, particularly involving 19- and 20-year-olds, it's easy to lose focus, O'Brien said.

With Penn orchestrating the offense, O'Brien wasn't too concerned about his team having a mental lapse. But when Penn went down against Penn State, O'Brien's heart skipped more than a few beats. He knew it would be difficult to survive even last-place Illinois with an ailing Penn.

The Buckeyes, like every other team in the Big Ten, wanted to come to Chicago with high hopes and a feeling of invincibility about them. Instead, the Buckeyes appeared out of sorts. They looked as if the strenuous 29-game season had zapped them of their energy. O'Brien needed to find new blood; he needed to conjure up new ways to motivate his overachieving Buckeyes. At St. Bonaventure and Boston College, he had created innovative and thought- provoking ways to extract from his players their absolute best efforts.

"The one thing OB does well is manage people," Biancardi said. "He keeps everybody in check. He relies on people in different ways, and that's the way he builds his team. He does it through honor and hard work. He has that ability to bring people together to play for all the right reasons. He motivates people through pride. It's why these kids play hard for him. There have been times when we've played our best basketball when it looks as if things are going bad. It's about getting every player to believe in your system and to believe in themselves."

At 3:30 p.m., just three hours before their scheduled tip-off against Michigan in a first-round game, the Buckeyes' team bus arrived at the United Center without a police escort. The Buckeyes walked briskly into the players' entrance. They ignored the clamoring of Michigan fans, who warned that the Wolverines had pulled themselves together and that the Buckeyes would melt under an unfamiliar national spotlight. The Michigan fans saved their jeers mostly for Redd and Penn, but neither acknowledged them.

The Buckeyes weren't worried, because they had conquered their fears of playing in big games away from Value City Arena. Although the Buckeyes claimed not to be superstitious, they followed their same pregame ritual, which had enabled them to hold it together mentally. They boarded the bus in exactly the same order they had during their trip to the arena in Puerto Rico. They listened to the same music—on the same boom box belonging to Penn. They entered the arena in the exact same order for warm-ups—Penn first, Johnson last. Any deviations, the Buckeyes figured, would alter the alignment of the stars.

"When you get right down to it, we all have our quirks," Johnson said. "If it worked once, it will work again. I think our doing that has also helped us develop camaraderie. When you're on the floor, all that matters is who's ready to play and who wants it most. It's not about mind games. It's all about hard work."

The Buckeyes had seemed intimidated by the Chicago crowd at the United Center during the inaugural conference tournament in 1998. This time, they were a more confident-looking team. They were a more talented team, too. Singleton and Coleman, playing in their second Big Ten Tournament, provided both focus and experience. They weren't nearly as taken by the surroundings as their younger Ohio State teammates. They gazed at Jordan's statue, too, but kept on walking. Ohio State had come too far to be distracted now.

"We've always believed we could win this tournament the moment we won the Puerto Rico tournament," said Singleton, a graceful 6-foot-5 small forward. "We stood up against every team in our conference. We beat every team that had beaten us for years. We didn't come to Chicago to make a good showing. We came to win."

The Buckeyes didn't come to watch, either. They arrived in time to watch Michigan State's fans wipe clean their green-and-white-painted faces, as underdog Northwestern made the Spartans sweat it out in a surprisingly close game. The Spartans had blown away the Wildcats 65-48 in the regular season. But with Big Ten Player of the Year, guard Mateen Cleaves, and the conference's best sixth man, forward Morris Peterson, scoring only a combined 11 points on 5-for-17 shooting, Michigan State limped away with a narrow 61-59 victory.

Suddenly, the Spartans looked vulnerable despite ending the regular season with a 15-game winning streak. If the Buckeyes ever doubted that most anything can happen and will happen in these postseason tournaments, they were believers now. "We'll be ready," Penn said days earlier. "We're not trying to prove anything, but we need to show everyone that we belong. You can't do that by letting your guard down."

For the first time in seven years, the Buckeyes had an opportunity to accomplish something special. The previous year, no one expected them to win a game in the conference's postseason tournament. They were the biggest of underdogs in 1998, having come to Chicago sporting only a single victory in conference play, thus being tagged with the unenviable 11th seed. Now, things were different. The Buckeyes had turned the conference on its head, challenging Michigan State for the regular-season championship before finishing as conference runner-up. Still, there was some doubt about Ohio State. Penn's injured hip dominated the pregame discussions. The feeling was: As Penn goes, so goes Ohio State. O'Brien, however, was counting on his role players, particularly Singleton and Coleman, to strengthen the link in Ohio State's chain that had been weakened by Penn's injury.

Singleton and Coleman inspired their teammates, in part because of what they had gone through during their first three years in Columbus. "Neshaun and Jason deserve to win," Redd said. "They've been cheated the last three years."

At 6:10 p.m., Singleton and Coleman jogged onto the court—led by Penn and followed by Johnson. The Ohio State contingent—estimated at

8,000—welcomed the Buckeyes with a thunderous ovation as the Ohio State cheerleaders yelled, "Go, Bucks." The Buckeyes seemed to go through their pregame warm-up drills in near-perfect cadence with the pep band. The Buckeyes appeared too loose. The Wolverines, their pride rejuvenated after a first-round win, seemed confident. Michigan's entrance into the arena triggered a roar from the Wolverines' fans. The Buckeyes' fans booed the Wolverines just as they would on some misty, mid-November football afternoon. After years of having its pride wounded by the Wolverines—on the football field and on the basketball court—Ohio State was motivated by revenge and a desire to exorcise its maize-and-blue demons.

At 6:19, awaiting the cue of an ESPN director, the Buckeyes stood at center court looking anxious to get it on. O'Brien, flanked by Biancardi and Boyages, appeared remarkably calm. He shouted out some last-second instructions as he made contact with Penn. Penn instinctively massaged his tender hip, then pointed his teammates in position as referee Ted Hillary stepped in to put up the jump ball.

Michigan, which won the 1998 Big Ten Tournament, was surprisingly fresh after battling Purdue in an overtime session in the first round. The Buckeyes wanted to get out and run. They wanted to wear down the Wolverines in the first half and make Coach Brian Ellerbe use more of his short bench than he wanted. O'Brien knew, as Ellerbe did, that at least four of Michigan's starters—including guards Robbie Reid and Louis Bullock—would have to play nearly the entire 40 minutes. If so, they would have a difficult time matching up with Penn and Redd down the stretch.

The Wolverines weren't hesitant to run. Yet, their transition game was expected to be hindered some because Ohio State was using a three-guard lineup that enabled them to better defend in the open court. During an 84-74 win over Ohio State on Jan. 16 in Ann Arbor, the Wolverines—with Reid and Bullock both playing 37 minutes—had beaten the Buckeyes in transition, scoring 18 fast-break points. O'Brien had unloaded his bench, giving extensive minutes to three back-up guards—Boban Savovic, Brian Brown, and Neshaun Coleman.

In their February 9 rematch in Columbus, O'Brien used five guards to slow down Reid and Bullock in transition. The strategy worked as OSU won 74-69, limiting the Wolverines to seven points in transition.

No sooner had the crowd of 20,297 settled into their seats at the United Center, than the Buckeyes had to dig deep again. The Wolverines rolled out of the starting block in full stride, while Ohio State tried gathering its legs. Michigan, ignited by Reid and Bullock, sprinted to an early 16-7 lead. O'Brien didn't wait for a television timeout. He summoned his players to the sideline. He didn't draw up some complicated schemes to combat Michigan's momentum. Instead, he looked into the eyes of his players and implored them to make yet another gut check.

The Buckeyes could hardly hear O'Brien, whose high-pitched screams were barely audible inside the loud, raucous United Center. The banging of drums and blaring of the Michigan brass section forced the Buckeyes to tighten up their huddle. O'Brien was used to the noise, especially at Madison Square Garden, where his Boston College teams had competed in the Big East Tournament. For the most part, this was a more serene setting. But most of his players weren't used to the unyielding, garish echoes that reverberated off the walls. Even as the Buckeyes were steamrolling past their Big Ten opponents at home, the needle on the noise meter rarely swung far to the right.

Now, Penn had to become a coach on the floor. His leadership surely would be tested; the Wolverines flirted with turning this quarterfinal game into a blowout unless the Buckeyes could find the internal drive that powered them to a Big Ten-record 11-win turnaround in conference play. As Michigan focused on denying Redd and Johnson the ball, Penn looked to get the rest of his teammates involved. Five minutes into the game, the Buckeyes were still looking for a lift, for someone to light their fire.

Ohio State's title chances seemed to depend on two freshmen, Brown and Savovic. They were ushered to the scoring table by O'Brien. The two first-year players weren't expected to put the ball in the basket. But as the season progressed, they began not to fear shooting from the perimeter when defenders dared them to fire away. Brown, a New Yorker, and Savovic, a Serbian, may have had difficulty understanding one another at times, but they understood their roles perfectly.

Savovic and Brown were affable understudies to Penn and Redd. They were neither media darlings nor hyped-up blue-chippers with gaudy, exaggerated high school numbers rolled up against inferior competition. They were lunch-bucket-toting, blue-collar role players thrust into the spotlight. Brown, a 6-foot-3 guard, rarely raised his voice above a whisper. On this night, he demanded to be heard. "Brian does everything well," teammate George Reese said. "We could sense at some point in the game, he would do something that would go unnoticed, but something we understood that would make a difference."

Brown was far more substance than flash. He sacrificed style points by doing the dirty work inside the paint. He snatched down an occasional rebound, then tossed it into the basket with his arms sometimes flailing wildly. "I've never been the first or second option in our offense," Brown said. "I'm sure there will come a time in the tournament when someone else will have to be more productive offensively." That time came early in the first half for both Brown and Savovic. They proceeded to make the plays that counted as Ohio State roared from behind. With Ohio State twice falling behind by nine points, and with Penn limited to three points in the first half, Brown and Savovic helped chip away at Michigan's lead. Savovic sparked a scoring spurt that trimmed Ohio State's deficit to 25-21 by hitting both ends of a one-and-one. Brown and Savovic forced back-to-back turnovers that led to field goals by Redd and Johnson. Then Savovic made a pair of free throws to give Ohio State a 32-29 lead. The Wolverines staggered toward the locker room at halftime, trailing 34-31.

The Buckeye freshmen played with uncanny poise. They were the unsung, unknown heroes who stepped up when all appeared lost against Michigan. Said O'Brien, "We did a good job to get back into the game at the end of the first half. We got a lot of contributions from a lot of different people." No one, however, contributed as much as Brown and Savovic.

It was obvious the Wolverines were fighting to hold on after the first half. Ohio State had the fresher legs. The Buckeyes were getting far more mileage out of their bench. Ultimately, Reese would play 28 minutes, and Brown would be afforded a season-high 20 minutes. The Buckeyes would have four reserves play at least 11 minutes, while only two Michigan backups would get more than four minutes of court time. In the battle of attrition, the Wolverines didn't have enough firepower to stave off Ohio State's imminent charge. Michigan would cut the Ohio State lead to 45-41 on a Bullock three-pointer with 16:17 to play, but that was as close as they would come.

The Wolverines were exhausted. Their season was nearing its futile end. "I think that Michigan got a little fatigued at the end of the game," O'Brien said. "When you get into the tournament, you have to be physically and mentally prepared to compete. I think our guys were, and I credit our bench for that."

When Savovic and Brown forced two more Michigan turnovers to help Ohio State put together a 14-5 run to take a 59-46 lead with 11:09 to play, the Wolverines chugged up and down the court like a broken locomotive. They couldn't keep their wheels on track, and when Ohio State outscored them 13-7 to take a 77-58 lead, the Wolverines ran out of steam. The Buckeyes led by as many as 24 points in wearing down Michigan for the second time in six days.

In the end, Brown and Savovic would combine for impressive statistics: 18 points, seven assists, eight rebounds, and five steals in 35 minutes. Not bad for a pair of freshmen who weren't supposed to contribute until the 1999-2000 season. They were the perfect complement to Penn and Redd, who finished with 14 and 19 points, respectively, as Ohio State advanced to the semifinals with a thoroughly efficient 87-69 victory—the school's first-ever Big Ten Tournament win.

O'Brien left the United Center floor knowing he would likely face his friend Bobby Knight and the Indiana Hoosiers in the semifinals. The third-seeded Hoosiers came in with a 22-9 record and were heavy favorites to oust the young Fighting Illini. Most everyone expected Illinois to be satisfied with its first-round upset of Minnesota, which was a Final Four participant in 1998 (a Final Four appearance nullified in 2000 because of NCAA violations).

In reality, the upstart Fighting Illini were confident victory was within their grasp. They had lost by 11 points to Indiana in the teams' first regular-season meeting, and they had pushed the Hoosiers into overtime before falling 70-64 in their season finale. So Illinois had no fear of Indiana. Instead, the Hoosiers cracked like a soft eggshell, as Corey Bradford, Damir Krupalija, and Sergio McClain led the Fighting Illini to a relatively easy 82-66 win to earn a shot at avenging a 64-61 loss to the Buckeyes in their unforgettable clash at Assembly Hall in Champaign earlier in the season.

The Buckeyes didn't stick around the United Center long enough to watch Illinois pull the upset. They hurried back to their hotel to watch the finish on television. The Buckeyes didn't want to look ahead, but the way they figured it, a rematch with Michigan State was inevitable. The Spartans had taken care of Northwestern earlier in the day, moving them into the semifinals opposite No. 4-seed Wisconsin, which had defeated No. 5 Iowa in the first of four quarterfinals.

"We don't care who we play," Penn said. "But we would like another shot at Michigan State."

O'Brien knew the Buckeyes had to guard against complacency. Most of all, he said, Ohio State had to focus only on Illinois. The Fighting Illini were paying attention to every word that filtered out of Ohio State's camp. There was a sense, Illinois' McClain said, that Ohio State wasn't taking them seriously. "We know Illinois is capable of playing very good basketball," center Ken Johnson said. "If we're at the top of our game, it won't matter what they do. We have to play our game. I'm sure they will play their game, too."

Admittedly, the Buckeyes came here with hopes of playing Michigan State; and the Spartans wanted another shot at the Buckeyes. Of course, a rematch was what the Big Ten desired. It would help CBS, which needed a ratings boost in this prelude to March Madness. It would be a game featuring the top two point guards in the country and the top two teams from the most competitive conference, which was ranked first in the Ratings Percentage Index.

But the television ratings didn't mean a thing to the Fighting Illini. Kruger's young crew had only one chance of advancing to the NCAA Tournament. There was no at-large berth awaiting them, even if they finished second. They weren't going to get a sniff at an NIT bid, either. If not for their sometimes-overzealous nature, they could have easily won a few more games. Illinois resembled some of O'Brien's Boston College teams, only slightly more athletic. While most of the media portrayed the Fighting Illini as the tournament's surprise, the Buckeyes knew better. They had tangled with Illinois in a wild game earlier in the season, and survived only when Johnson rejected a Victor Chukwudebe shot in the final seconds.

Michigan State drew Wisconsin in the semifinals. The Badgers were the only team to beat the Spartans in Big Ten play. If Ohio State was worried some about Illinois, Michigan State had every reason to respect the Badgers, who won convincingly in the team's first meeting of the regular season, 66-51, in Madison. Still, the second-ranked Spartans were all but penciled in to the championship game. They entered the tournament with the most balanced attack in the conference. Along with Ohio State, they were also ranked among the best defensive teams in the country, holding most opponents to less than 35 percent shooting.

The Fighting Illini looked comfortable playing before the United Center crowd. Because the ride from Champaign to Chicago is just over two hours, this was essentially a home game for Illinois. The Buckeyes, despite their rather easy win over Michigan in the quarterfinal, came into this game wobbling slightly. There remained doubt about Penn's fitness. What troubled Ohio State's fans most was Penn's late-season shooting slump.

O'Brien, though, never appeared worried about his clutch-shooting point guard. He figured it was only a matter of time before Penn rediscovered his shooting touch. Against Illinois, Penn put up 15 shots, but he couldn't recapture the magic. He made only three shots—all from three-point range.

As bad as he looked, Penn still scored 15 points and had eight assists. But not even Michael Redds's career-high 32 points could keep the Fighting Illini from pulling off their third upset in the Big Ten Tournament.

Illinois, which had already eliminated Minnesota and Indiana from the tournament, now moved within one victory of qualifying for the NCAA Tournament with a losing record, thanks to its 79-77 upset of Ohio State. "Illinois is the best last-place team in the country," O'Brien told reporters during a solemn postgame press conference.

The Fighting Illini were the Cinderella team of this tournament, but O'Brien wasn't too surprised that the Buckeyes fell prey to an Illinois squad that seemed to be reaching its peak prior to the tournament. The Fighting Illini had won only three of their 16 regular-season conference games. Kruger, though, was patient because he trusted that his young players would eventually take advantage of their athleticism. At least on this night, the Buckeyes didn't have enough athletes to keep up with Bradford and Chukwudebe, who combined for 30 points.

At first, it appeared as if this would be a long night for Illinois. The Fighting Illini didn't have an answer for the mercurial Redd, who was too much to handle when he got the ball inside 15 feet. Redd simply beat the Illinois defenders off the dribble, blowing past them for layups and short-range jumpers. When the Fighting Illini shut down the baseline or sealed his path to the lane, Redd stepped back beyond the three-point line to make two of his four shots. In the end, Redd scored a career-high 32 points on 11-for-18 shooting, and he was an uncharacteristically solid 8-for-11 from the free-throw line.

Indeed, Redd saved his best for last in the conference's prime-time tournament. His numbers were good across the board. He added three steals, soared for seven rebounds, and had three assists. "You always want to play your best game in big games like these," Redd said. "I guess I would feel better about it if the outcome had been different."

Redd may have been hotter than a bonfire, but his backcourt mate, Penn, didn't sizzle the way he had most of the season. He continued to deny it, but his teammates knew his hip injury was affecting his performance. "Scoonie is the toughest guy I know," Coleman said. "Scoonie and I have been up and down physically, but it'll take more than a sore backside for him to miss a game." But this was not the same All-Big Ten point guard whose leadership, grit, and court awareness transcended raw numbers and computer-generated data. The numbers, though, weren't good—and were hard to overlook.

The Buckeyes trailed 32-27 at the half, mostly because they were lacking continuity in their half-court offense; they also shot only 34 percent from the field. O'Brien's team played more like an uncertain 11th-seed. The Buckeyes took shots that made the crowd shake its collective head. They tripped over themselves like pigeon-toed tap dancers, committing nine turnovers and allowing Illinois to score eight fast-break points in transition. The Buckeyes botched all but one of six fast-break chances, throwing the ball aimlessly off the glass or throwing it away.

O'Brien stopped the clock twice to get the Buckeyes' attention. On a road traveled too many times by the Buckeyes, they didn't shoot free throws well, making only 15 of 23 attempts. The Fighting Illini made 22 of 30 free throws, including a 6-for-6 effort from Bradford, and the Illinois bench made 11 of 15 free throws. O'Brien shuffled players in and out in a desperate attempt to find the right substitution pattern. While he kept hoping for something to click, the Fighting Illini seized the spotlight. They were the underdog and the tournament Cinderellas, assuming the role Ohio State had been cast in before the season began.

The Buckeyes lumbered up and down the court as if someone had sabotaged their $200 Nike shoes. They were slow to get back on defense, looking flat-footed and listless for the first 30 minutes. Bradford and McClain looked like the first and last legs of a sprint relay team, dashing into the open floor with no one between them and the basket. Now, Ohio State was hoping to be the tortoise that would catch the hare at the end. The Buckeyes, though, fell behind by 11 points. Considering they were barely shooting 30 percent from the floor, 11 points seemed an insurmountable deficit.

Again, as they had done so often, the Buckeyes, with O'Brien preaching and pleading, cut methodically into the Illinois lead. Illinois coach Lon Kruger began stomping the sideline, his face a picture of urgency. He had watched his young team fold down the stretch, giving games away only because they didn't know how to win. The Fighting Illini were much like the Ohio State team that limped to the finish of the 1997-98 season like a tired mule in compiling an 8-22 record.

Only 4:31 remained on the clock when O'Brien squeezed into a huddle to talk with his players. He didn't carry a clipboard into the huddle. He didn't talk Xs and Os. He looked into the eyes of his go-to players, Penn and Redd, and demanded they not let this chance at a rematch with Michigan State get away.

Redd, playing as if he had been touched by Michael Jordan's majesty, staged a one-man magic show in pulling the Buckeyes into a 70-70 tie with 1:53 to go. The Fighting Illini respected Redd enough that they left Coleman and Brown alone at the perimeter, and the backup guards answered with a couple of long-range jumpers to make it a game. The Buckeyes seemingly had the advantage in an emotional roller coaster that left both Kruger and O'Brien exhausted. The players, too, were running out of gas. They would creep and crawl to the finish, running only on fumes.

The leg-weary Buckeyes were caught reaching and grabbing as they played defense more with their hands than their feet. And the officials were unforgiving, calling fouls on almost every Illinois possession. If the foul line was Ohio State's albatross, it was Illinois' harbor of refuge. Bradford, who scored 12 of his 17 points in the second half, and Nate Mast made six free throws to put Illinois ahead 77-72 with 32 seconds remaining.

To most everyone in the United Center, this game appeared lost for Ohio State. The Buckeyes' pep band began packing up its gear. Jim Nantz and Billy Packer, the CBS broadcast team, talked about the improbable matchup between the tournament's No. 1 and No. 11 seeds. Redd tiptoed baseline to hit a layup over a flat-footed Luke Johnson to cut the Illinois lead to 79-76 with only 23 seconds remaining. Still, the Illinois lead appeared safe. The clock had turned its back on Ohio State, leaving the Buckeyes in the undesirable position of hoping time would stand still. The Illini had time on their side, but their inability to make a game-clinching free throw made those 23 seconds seem like an hour for Kruger. McClain, who scored only seven points in 30 minutes, had a chance to put the game away by converting both ends of a one-and-one. Instead, his missed free throw with 19 seconds to go kept Ohio State's pulse pumping.

Suddenly, the Buckeyes had the ball back with a chance to force overtime. Kruger and O'Brien were again matching strategies in another pulsating finish. The pumped-up Illini fans were up on their feet with their fingers and toes crossed.

Penn had expected Illinois to pressure him in the backcourt. Instead, the Fighting Illini turned back to defend the perimeter. O'Brien skipped along the sideline, motioning the Buckeyes to hurry as time slipped away. Penn pushed a pass to Brown, who kicked the ball back to Penn three steps beyond the three-point arc. Penn, with Bradford and Johnson flying toward him with their hands in his face, released the trey with the clock showing six seconds to go.

O'Brien got up on his toes, leaning with Penn's shot. The chances were always good that Penn would rescue the Buckeyes—in this case, saving them the embarrassment of losing to the last-place team in the conference.

Penn's shot looked good as it rotated toward the basket. The ball hung on the rim for a split second as all five of Illinois' players hurried toward the basket. O'Brien was still leaning, still hoping for another magical comeback.

The ball rolled off the rim and through the hands of two Illinois players, then off the foot of another. The Buckeyes were given one more chance to send a chill up the backs of the Illinois faithful.

Penn was fouled quickly on the inbound pass. The strategy was simple. He would make the first, then miss the second on purpose, hoping the Buckeyes would recover the loose ball, score, and send the game into overtime. It was a perfectly executed strategy. Penn made the first shot, and—after Penn intentionally missed the second attempt—Redd slipped in between a mass of players to secure the loose ball.

As Redd leaned back with his shooting hand cocked, O'Brien was still leaning. Kruger was now on the floor, watching with his eyes wide open. Redd's shot dropped just inside the rim at the horn, then spun out, as Redd, stretched out on his back, looked on in disbelief.

"I had a good look at the basket," said Redd, who sat there on the United Center floor as the Fighting Illini circled the court in a frenzied celebration that spilled into the stands. "It looked good to me as I was falling down."

It looked good to O'Brien, too. By the time he straightened up, Ohio State's Big Ten Tournament title aspirations had vanished. The rematch with Michigan State was never going to take place. The chance to show the entire country that the OSU program was back had been lost.

The Buckeyes came to Chicago lacking confidence, so hardly anyone appeared too surprised when they were ousted from the tournament. On the short flight back to Columbus, O'Brien knew his young team was at a crossroads. The Buckeyes could dust off the Illinois loss or feel sorry for themselves because they didn't reach the tournament championship game.

"We rededicated ourselves and prepared to play what would be the biggest games of our guys' lives [in the NCAA Tournament]," O'Brien said. "That is what we worked hard to achieve. Everyone wants to win the Big Ten championship, but the chance to play on into March was all the motivation our guys needed to put the Illinois loss behind us."

As for the Fighting Illini, their fascinating, awe-inspiring quest to secure one of the 64 NCAA Tournament bids ended with a loss to Michigan State in the tournament title game the next day. The Spartans, behind the solid play of guard Mateen Cleaves and swingman Mo Peterson, guaranteed themselves a No. 1 seed in the NCAA Tournament by winning the first of back-to-back Big Ten Tournament titles.

12

REVVING IT
UP IN INDY
How Sweet It Is

The Buckeyes hung around the United Center only briefly after their loss to Illinois in the semifinals of the Big Ten Tournament. They did not have time to sulk. They knew for the first time in seven years that they would begin a new season in March. While Michigan State was taking care of Wisconsin in the other semifinal, the Buckeyes headed back to their hotel. They grabbed a bite to eat, then left immediately to take a charter flight back to Columbus.

The Buckeyes were not bitter about losing to the Fighting Illini. They were, however, disappointed in not getting another shot at Michigan State. If fate or luck were on their side, perhaps that chance would come in the NCAA Tournament. The Buckeyes wanted to show the entire country they were for real. With 23 wins to their credit, they were no longer a surprise. With the exception of a few games on ESPN regional telecasts, the Buckeyes had not been on national television all season. They craved some national exposure. It had been five years since the Buckeyes were the focus of any network's attention. They had come so close to playing in the spotlight on Sunday. The comeback season would have taken another long stride if they could have made it into the tournament championship game.

On Sunday morning, O'Brien made his way to the Schottenstein Center. He wanted to sift through some papers and look at some game film. He couldn't do much of anything, really. He was too anxious, too wired to think of anything other than the NCAA Tournament selection show. O'Brien knew the Buckeyes were going to be a part of March Madness. He wondered if the Buckeyes would get any respect from the committee members. Surely, they could not leave OSU out of the tournament mix. Yet, there had been teams with 20-plus wins that had to settle for NIT bids. O'Brien's fears dissipated when he remembered that the Buckeyes had finished second in the Big Ten regular-season standings behind Michigan State, and that the Big Ten, because of its No. 1 ranking in the RPI, would likely get six or seven tournament bids.

Now, O'Brien began to focus more on the NCAA Tournament seedings. He would be satisfied with a fourth or fifth seed. However, a lot depended on the results of the other major conference tournaments finals—including the ACC, the Big East, and the SEC. All of those conferences would have teams vying for the top four seeds in the four regional tournaments.

"If you had told me that we would be in this position at the start of the season, I would have settled for whatever we could get," O'Brien said. "We knew we were going to be in the tournament, so at least we didn't have that to worry about. We didn't think much about where we might end up. We really didn't care. We were in, and that was good enough."

Still, O'Brien paced about Value City Arena in anticipation of the selection show. He had time to reflect on just how far Ohio State had come. A year ago, the Buckeyes were mired in a 17-game losing streak. They were the laughingstock of the Big Ten. It didn't seem possible they would be gathering around a television set inside Value City Arena, waiting to see who their first-round opponent would be in the NCAA Tournament.

"It was just a very difficult stretch where we were constantly losing games in my first year," O'Brien said. "That part of it was not enjoyable, but this part is what makes it a lot of fun. That's why I continued last year to give our guys credit, because through all the losing, they stayed very positive, and they continued to keep coming back and back and back."

Hardly anyone expected the Buckeyes to be back in the tournament mix—not after just two years into a major reclamation project. Nothing like that had been done before. There was no precedent. Several other teams had advanced to the NCAA Tournament after compiling losing records the year before, but absolutely nothing like this. The Buckeyes had overcome the greatest odds of all.

"I was a little surprised that we did that well," O'Brien said. "The key for us was to keep everything in the right perspective. Everybody said, 'Well, you're going to do this and you're going to do that.' We knew how quickly things could turn around. I was a little bit surprised that we played so well. When you think in terms of how hard our guys worked and how hard they practiced, then maybe you can understand. We improved significantly over a year ago, and there are many reasons for that."

Michael Redd and Scoonie Penn were the biggest reasons behind the Buckeyes' unparalleled improvement. They were the pistons that kept the engine running. They were perhaps the best one-two punch in the Big Ten. Yet, if O'Brien were handing out an unsung-hero award, center Ken Johnson would have been an easy choice.

Johnson spent much of the regular season learning how to get the most out of his talents. Even though he averaged 14.1 points and 13.5 rebounds as a senior at Henry Ford High School, Johnson didn't get much attention from major-college programs. His recruitment status was influenced some by the fact that his high school team had a losing record during his senior season, which is uncommon among major-college prospects. The college scouts spent plenty of time checking out players in the Detroit Public School League, which is among the most competitive high school leagues in Michigan.

Johnson, the scouts concluded, may have been too frail to compete at the next level. He ran the floor well, but lacked the court awareness to flourish in transition. He did not have a shot he could call his own. He did not have a shot, period. The scouts wondered, too, if he had the mental toughness to compete at the Division I level. They noticed he had trouble willing— or wheeling—himself into the paint, where he could take advantage of his six feet and 11 inches. Johnson was considered too soft to get it on against the likes of Michigan's Robert Traylor and too passive to develop an instinctively aggressive game that was paramount to success in the typically physical Big Ten.

Johnson may have had his shortcomings, but Ayers liked him. After recruiting so many troubled players, Ayers found Johnson likeable and personable. He did not do many things particularly well, but Ayers insisted his potential was immeasurable. Johnson, shunned by his hometown school, Detroit Mercy, headed to Columbus with no great aspirations. He would have to sit out his first year and focus on solidifying himself academically. However, many observers were skeptical that this stringy-legged kid with rail-like shoulders would ever suit up at Ohio State. Of course, there were reasons to be skeptical, considering all that had happened to the Ohio State program over the past five years.

Johnson, though, never doubted himself. He never doubted, as he sat behind the bench during the 1996-97 season, that there were good times ahead. He did not know, of course, that Ayers would not survive another year. But when O'Brien arrived and began cleaning house, Johnson somehow still felt secure. Even if he had to play behind Jermaine Tate, he was going to stick it out.

Then, when Tate was among those asked by O'Brien to find another school, Johnson inherited the job in the post. Finally, he would have his chance to prove that he was among the best players in the Detroit Public School League.

At the start of the 1997-98 season, Johnson looked unsure of himself. He was uncomfortable in the paint and had a difficult time catching the basketball in traffic. If he had been a wide receiver, any quarterback would have been hesitant to throw him the ball. Johnson committed careless turn-overs, mostly because he was slow to recognize double teams and the mixed bag of zones the opposition used to force the Buckeyes to beat them from the perimeter.

Johnson's skills began to develop midway through the Big Ten season, which was one of the few positives during O'Brien's first season at OSU. Johnson also appeared more mature and patient. He was not trying to force things to happen. Instead, he was letting the game come to him while doing what was necessary. That, of course, is what O'Brien and his coaching staff had hoped to see of Johnson when it became clear near the end of the 1998-99 regular season that the Buckeyes would get an NCAA Tournament bid.

Despite the Buckeyes' disappointment at the Big Ten Tournament, Johnson strolled confidently into the Schottenstein Center the day after the loss to Illinois. He waited along with his teammates to see where they would begin their NCAA Tournament trek. At 5:30 in the afternoon, the Buckeyes made their way into an upstairs lounge to learn their fate. In the past, this had been an annual gathering for the Buckeyes, but now they were watching as anxiously as other programs that frequently lived on the tournament bubble. Unlike players from Duke, North Carolina, and Kentucky, Ohio State's play-ers and coaches were somewhat restless. They had reason to be excited, con-sidering that none of them—except Penn—had ever played in an NCAA postseason tournament. Penn was making his third NCAA Tournament ap-pearance—the first two with Boston College.

O'Brien knew that the Big Ten Tournament winner, if it was Ohio State or Michigan State, would likely get a No. 1 seed in either the South or Midwest regional. At 6:15, the selection show was midway through its brack-ets. Johnson crept closer to the television set. He seemed most anxious of all, waiting to see where the Buckeyes would land in the tournament draw. The fact that the Buckeyes were going to the tournament at all was reason enough for Johnson to get excited. He had not made any All-American teams or even honorable mention in the Big Ten, but O'Brien insisted that Johnson's pres-ence influenced the Buckeyes' fate. It was easy to overlook Johnson, said O'Brien, when the spotlight shone the brightest on Penn and Redd.

However, the numbers that dazzled O'Brien most when he studied Johnson's portfolio were the 9.5 shots he blocked per game while a high school senior. At Boston College, O'Brien had a grinder in the post in Bill Curley, whose shooting and rebounding skills far exceeded Johnson's. With his spider-like arm span and uncanny mobility, Johnson established himself as the most intimidating defensive stopper in the Big Ten.

"Ken is the guy who erases everybody's problems," O'Brien said. "You can talk to Ken until you're blue in the face, and he's not going to front the post. It's hard for him. You give that up knowing you are going to get the rest of it. The one thing we never had at Boston College was a guy like Ken—a guy who is a dominant shot blocker."

The selection show was winding down, and the Buckeyes were still sitting, standing, and waiting. Finally, after biting their nails and shifting in their seats, the Buckeyes leaped for joy as they clinched the No. 4 seed in the South Regional in Indianapolis, where they would face 13th-seeded Murray State at the RCA Dome.

The Buckeyes, after suffering through hard times, were back.

"This is something I waited four years for," said Neshaun Coleman, his voice cracking amidst his joyous tears. "After all we've been through, we deserve this. No one will ever know how hard Coach O'Brien worked and how much he wanted this for us."

"We expected to be a three or four seed," Redd said. "I think our losses to Penn State [in the regular-season finale] and Illinois [in the Big Ten Tournament] may have kept us from getting an even better seed."

As it turned out, the loss to Illinois was a blessing in disguise. The Buckeyes were going to be playing closer to home—a three-hour drive from Columbus. They were going to be joined in Indianapolis by No. 1-seed and SEC regular-season champion Auburn (27-3), while No. 2-seed Maryland (the ACC runner-up) and No. 3-seed St. John's (the Big East Conference runner-up) were sent to the other subregional.

Predictably, the selection committee made Duke (32-1), riding a 32-game winning streak, the No. 1 seed in the East. Connecticut (28-2), the Big East champion, was tabbed the No. 1 seed in the West, while Michigan State (29-4), the Big Ten regular-season and Big Ten Tournament champion, got the No. 1 seed in the Midwest.

The committee was unpredictable, too. It seemingly invited some undeserving bubble teams: Alabama-Birmingham and New Mexico. It crushed the postseason-tournament aspirations of teams that seemed to be more deserving, such as Xavier, Toledo, and Mississippi State. The nine-member selection committee had been accused of slighting deserving teams many times before, so this was not an exceptional year. Again, the committee followed conventional wisdom by catering to the major conferences while at the same time defying logic.

That logic left Xavier coach Skip Prosser (now at Wake Forest) scratching his head, partly because his 21-10 Musketeers beat tournament qualifiers Temple and George Washington, their Atlantic 10 rivals. Toledo's Stan Joplin voiced his opposition because it was hard for him to understand how his team's 20 wins weren't good enough to earn it a tournament bid, especially considering that Toledo had beaten four qualifiers—Kent State, George Mason, Miami of Ohio, and Ohio State.

Ohio State, ranked 11th in the final regular-season Associated Press poll, was 11-2 against tournament qualifiers. The Buckeyes would be facing a 27-5 Murray State team that earned its way into the tournament by winning the Ohio Valley Conference championship. The Buckeyes, some basketball analysts predicted, would be handicapped by Penn's tender hip. They were also heading to Indianapolis having lost two of their past three games. So often, postseason success is rooted in late-season momentum and the luck of the tournament draw.

The Buckeyes were in the same bracket with No. 1-seed Auburn, which many predicted would advance easily to the national semifinals. The Buckeyes were not given much of a chance to survive. The UCLA Bruins, though the No. 5 in the South Regional, were expected to give Auburn the most trouble, if they could survive Detroit Mercy.

On the eve of their first-round game against Murray State on March 11, the Buckeyes heard their doubters again. They heard talk that the Racers could pull the upset—that the Buckeyes had reached their peak, that even if they escaped the usual wave of first-round upsets, UCLA would be waiting to send them back down Interstate 71 to Columbus.

After the pregame press conferences, Neshaun Coleman felt compelled to remind his teammates of just how far they had come. Now was not the time, he said, for the Buckeyes to take the Racers lightly. He reminded them that Penn State and Illinois were not supposed to beat them down the stretch.

"We see the Illinois loss as a lesson," Coleman said. "You can't lose focus in a tournament. "We cannot expect Murray State to be afraid of us. We have to play hard for 40 minutes, and that's something we didn't do against Illinois and Penn State."

The Racers did not have a sparkling tournament history. They were only 1-9 in previous tournaments, including a loss to Rhode Island in 1998. The oddsmakers did not flinch in making Ohio State as a huge favorite. This was a familiar scenario for Ohio State, which had been an overwhelming pick to advance to the championship game of the Big Ten Tournament. "Murray State won their conference and they have tournament experience, so we can't take them lightly," Redd said. "Anything can happen in the tournament. They will be hungry and so will we."

Long before Ohio State and Murray State stepped onto center court, the RCA Dome seats were filled mostly with Buckeye fans. They had gotten to the arena early to tailgate, as if this were a fall football game at Ohio Stadium. The Buckeyes' fans had waited seven long years for this moment, and they weren't going to be late for the party.

Though in the first eight minutes of play, the Racers weren't impressed with Ohio State or intimidated by Ohio State's fans. Murray State exchanged blows with OSU in taking a 10-7 lead. The smaller Racers were able to keep Ohio State off the offensive glass, and they hit a couple of short jumpers, choosing not to challenge Johnson inside. Johnson, though, had discouraged the Racers by slapping away two shots. "I tried to stay positive," Johnson said. "Coach O'Brien always says to stay out of foul trouble and stay on the floor. I think that I have to play aggressive and still block shots."

The Buckeyes had trouble finding their rhythm offensively. Penn would struggle throughout, as he made only 2 of 12 shots from the floor—including 1 of 8 from three-point range. Penn, a 74 percent free-throw shooter, was only 2-for-4 at the foul line. He had three turnovers and only four assists, and the numbers reflected how well the Racers defended the Buckeyes in transition. "Physically, I felt good," Penn said. "I was fighting myself mentally. I am confident I'll find my shot. All I can do is keep shooting."

While Penn struggled, the Buckeyes endured some long scoring droughts, but Redd scored on a layup with 11:26 remaining in the first half to cut the Murray State lead to 10-9. The Ohio State contingent went wild, and suddenly this had the making of a home game for the Buckeyes. "We used the expression, 'This is our house,' " O'Brien said of the RCA Dome, which is home to the Indianapolis Colts. "We had a lot more people supporting us in Indianapolis than any of the other [eight] schools combined. We turned that into our advantage. We kept telling them this was our place. It seemed like everybody was with us, and that was a big advantage."

The crowd could not compensate for what was bothering Penn. Murray State coach Tevester Anderson figured his team could win if the Racers could rattle Penn and make Redd take low-percentage shots. Penn could not get up and down the court as he wanted. He wasn't nearly as fit as he had claimed, and Murray State guard Marlon Towns chased after Penn from baseline to baseline. The Racers had a more difficult time checking Redd, who scored 12 points in the first 18 minutes as Ohio State took a 30-15 lead with 2:24 to go in the first half on a slam dunk by Jon Sanderson, who had been replaced in the starting lineup by freshman guard Brian Brown.

Just when it appeared the Buckeyes were about to put the game away, Murray State guard Aubrey Reese buried a three-pointer and then stripped Brown of the ball at mid-court and scored a layup to cut the Ohio State lead to 30-20. The Buckeyes had counted all season on Penn to stop an opposition's run with a timely basket or a steal. It wasn't happening this night. Penn barely drew iron with a 15-foot jumper, and a three-point attempt bounced off the front of the rim with 51 seconds to go before halftime.

The Buckeyes could have shifted into cruise control midway through the second half if they had hit more free throws. Murray State stayed within shouting distance by not allowing Ohio State to get into the open court.

They controlled the tempo by forcing Ohio State to rely mostly on its half-court game. Penn and Redd got the ball inside to Johnson, who ignited a 6-0 run at the start of the second half as Ohio State widened its lead to 17 points, 38-21.

Johnson did the unthinkable. He parked himself down low and spun around center Duane Virgil for a couple of half hooks. Finally, O'Brien was getting what he wanted from Johnson.

As Ohio State seemed ready to close the deal, back came Murray State. The Racers leaned on Reese, who scored seven straight points to help cut the Ohio State lead to 38-28 with 16:55 remaining. The Buckeye faithful were silenced some. They could sense something was going wrong. The Buckeyes began playing like a team that had not been to the NCAA Tournament in seven years. They looked nervous and unsure of themselves as Murray State, playing like an underdog with nothing to lose, kept throwing its best shots, hoping the Buckeyes would buckle. In a game of emotional ups and downs, the Buckeyes put together another 6-0 run to lead 50-33; then Murray State chipped away at that lead to close to within 10 points, 51-41, on a couple of three-pointers by Towns.

Now, the clock had become Ohio State's ally. The Buckeyes could afford to be more conservative with a double-digit lead. The Racers went after the Buckeyes' weakness: free-throw shooting. O'Brien dropped to his knees every time a Buckeye stepped up to the foul line. He didn't want his team exiting the tournament like this. It was all right to be hammered on the boards, or if Murray State shot the lights out from the floor, but it was inexcusable to lose at the foul line—as Georgetown did in losing to Villanova in the 1985 national championship game.

O'Brien put his hands on his chin. He knew his team's fate rested at the charity stripe. He could filter through all the numbers, but Ohio State's losses to Penn State and Illinois were mostly the result of poor free-throw shooting. O'Brien didn't want to sweat it, but he knew the free-throw line would give Murray State a wide-enough crack in the door to get back into the game.

Only this time, the Buckeyes made their shots. They made six of eight free throws to turn back the Murray State charge. Johnson clinched Ohio State's first tournament victory in seven years with his fifth blocked shot of the game with 26 seconds to go. "He's a real great shot blocker," Virgil said. "You have got to try and shake him, but it didn't work, so he made it difficult for us to get anything in the post."

O'Brien, with Penn and Redd in tow, made his way toward the interview room with a wry smile on his face. He was happy to be moving on, but the Racers had hung around long enough to make him feel a bit uneasy. Still, the Buckeyes won handily, 72-58.

"I think that Murray State did a very good job of guarding us," O'Brien said. "We didn't shoot the ball very well, especially from the free-throw line. I thought we were excellent defensively. I think some significant numbers were the fact that they came in averaging just less than 80 points a game, and they ended up with 58. I think defensively is where we won this game. I think that when you get in the tournament, it is about survival."

Tevester Anderson wasn't interested in surviving. He thought this was the perfect time for his team to win its second tournament game in 10 appearances. "We wanted to win some games in the tournament," said Anderson, who was in his first year after replacing Mark Gottfried, who left for Alabama. "I thought this year's team had a chance. I realize Ohio State is a very good defensive team, and I never thought that a team was out there that could force us to shoot 27 percent from the field."

Ohio State created problems defensively by mixing a man-to-man with a combination of zone defenses. The Racers were handcuffed shortly after tip-off when forward Isaac Spencer sustained a back injury that limited his effectiveness around the basket and on the boards. Spencer tried to go, but he grimaced noticeably as the game progressed. Anderson shuffled him in and out, but the team's trainer could not keep Spencer's back from stiffening up as he sat on the bench.

"Isaac is the guy we looked to to help us out when we needed a basket," said Reese, who scored 26 points in 35 minutes. "The shots just weren't falling for us. When a player gets hurt, the rest of the team has to step up."

Although each team had one of its stars slowed by injury, in the end, Ohio State's depth dictated the outcome. No one, however, played a more prominent role in the outcome than Redd. The rest of Ohio State's starting five combined to make only seven of their 27 shots. Redd beat the Racers off the dribble and in transition, taking an inordinate number of high-percentage shots. He finished with 26 points on 10-for-20 shooting and refused to step out to the perimeter. A much more disciplined Redd took only one three-pointer, but he was 7-for-12 from the free-throw line because he attacked the undersized Racers, who tried to defend in the paint. The Racers, unlike Illinois, opted not to step out to challenge Redd and Penn from the perimeter.

"Teams look at Scoonie and me as the main scorers and try to shut us down," Redd said. "Plus, it's tournament time, and you really don't want the season to end." Anderson tried a matchup zone and man-to-man defense to stop Redd, but the strategy failed because of Redd's ballhandling skills.

"We thought we could slow him down," Anderson said. "Marlon Towns probably did the best job he could on Redd. When you play a guy who plays that well off the dribble, it's hard to contain him. We ran into a buzz saw."

The Racers did not lose for lack of effort. They gave O'Brien something to worry about as they snatched 21 offensive rebounds, but they could not translate that hard work on the boards into many points. Murray State probably would have dominated the glass even more if eight of forward Jason Singleton's team-high 10 rebounds had not come off the defensive glass. Singleton was the only other Buckeye to score in double figures, netting 10 points, and he was one of three Ohio State players—including Brown and Johnson— to make four of six free throws.

The Buckeyes celebrated their first NCAA Tournament win since 1992 —a drought that was the longest in school history. However, their enthusiasm may have been tempered some by the fact that Penn's struggles, particularly his shooting, continued.

"It's been like that for Scoonie the last four games, but we're confident he'll get it together," Redd said confidently. "It was time for me to step my game up to another level. However, we cannot get too far into the tournament without Scoonie and the other guys getting it done offensively. They did everything to shut Scoonie and me down, so it was important for the other guys to contribute." The Buckeyes' bench players—Reese, Savovic, and Sanderson—scored 15 of their 16 points in the second half.

O'Brien wasn't nearly as concerned about Penn's shooting woes as he was about some other disturbing numbers. The Buckeyes missed 14 layups and converted only two of their nine offensive rebounds into points. Again, they didn't shoot free throws well, making only 21 of their 35 attempts from the line. "I'm just worried that's going to hurt us," O'Brien said during a postgame press conference in which he looked more relieved than satisfied.

O'Brien, though, wasn't nearly as disappointed as UCLA coach Steve Lavin, whose UCLA Bruins, the No. 5 seed, were upset by the No. 12-seeded Detroit Mercy Titans in an earlier first-round game at the RCA Dome. Redd had suggested the day before that the higher-seeded teams were vulnerable if they came in unprepared against the tournament underdogs. The Bruins did not take Redd's warning to heart. They showed a lot of flash, but were missing much substance in being booted from the tournament. The Titans, who came into the tournament with a 24-5 record, stunned a higher-seeded team for the second year in a row, having knocked out St. John's in 1998.

If nothing else, the Titans got Ohio State's attention. But no one noticed more than Johnson, who didn't get a scholarship offer from his hometown school—Detroit Mercy. So Johnson had every reason to be fired up for Murray State, knowing a win would give him a chance to face some of his old high school friends from the Motor City.

The next day, on March 12, the Buckeyes were fans like all the rest of the paying customers inside the RCA Dome. They were the typical basketball junkies, watching game after game. They talked with the media briefly before spending two hours preparing for second-round foe Detroit Mercy. Johnson talked mostly about his reunion with several Detroit players he either played with or against while in high school. That was the story line in this matchup.

The matchups on the floor didn't seem to matter much, mostly because Ohio State was expected to have a runaway victory.

During the morning shoot-around, Penn stretched from side to side, trying to limber up his still aching hip. His lateral movement was better and he appeared far more energetic as well. Penn was more concerned about his shot. While the rest of his teammates worked on free throws and intermediate jumpers, Penn fired countless three-pointers in a desperate attempt to find the shooting touch that deserted him prior to the Big Ten Tournament.

Ultimately, it was not Penn's shooting that O'Brien hoped would carry the Buckeyes into the Sweet 16. Rather, it was his court savvy, toughness, and willingness to fight among the wide bodies.

"If my shot is not on, I will not be too concerned about it as long as I can help my team out in other ways. I can be a floor leader," Penn said. "What I have to do to win I will do. If I am not scoring points, it doesn't make a difference."

Penn and forward George Reese influenced the Detroit Mercy game by crashing the boards. The Titans were so anxious to get out in transition, they practically ignored Reese, who slipped in the back door to pull down 15 rebounds—including seven offensive rebounds that enabled Ohio State to secure a 16-2 advantage in second-chance points. Penn masterfully maneuvered his way through the big men to rip down a career-high 12 defensive rebounds. "I think 12 rebounds is the most I have ever had in my life at any level," Penn said. "We finally came up on a team that is not bigger than us. All season in the Big Ten, the teams have been bigger than us."

Penn put up some impressive numbers, reminding everyone that he was among the premier players in the country. He did not make that many more shots than he had against Murray State, but he scored 15 points by hitting three of his eight three-point attempts, which set a single-season school record of 79. Penn was tough on defense, too, shadowing guard Rashad Phillips, who made only four of 10 shots for nine points. "I thought our guys were good on defense," O'Brien said. Actually, the Buckeyes were dominating on defense. The Titans shot 30 percent for the game, including 20 percent in the first half, as they trailed 25-12. The Titans may have intimidated UCLA in their opening-round upset of the Bruins, but they delivered a heavy blow to Ohio State—an elbow that bloodied Penn's chin. Despite being knocked to the floor a couple of times, Redd picked himself up to score 15 points. Redd, with a scarlet towel draped around his neck, could barely stand up. He could hardly talk, really. "It's awesome," he said after the game, breathing unevenly. "My voice is hoarse after all the yelling."

Redd's pain was soothed some by the ease with which the Buckeyes registered their 75-44 victory over Detroit Mercy before a crowd of 32,758 – most of whom were wearing scarlet and gray.

While Penn and Redd were the focus of most everyone's attention, Johnson harassed his neighborhood friends, who simply did not have enough depth or talent to compete in the final 20 minutes. Johnson totaled only eight points and three rebounds, but his dominating presence inside caused the cold-shooting Titans to rely more on their perimeter game. Johnson played in-your-face defense, blocking six shots and frustrating his playground nemesis, 6-11 Detroit Mercy center Walter Craft, who scored a season-low two points.

"I think we were motivated some by all the trash talking," Johnson said. "We wanted to take it to them early and show them that we weren't going to be intimidated. This was an emotional game for me. It was fun playing against these guys, but nothing motivated us more than winning another tournament game. It wasn't pretty, but it was good enough."

The Buckeyes had won many games like this all season. In the NCAA Tournament, each victory is a thing of pristine beauty. This was one of the sweetest victories of all, one that put the Buckeyes into the Sweet 16 in Knoxville, Tennessee.

13

STILL DANCING
A Party in Knoxville

A day after the Buckeyes defeated Detroit Mercy in the second round of the NCAA Tournament, Jim O'Brien went back to work. Twenty-four hours was time enough for him to absorb himself in the euphoria of OSU advancing past the first weekend of tournament play. In three days, the Buckeyes would be making the trip to Knoxville, Tennessee, leaving them little time to savor their early-tournament success.

O'Brien met with his coaching staff early that Sunday afternoon to begin plotting a strategy for Ohio State's next opponent—the Auburn Tigers, who were the No. 1 seed in the South Regional. The Tigers, having compiled a 29-3 record, survived a late second-half letdown to gut out an 81-74 win over a stubborn Oklahoma State in the second round.

The Buckeyes and Tigers were joined in Knoxville along with No. 2-seed Maryland and No. 3-seed St. John's. Maryland, behind an 18-point effort by All-American Steve Francis, moved on after beating Creighton 75-63. St. John's earned a shot at the Terrapins by handing Bobby Knight's Indiana Hoosiers their worst-ever defeat in the NCAA Tournament, 86-61.

On Monday morning, O'Brien arrived at his office shortly before eight. He hadn't slept much the night before. He was up thinking of ways to contain Auburn's All-America forward Chris Porter and 7-foot center Mamadou Ndiaye. Porter and Ndiaye had given Oklahoma State fits by dominating the offensive boards. That was a major concern for O'Brien, considering Big Ten opponents hammered the Buckeyes on the offensive glass. Even though Ohio State outrebounded Detroit Mercy 51-25, O'Brien didn't allow himself to feel comfortable. Besides, the Titans weren't strong enough to compete with the Buckeyes for 40 minutes. The Tigers had more depth on the bench and were used to playing a physical brand of basketball in the Southeastern Conference.

If O'Brien was worried about his front-court players having trouble against the Tigers, Auburn coach Cliff Ellis tossed and turned as he tried to figure out a way to keep OSU's explosive backcourt – Penn and Redd – from having a field day against Auburn's Scott Pohlman and Doc Robinson.

O'Brien and Ellis were playing head games long before their March 18 tip-off at Thompson-Boling Arena on the campus of the University of Tennessee. O'Brien suggested that if the Buckeyes find themselves being mauled on the boards, he might be forced to decide whether or not to dump his three-guard offense and beef up his frontcourt. Ellis, on the other hand, suggested that if the Tigers couldn't keep up with Penn and Redd, he might have to scale down his frontcourt in an effort to match the Buckeyes' speed and quickness, especially in transition.

On paper, the OSU-Auburn regional semifinal looked like a toss-up. The Tigers, despite losing to Kentucky in the SEC Tournament title game, 69-57, was still considered by many to be the favorite to get out of Knoxville unscathed, therefore earning a Final Four berth in St. Petersburg, Florida.

O'Brien, though, had reason to feel confident. The Buckeyes had gathered plenty of momentum in Indianapolis. They seemed to be peaking at the right time. The Tigers had stumbled some near the end of the regular season and weren't nearly as sharp in their first two NCAA Tournament games. O'Brien's task was to keep his players on the charge, while Ellis focused on chipping away the complacency from an Auburn team that looked as if it had peaked to soon.

There would be some intriguing matchups on the floor. However, the matchup between O'Brien and Ellis—the leading Coach of the Year candidates ,appeared just as interesting. While O'Brien was turning things around in Columbus, Ellis was energizing an Auburn program that had fallen far behind Kentucky and Arkansas in the SEC. They were both named Coach of the Year in their respective conferences, partly because they turned also-ran programs into conference contenders.

"I can't find adequate-enough words to describe the wonderful job that Jim has done at Ohio State," Ellis said. "He has gotten the most out of his kids."

Ellis didn't do too badly, either.

"[Ellis] has gotten his players to believe in his teachings," O'Brien said. "You have to be impressed with the way they have improved and the way they compete."

This regional semifinal game had the makings of a chess match. Ellis wanted to force O'Brien to dump his three-guard offense for a bigger team that couldn't possibly defend Auburn on the perimeter. The Tigers wanted to force O'Brien's hand by wearing down the Buckeyes on the glass. Auburn, like Ohio State, had a solid backcourt tandem in Pohlman and Robinson. O'Brien figured the backcourt matchups favored the Buckeyes, so he focused his attention on forwards Jason Singleton and George Reese being able to frustrate Porter.

O'Brien got just what he wanted in the first 14 minutes and 16 seconds of the game. Porter couldn't shake Singleton long enough to get into a rhythm offensively. The All-SEC forward slipped inside for a layup with 14:55 remaining in the first half to cut Ohio State's lead to 7-5. Even as Porter struggled, the Tigers led 17-15 after Daymeon Fishback dropped a trey from the top of the key with 8:59 left.

While Porter found himself sitting next to Ellis on the bench, Redd lit up the Tigers. He scored seven of OSU's first 15 points, including a long three-pointer from the right wing. Ellis sprang from the bench, demanding that someone put a glove on Redd, get in his face—do something to disrupt his rhythm. Redd, though, was feeling it this night. After Penn hit a 12-footer to tie the game at 17, Redd used his quickness to beat the Tigers off the dribble, and scored on two slashing layups to give Ohio State a 21-20 lead.

Although most in the crowd of 23,898 were SEC fans, the Buckeyes had the look of a confident home team. The Tigers were staggering before Ellis called a timeout at 4:49 to calm his team's nerves. Ellis didn't get into his players' faces. Instead, he challenged them to take the game to OSU. The Buckeyes were playing the more physical game in the first half. Still, the Tigers were winning the battle of the boards, 26-17—including 11 to six in offensive rebounds. Inexplicably, the Buckeyes were holding a 4-1 edge in second-chance points, mostly because the Tigers were rushing their second shots.

Ellis lit a fire under the Tigers. They came out with more energy, and regained the lead, 24-21, as Fishback made a three-pointer and hit one of two free throws. Then, O'Brien stormed toward the edge of the court, and signaled to Penn to slow things down. The Buckeyes were saved by an official timeout, which seemed to drain Auburn of its energy and momentum. The Buckeyes responded to O'Brien's demands, and scored seven straight points – including a Brian Brown three-pointer from the right wing with 2:12 remaining in the first half to take a 28-24 lead.

Finally, Porter resurfaced with 1:21 left in the half. He hit one of two free throws to cut the OSU lead to 28-25. In the final 31 seconds, the Tigers opted to double-team Redd, who had scorched them for 11 points on 5-for-9 shooting. But they turned their backs on Penn, who shook himself free of Pohlman to knock down a trey from 22 feet and give OSU a 31-26 lead at halftime.

O'Brien had a leg up in his battle with Ellis. Yet, as he trotted into the locker room behind his players, O'Brien didn't appear to be in a mood to celebrate. Instead, he was discussing second-half strategy with his assistant coaches even before leaving the floor. Ellis was trying to devise a strategy that would get Porter and N'diaye more involved in the offense. Porter was a workhorse on the boards, grabbing eight rebounds, but he scored only six points. N'diaye was 0-for-2 from the floor and 1-for-2 at the foul line.

The Buckeyes held the lead for the first 7:34 of the second half before Pohlman put Auburn ahead 45-44 with a pair of free throws. Now, the Buckeyes were stumbling and trying to gather their tired legs. The Tigers accelerated the tempo, which allowed Robinson to put down two short-range jumpers in transition and Fishback to drill a trey to give Auburn a 52-46 lead with 10:17 to play.

In the final minutes, Xs and Os wouldn't determine the outcome of this semifinal as much as the coaches' gut feelings and their management of both the clock and their personnel. O'Brien and Ellis eventually had to make critical decisions about when to put in their star players—Penn and Porter—each of whom was saddled with four fouls. With a large contingent of SEC loyalists pulling for Auburn, Penn was sitting next to O'Brien with 10:14 to play when OSU called timeout.

The Buckeyes, with O'Brien constantly juggling his lineup, were about to reach the point of no return. They had given Auburn too much cushion down the stretch. It was an unsettling feeling for O'Brien because he knew the Tigers had a way of putting teams away.

The Tigers had problems of their own, particularly Porter's foul trouble. Ellis ran him in and out of the lineup, trying to keep Porter fresh so he wouldn't commit a fatigue foul. Penn, his shooting touch golden again, had an immediate impact upon his return. He came off the bench and drilled a three-pointer from the top of the key to cut the Auburn lead to 52-51.

"We tried to hang on as much as we could with Scoonie on the bench," O'Brien said. "But we felt the game slipping away. You don't want to lose with your best player on the bench. I knew Scoonie would play smart. I knew we had a chance with him on the floor."

The Tigers, on the other hand, didn't have much of a chance with Porter sitting next to Ellis. He had played aggressively, despite foul trouble, challenging Johnson and Reese on the baseline. Back in the game, he hit a 12-foot turnaround to give Auburn a 54-51 lead with 7:15 remaining. Singleton scored six of his seven points in the last 6:45, including a layup that gave Ohio State a 55-54 lead. When the games were close, Porter had been Auburn's go-to man. Moments later, he committed his fourth and fifth personal fouls in a span of two minutes. The last one sent Redd to the foul line, where he dropped both shots to give Ohio State a 64-61 lead with 1:57 left.

Ellis, with his blue sweater still buttoned, put his arms around a beleaguered Porter. They both glanced at the scoreboard. They had not imagined the Tigers fighting for tournament survival with Porter in the role of spectator. Their worst fears had come to pass—Penn and Redd were making things happen down the stretch.

Redd hit two free throws. Penn made a 16-footer. Then Redd capped off a 22-point night with a steal and breakaway slam dunk with 1:01 remaining to give Ohio State an insurmountable 68-61 lead. Doc Robinson hit a three-pointer that Ellis hoped would jump-start a miracle rally with 65 seconds to go, leaving Auburn with a 70-64 deficit.

After an Auburn timeout, Penn, who had delivered so often in the clutch during the regular season, banked in a 12-footer with Robinson chopping down on his arm. Penn scored the last of his game- and NCAA Tournament-high 26 points on a free throw with 55 seconds left to cement a 72-64 victory.

"We kept our heads above water by not giving them too many second-chance points," said O'Brien, who watched as his Buckeyes held their own on the offensive glass, battling to a 14-all tie. "I had confidence that Scoonie and Michael would turn things around."

O'Brien, though, had already begun the turnaround. It was good enough to make him the National Association of Basketball Coaches (NABC) co-Coach of the Year with Duke's Mike Krzyzewski. Ellis's consolation prize was being named the Associated Press Coach of the Year.

While the Buckeyes had a hard time shaking Auburn, the St. John's Red Storm smoked Maryland early to take a 38-19 lead at halftime before cruising to a 76-62 win and gaining a spot in the regional final opposite Ohio State. The Red Storm were led by freshman point guard Erick Barkley, who tallied a game-high 24 points and nine assists. St. John's big guns, guards Ron Artest and Bootsy Thornton, combined for 22 points.

On the eve of the regional final, Penn and Barkley tried to downplay what many figured would be the pivotal matchup. Aside from the point-guard battle, the Buckeyes didn't appear to match up well against the more athletic Red Storm. St. John's had gotten O'Brien's attention, but Penn wouldn't allow himself to be overly impressed. "We felt like we could play with anyone," Penn said unblinkingly. "We had come too far to settle for just being there, so we were not going to be intimidated."

On March 20, the Buckeyes were looking to write another sterling, yet unfathomable chapter of a storybook 1998-99 college basketball season. If a screenwriter had submitted this improbable plot to a Hollywood studio, it would have been trashed. Even in the make-believe world of fairy tales, Ohio State's rise from the gutter to the Final Four appeared the most implausible of scenarios.

The Buckeyes, constantly reminded of their seven years of bad luck and bad play, were the leading men in a bad movie. The story line had been accentuated by a strange twist of irony. As the story weaved through a maze of unbelievable plots from Columbus to Knoxville, Tennessee, even O'Brien was left shaking his head.

The Buckeyes had gone to the RCA Dome in Indianapolis and dominated Murray State and Detroit. Only then did it seem that anyone was taking the Buckeyes' charge down the NCAA Tournament trail seriously. They were not supposed to make it past the second round—not with the tradition-rich UCLA Bruins in town. They were supposed to be ripe for the picking against a defensive-minded Murray State team that intended to make anyone other than Redd and Penn beat them. The Buckeyes were a nice story, even though most Sweet 16 sensations are usually written out of the script in the third or fourth round of the tournament. The Buckeyes, though, were sitting behind the wheel, preparing for an unexpected climax.

Forget *Hoosiers*. This stuff was real.

The Ohio State basketball program, one that had been so far gone that a search party couldn't find it at the beginning of the season, had risen above its deplorable past to come within a victory of advancing to the Final Four. If anyone had suggested that the Buckeyes would be playing St. John's in the South Regional championship game in the heart of Dixie amid the heightened anxieties of March Madness, he or she would have been laughed out of town.

The Buckeyes led comfortably, it seemed, by 13 points midway through the second half. Then the Red Storm was given new life when Redd and Brown each missed the front end of a one-and-one.

The Buckeyes were leading 73-64 with 2:50 remaining when Singleton took a baseline pass from Penn and laid it off the glass. The Ohio State fans jumped out of their seats, but O'Brien didn't change the stoic expression on his face. He had been here many times before with St. John's in several memorable Big East battles, so he told his players again and again to keep working. There was too much at stake for the Red Storm to quit now. Coach Mike Jarvis had proven that he was a master at late-game strategy at both George Washington and Boston University.

With 1:58 left in the game, the Red Storm's fate appeared sealed when Barkley picked up his fourth personal foul and the team's fourth. Barkley has an aggressive nature on the floor, but with four fouls, he couldn't afford to try to break down the Ohio State defense to set up medium-range jump shots for Artest and Thornton. Barkley would have to think twice about taking on Johnson, the tournament's best shot-blocker, by driving the lane to put up one of his acrobatic layups.

The clock had turned on St. John's. It was down to a precious 97 seconds, and Ohio State had possession of the ball. After Thornton stole the ball from Singleton to keep hope alive for the Red Storm, Johnson apparently swatted away the Red Storm's fading hopes when he blocked Barkley's running eight-foot jumper at 1:32. The Buckeyes, though, weren't around to claim possession. Thornton picked up the loose change, then cashed in two points despite being smacked across the forehead by Johnson, whose third foul sent Thornton to the line with a chance at a three-pointer. Thornton made the free throw to cut the Ohio State lead to 73-67 with 1:28 to play.

Suddenly, the difference was a couple of three-pointers. The Buckeyes' apparent blowout had become the proverbial nail-biter. It was time for the wheels to turn. O'Brien and Jarvis would have to match strategy and hope they had the better substitution pattern.

In the next five seconds, both teams suffered through big-game jitters. Savovic, ushered in to replace Johnson on the offensive end, committed a turnover. St. John's forward Reggie Jessie traveled, giving the ball back to Ohio State.

O'Brien valued Johnson more on the defensive end with the game tighter. He shuffled Johnson and Savovic on and off the bench with almost every change of possession. Artest, though, beat Johnson off the dribble to hit a four-foot jumper off the glass to trim the Ohio State lead to 73-69 with 48 seconds left.

The Red Storm, with their season of great expectations drifting into the murky waters of tournament upsets, could no longer fear Johnson. They had to fight like mad ticks with summer itch and challenge Johnson inside—in part, because Artest and Thornton weren't knocking down their shots from the perimeter.

When the Buckeyes met with reporters the day before, there were concerns that St. John's athleticism and ability to penetrate would leave Johnson in a perilous situation. The Red Storm was too quick for him to defend if they got inside the paint. Instead, a vastly improved and more mature Johnson frustrated the No. 2 seed. He altered the Red Storm's shots, made them make one more pass than they wanted and caused them to hurry shots.

Johnson was the intimidator. He was the enforcer. He was the difference. Johnson blocked a tournament-high seven shots and changed the direction of eight other shots. The man who was considered an offensive liability chipped in with 12 points on 6-for-9 shooting.

With only 48 seconds remaining in the game, the Red Storm's focus wasn't on Johnson. They had to foul Ohio State and hope the Buckeyes followed their season-long script of missing free throws. Here they were again, with the time bomb ticking. O'Brien summoned his coaches a few steps from the bench to discuss strategy during a timeout. It didn't take a basketball guru to figure out that Ohio State's brain trust wanted the ball in Penn's hands down the stretch. Penn had been the most reliable Buckeye when it came to shooting free throws. Surely he would not commit a costly turnover when pressured.

The Buckeyes, of course, didn't foul up their lines in this tournament melodrama. They stayed true to form, except when Penn hit two clutch free throws to put Ohio State ahead 75-69. St. John's countered quickly with a layup by Chudney Gray to make it 75-71.

When Redd missed the front end of his one-and-one attempt with 34.9 seconds left, Artest sprinted into the open court. In a rare defensive lapse, the Buckeyes were caught flat-footed in transition—as Artest scored a fast-break layup to cut what was one a huge deficit to two points, 75-73, with 17.9 seconds left.

In an instant, the scarlet-and-gray pom-poms that the OSU cheerleaders were pumping feverishly into the air, as if victory had been secured only 60 seconds before, were stilled. The Ohio State fans began to sweat. The Red Storm fans, even those who had been ready to beat the traffic midway through the second half, straightened up as if they were zapped with a defibrillator. Ohio State had controlled this game throughout, but its 45-28 halftime lead had dwindled almost to nothing.

The Buckeyes looked as though they had run smack into a wall. Jarvis pinned the Buckeyes' faces against that wall and made them confront a familiar foe: the foul line.

Gray tagged Brown without the clock rolling off a second. Brown, who had taken only one shot in 27 minutes, had to make his first free throw of the night to get a bonus shot. Brown had said the day before that this was the kind of pressure he expected when he signed on with Ohio State. It was only a free throw. All that was riding in his young, sweaty hands was a ticket to the Final Four.

Brown took a deep breath. He bent his knees smartly. The ball rolled smoothly off his fingers.

The crowd of 24, 248—most of them unnerved Ohio State fans—knew everything could depend on this shot. The St. John's fans were hooting and hollering, trying their best to distract Brown. The Buckeyes' fans could only hold on tight and say a little prayer.

Brown's free throw bounced off the back of the rim and into Postell's hands. Incredibly, the Red Storm now had a chance to win the game. The Buckeyes, haunted again by poor free-throw shooting, had to rely on their defense—and the fact that St. John's didn't shoot that well from the foul line, either. In the end, the Red Storm made only 15 of their 23 freebies, but when Reese fouled Gray with 12.5 seconds to go, they had a chance to wipe the slate clean.

Gray promptly missed the first free throw. O'Brien, yelling for a 20-second timeout, wanted Gray to think about the importance of his next shot. He put Johnson and Savovic back into the game, hoping Johnson could snatch down a defensive rebound. But Gray sank his second shot, making the score 75-74 with 12.5 seconds left.

Now, it was Jarvis's move. He called a full timeout to draw a simple picture for his team. He wanted his players to press full court in the hope of forcing a turnover or getting the quick foul. Again, the clock didn't move, as Gray chopped Penn across the arms, sending the Buckeyes' captain to the foul line.

This was far too much excitement, even for Andy Geiger. He hadn't counted on making the Final Four only two years after hiring O'Brien from Boston College. Geiger had managed athletic programs at three prestigious universities: Brown, Stanford, and Maryland. Yet, he hadn't experienced anything like this.

"We were all caught up in it and were very excited, almost breathless about what we saw as a possibility to achieve something special," Geiger said. "I marveled at Coach O'Brien's calmness and his stability. He was even-tempered through the whole thing, and you could tell it was a big deal and a lot was at stake."

With the Ohio State lead down to a single point, O'Brien put his best free-throw shooters on the floor. Reese substituted for Singleton, and Sanderson replaced Johnson. He wanted Penn at the line. Nothing had changed since their days together in Chestnut Hill. Penn would get two shots because Gray's foul was the 10th on St. John's, putting it over the limit.

Penn had outdueled Barkley. He had played a complete game. (He would finish with eight rebounds, eight assists, and two steals.) However, all that mattered now was how he would handle himself at the foul line with the tournament heat turned all the way up.

Penn missed the first free throw. O'Brien dropped to his knees. The Ohio State fans folded their arms across their chest and sighed heavily. The St. John's fans were simply clinging to whatever semblance of hope that remained.

Penn then made the second free throw to leave Ohio State with a 76-74 lead. O'Brien stood up quickly and then motioned in his defensive stoppers—Brown, Singleton, and Johnson.

Jarvis and the Red Storm had seemingly always put their fate in the hands of Artest. Jarvis knew, however, that Singleton would go after Artest like a fat rat in a cheese factory. Singleton wouldn't let Artest see his own shadow, let alone a shot at the basket. With the clock winding down, a duel of point guards ensued. Barkley hurriedly pushed the ball upcourt with Penn riding him every step of the way. Barkley looked for Artest and then glanced at Thornton, but neither was open. As Barkley made his move toward the basket with a right-hand dribble, Penn reached in to deflect the ball. The ball popped free, and Redd retrieved it near the baseline. Redd was fouled immediately by Artest with nine-tenths of a second left on the clock.

"I don't know what happened," said Penn, who finished with 22 points on 7-for-13 shooting and was named the South Regional Most Outstanding Player. "I just heard the crowd go crazy."

Redd, who finished with 20 points and six rebounds, needed to make both free throws to render a St. John's Hail Mary heave useless. He made the first free throw, but missed the second. Then, as the horn sounded, Barkley launched a 70-footer that drifted wide right of its target. The Buckeyes had stunned most everyone with a surprising 77-74 victory.

O'Brien sighed.

Geiger leaned back in his seat.

The Ohio State fans lost it.

The Buckeyes gathered at center court and did the Dirty Bird—a jubilant, triumphant, and imperfectly choreographed four-step routine created by the Atlanta Falcons, whom the Denver Broncos had beaten in the Super two months earlier.

"Can you believe it?" Penn shouted as he rushed to embrace O'Brien.

"You gotta believe," Penn shouted as he fell into the arms of his mother, Allegra Penn. "I can't believe it."

The Buckeyes, wearing Final Four caps, celebrated more than a victory. It was time to celebrate the rebirth of a basketball program steeped in a long history of success.

As the Buckeyes continued to skip around the court, the sometimes-stoic O'Brien considered cutting a few steps, too. It is not his nature to celebrate openly. In the back of his mind, he was already thinking about Ohio State's next opponent—Connecticut, the No. 1 seed in the West Regional, which exorcised its regional final demons with a 67-62 win over another NCAA Tournament surprise, Gonzaga.

O'Brien couldn't contain his euphoria. Finally, he leaped for joy as his daughters, Erin and Amy, made their way down to the arena floor. The O'Briens, standing in the middle of a scattered celebration, hugged and kissed. Together they shared a dream they talked about, but rarely envisioned coming to fruition. O'Brien grabbed his daughters' hands. Unlike his reaction to the Buckeyes' second-round win over Detroit Mercy, O'Brien appeared more thrilled than relieved. In his 17th year as a head coach, the former ABA point guard was taking a team to the Final Four for the first time.

"In any of our lives, when you experience something special, you want special people to share it with you," O'Brien said. "It's why we all got emotional. In a setting like that, it was as special as it gets. The fact that Erin and Amy were there to share it is something we will remember all our lives. No matter what happens, we can point to that day, that whole atmosphere, and ask, 'Do you remember this?' When we look at the tape, we will have some vivid memories.

"I was lucky they were able to be there. It was an incredible feeling. There have been some very good coaches, outstanding players and guys who have coached their entire lives in college—and with remarkable success—that have never gotten to the Final Four. So you look at those teams and ask yourself, 'How lucky am I?' If you ask any college basketball coach what he would like to accomplish, his first response would be to win a national championship. If you can't do that, then the second reaction is getting into the Final Four. It is like getting to the highest step of your professional ladder and one step removed from winning it all. When you think about getting to the Final Four, it sometimes seems inconceivable. It's like being in the Super Bowl or the World Series."

O'Brien's Final Four dream was realized, in part, because of the intimidating presence of his once-awkward 6-11 center Ken Johnson. Redd and Penn produced all the highlight-reel stuff, but Johnson did most of the dirty work before doing the Dirty Bird.

"I knew the game would be decided inside," Jarvis said. "We had to take control of the paint right away, but he wouldn't let us. We didn't attack him the way we planned. Let me tell you, they don't win the game without him. He did what he wanted to for much of the game."

St. John's forward Lavar Postell, who would score a game-high 24 points, tipped his hat to Johnson, too. "I've got to give him credit. I didn't know he was that good. He scored, pulled down some key rebounds, and blocked a lot of shots."

Johnson played an intelligent 37 minutes and exhibited the poise and patience that was absent in the regional semifinal victory over Auburn, a game in which he was plagued by foul trouble.

"It was really hectic in the paint," Johnson told a small group of reporters who gathered around him in the Ohio State locker room. "I think things turned out better than I thought they would. I knew I had to have a presence for us to be successful. I had to make something happen. I just did my thing. I've been going up against guys in the Big Ten who are bigger and more physical than guys they face in the Big East, so I was confident that I could hold my own."

It was because of Johnson that St. John's fell behind and struggled. "We had momentum going for us when we made our run at the end." Jarvis said. "I'll be seeing Penn and Red in my sleep, but I'll have nightmares thinking about how Johnson controlled this game."

Jarvis had reasons to toss and turn all night. Johnson all but negated two of his big scoring threats, as Artest and center Tyrone Grant scored a combined 12 points on 5-for-15 shooting. The two had had off nights before, but nothing quite like this.

"I think Kenny started having a better feeling of himself, more confident and more conscientious about his own work habits," O'Brien said. "He grew up against St. John's and Detroit during the tournament. It's true that both of those teams had no one bigger than 6-foot-7. Whenever he had Artest guarding him, we were trying to exploit the advantage we had there. He still has some things to iron out. We didn't think he would be the automatic presence inside."

As a wave of Ohio State fans poured onto the floor of the Thompson-Boling Arena, O'Brien climbed quickly up a ladder to cut a string from the nets, a symbolic souvenir of the Buckeyes' rapid ascension to the top of the college basketball world. When O'Brien turned to embrace Ohio State president William E. Kirwan and Geiger, his players encouraged him to do the Dirty Bird. He shied away from them. However, Singleton and Penn wouldn't let him sneak into the postgame interview room without dancing. A smiling O'Brien let his hair down and rocked side to side as he tried to get with the rhythm of the Ohio State pep band. He didn't boogie down quite like his players, but the Buckeyes saw another side of the man who led Ohio State from an 8-22 season to the brink of a national championship.

"My guys have been trying to get me to do that all year, and I held out," a jubilant O'Brien said. "It was pretty obvious that nobody taught me."

It was obvious, too, that O'Brien had taught the Buckeyes how to win. While Ohio State fans clamored for his attention, trying to shake his hand as if he were a politician during an election year, O'Brien seemed more surprised than his players that they had taken yet another momentous step in completing the greatest turnaround in college basketball history. Already, no other Big Ten school had ever won only eight games and one conference game one season, then advanced to a regional final the next.

"Can you believe this?" O'Brien asked Erin O'Brien, who is the oldest of his two daughters.

"It's unbelievable," said O'Brien in a soft, raspy voice barely audible amid the loud screams of the Ohio State fans.

Few, it seemed, could believe that Ohio State had come to Knoxville, and defeated the South Regional's No. 1 and No. 2 seeds. The Buckeyes were given long-shot odds of beating Auburn in SEC country.

"It was like a bad novel," Geiger said. "My first reaction was, 'Who wrote this?' This is not real. This can't be going on. Yet, there we all were. It was amazing.

"I had gone up to the stands to get President Kirwan, so he could congratulate the team. Then, I danced a little off to the side. We can jump up and be elated, but that moment belongs to the players and coaches. When we won, I ran over to the other side of the arena just looking for anyone to hug. I thought about how that building [Thompson-Boling Arena] had been lucky for me. When I was at Stanford, we won the women's NCAA national championship there [in 1990]. I thought to myself that lightning does strike twice in the same place, at least in terms of my life.

"I was stunned by what happened. I did not expect it to happen. I don't know if I've ever been happier in my life or enjoyed anything more than the weekend in Knoxville, Tennessee. That trip to Knoxville and that regional victory was like a dream. It was just astounding."

"This is as good as it gets—for now," O'Brien said. "St. John's refused to go away nicely. If it wasn't for one or two plays we had to make at the end, who knows what would have happened? I think we played very well for 38 minutes and we were happy we were able to hold on."

It was a wild, furious ride to the finish.

"As the game went right down to the last breathtaking play, when Scoonie stole the ball, I was sort of sitting quietly," Geiger said. "I internalize a lot of those situations. You cannot do anything but hope and pray it all works out. You have to be lucky. Things have to break your way. You have to get a draw in a bracket where you can make it happen. I will always be grateful for that opportunity. Making it to the Final Four is something the vast majority of athletic directors will never get to see."

In a way, this was a complicated regional tournament for Geiger, who was torn by mixed emotions. There was a part of him that wanted to cheer for Maryland coach Gary Williams, whom he worked with before leaving for Ohio State in 1994. Williams had been at Ohio State from 1986 to 1989 before leaving for College Park, Maryland. O'Brien replaced Williams at Boston College in 1986.

The coaching careers of O'Brien and Williams have followed similar paths. They both were hired at Boston College and Ohio State. They have similar interests as well, including golf, and have even traveled to Scotland and Ireland together on golfing trips. They both possessed a competitive spirit and immeasurable desire to develop championship-caliber teams. However, O'Brien is more diplomatic while working with officials. Williams is much more demonstrative and demanding.

Geiger, a Dartmouth graduate, wasn't in a hurry to get to Thompson-Boling Arena for the first South Regional semifinal game on March 18. The St. John's-Maryland game interested him only because Williams was coaching. Geiger also didn't want to leave the slightest impression that he still had an emotional tie to Maryland. The Terrapins needed an emotional lift after St. John's ran them over in the regional semifinals.

"Instead of watching the first game, I went over to the hotel with the team," Geiger said. "When I got to the arena, St. John's was just pummeling Maryland. It was an interesting thing for me because I came here from Maryland. I didn't want to get caught up in any of that or be around it. Somebody might come over and ask me questions about that. I was at Ohio State—not Maryland. I stayed pretty much with the Ohio State people.

"I will never forget my meeting with Gary Williams after the game. Coming off the floor after what was a crushing disappointment for them, he went out of his way to wish us well. I knew he was hurting because they had high expectations. It's something about that night I will never forget. It had to be a doubly difficult moment because he had been at Ohio State. It was two paths coming together at one place at one time. It was a moving time for me. I was disappointed because Gary wanted it so bad. It meant so much to him. I don't have the language to explain what a competitor he is. He pours everything that he possibly can into his job. Working with Gary wasn't always easy, like working with me isn't always easy. I have tremendous respect for the incredible drive the man has. Jim and Gary are strong competitors, and they react to failure differently. Each has an enormous drive to be successful. Jim is very steady and very composed and conceals the fire. Now, Gary, everything is on his sleeve—and then some. So they are vastly different in style."

O'Brien's style is more to Geiger's liking. It got a little better after O'Brien put together something equivalent to a basketball miracle by engineering an 18-win turnaround and leading the Buckeyes into the Final Four for the ninth time in school history.

"It did not surprise me—not after Indianapolis," Geiger said. "Jim O'Brien is a great basketball coach. But I said every prayer I know at the end of the game. You can't imagine this would happen in two years. It's impossible to create this fantasy. You don't just turn on the switch and go to the Final Four. I've never seen anything like this. You have to be surprised that we've gotten this far. This has been a stunning season.

"It hasn't been easy turning things around. I'm so grateful for what these guys have accomplished. It's a great source of pride for our school and the state. It's incredible how much the players have matured and how they developed a sense of family."

Only three other teams can claim to have accomplished anything close to what Ohio State pulled off. The 1941 Wisconsin Badgers, the 1952 Santa Clara Broncos, and the 1974 Kansas Jayhawks all made it to the Final Four one year after winning fewer than 10 games.

Ohio State defied all the odds right from the opening tip of its first game of the season against Oakland University on November 13, 1998. It went on to prove many of the so-called experts and television analysts wrong. Dick Vitale of ESPN and ABC Sports scratched the Buckeyes from his office pool early. He predicted his former team, Detroit Mercy, would pull the upset. He predicted an Auburn blowout. He predicted St. John's would finally burst the Buckeyes' bubble and restore a sense of normality back to a wild, unpredictable NCAA Tournament. Only when O'Brien and Penn were doing the Dirty Bird at center court did Vitale concede, "They're for real, baby."

However, O'Brien didn't need anyone's affirmation of the Buckeyes' legitimacy. The Buckeyes battled their way into the Final Four despite a lifeless performance in losing to Illinois in the Big Ten Tournament. The Buckeyes grew up during the NCAA Tournament, learning a valuable lesson after losing to Illinois.

"No one would have predicted a Final Four—not even the NIT," O'Brien said. "We knew we were going to be better, but we didn't know how much better. We got hot at the right time. Our players were never satisfied with their accomplishments. We felt we could beat Auburn and St. John's."

The Fighting Illini, he noted, helped to rekindle the Buckeyes' fire. He said that the Illini loss, more than anything else, made Ohio State a more focused team going into the NCAA Tournament. "I am very thankful of having the opportunity to coach this group of guys," O'Brien said. "This is as good a group as I've ever been affiliated with in all my years of coaching. They have been respectful and considerate to everything we have asked of them all year. After the loss to Illinois, we asked them to play harder, play better, and don't give up."

For Redd, it was easy to explain the Buckeyes' unlikely journey to the Final Four.

"We were tired of losing," Redd said. "After we beat Indiana in Bloomington and Iowa in Iowa City, we felt we were as good as any team in the country."

14

THE FINAL FOUR

On a majestic spring evening in St. Petersburg, Florida, Jim O'Brien knelt courtside with his black and red silk necktie tightly snugged and his shirt neatly tucked. Just minutes before the 1999 NCAA Division I national semifinal game between Ohio State and Connecticut, O'Brien remained unflappable amid the staccato applause and incessant foot stomping of a vociferous March Madness crowd of 41,340 at Tropicana Field.

This was a maddening, yet exhilarating exercise in Final Four pressure. O'Brien, though, appeared unmoved. The so-called college basketball experts figured that every timeout, every dead ball would only prolong what seemed to be inescapable defeat for the underdog Buckeyes.

Ohio State's title-starved fans sat anxiously in their high-priced Final Four seats—some scalped for $1,000. They hoped O'Brien could conjure up more tournament magic, as he had in leading the fourth-seeded Buckeyes to surprising victories over No. 1-seed Auburn and No. 3-seed St. John's in the South Regional in Knoxville, Tennessee only a week earlier.

In just his second season at Ohio State, O'Brien was sharing center stage with three more visible coaches. Duke's Mike Krzyzewski, Connecticut's Jim Calhoun, and Michigan State's Tom Izzo were supposed to take their talented teams to sun-splashed St. Petersburg, Florida, where golf and windsurfing are far more popular than college basketball. Duke, Connecticut, and Michigan State hit a few speed bumps along the way. But their journey through the NCAA Tournament didn't have nearly the obstacles that Ohio State negotiated on the road to the Final Four.

The Buckeyes, who entered the game with a 27-8 record, survived emotional peaks and valleys against Murray State and Detroit in making it to the Sweet 16. They withstood a late flurry by Auburn to advance to the Elite Eight. Then St. John's nearly reeled them in during the waning minutes of the South Regional final. The Buckeyes didn't back into the Final Four. They earned every mile of this NCAA Tournament trip, one that began in Indianapolis and gathered unfathomable momentum in Knoxville.

Incredibly, one year after slamming a wrecking ball into the program by dismissing six players, O'Brien rebuilt the Buckeyes into national contenders. The Buckeyes were forged together by a basketball fundamentalist whose recruiting skills and innovative ways in which he motivated his players were the catalyst for revitalizing the Ohio State basketball program.

O'Brien and his overachieving Buckeyes had beaten the odds all season. However, the odds were stacked heavily against this Brooklyn-born Irish Catholic in the semifinal. O'Brien's teams hadn't beaten Calhoun's teams head-to-head in 18 consecutive games. O'Brien had read the newspaper accounts of his lopsided duels with the Connecticut coach. At every pregame press conference, he braced himself for the inevitable questions as to why Calhoun had had his number. As soon as he sensed a reporter was about to fire off the inevitable, O'Brien would force a dry, uneasy smile.

An hour before tip-off, O'Brien and Calhoun talked briefly as their teams went through their pregame drills. They didn't say much, really. They hadn't seen much of one another during the week, partly because the Buckeyes were staying 40 minutes from the arena at the Suites at Mainsail Village in Tampa. The Buckeyes, unlike the players at Michigan State, Connecticut, and Duke, arrived at this private, secluded condominium without fanfare. While hundreds of fans clamored for a mere glance at their Final Four heroes, O'Brien decided to keep the Buckeyes under wraps. If nothing else, the lone survivor among the tournament's Cinderellas, wasn't going to be distracted before reaching the big dance at Tropicana Field.

Considering his team's history against the Huskies, O'Brien didn't need any distractions, either. He knew Calhoun felt confident about his chances. But these weren't the Eagles of Boston College. Maybe this time things would be different.

"Jim Calhoun is obviously a wonderful guy, and we've become friendly down through the years," O'Brien said on the eve of the Ohio State-Connecticut semifinal. "But last night, we were together; there were the [Final Four] coaches. It was Mike and Tom, Jim and myself. When Calhoun sees Tom, he says, 'Tom, it's nice to see you. Mike, it's nice to you. Jim it's really nice to see you.'"

The joke had always been on O'Brien whenever his Boston College teams faced Connecticut in Big East Conference games. This time, the Buckeyes wanted the last laugh. They wanted to atone for being the laughingstock of the Big Ten for much of the 1990s.

The O'Brien-Calhoun matchup had become predictable. It was like the 1978 Triple Crown duel between Affirmed and Alydar. No matter how fast Alydar circled the turf, Affirmed was always better in the last furlong. The oddsmakers had to believe that if O'Brien's Buckeyes were challenging down the stretch in this national semifinal, his thoroughbreds—Scoonie Penn and Michael Redd—were likely to fade after a wild four-week tournament foray from Chicago to Indianapolis to Knoxville to St. Petersburg. Indeed, a breakdown, the experts concluded, seemed inevitable.

The indisputable fact remained that Calhoun had always gotten the best of O'Brien. Yet, when Ohio State center Ken Johnson and Connecticut center Jake Voskuhl stared down one another at center court for the opening tip-off, O'Brien's eyes glistened with confidence. Calhoun, well, looked even more confident. Few, if any, among the crowd gave the Buckeyes a chance of getting into the championship game.

No way were they going to buck the odds—again.

The Buckeyes had traveled this road before and unearthed a few miracles en route to winning 27 games—including their South Regional wins before a hostile, partisan Southeastern Conference crowd at Thompson-Boling Arena.

As O'Brien glanced down the sideline at Calhoun, another of his adversaries, Michigan State's Tom Izzo, was discussing strategy with his Spartans in the locker room. O'Brien knew his Buckeyes wanted another shot at Michigan State, the Big Ten champions. The Spartans had defeated Ohio State in East Lansing in their only meeting of the season, and their expected rematch at the Big Ten Tournament never materialized, as long-shot Illinois upset Ohio State in the semifinals at the United Center in Chicago on March 6. O'Brien felt bad for his players. He wanted them to leave this place understanding how much they had narrowed the gap between themselves and the country's college basketball elite. Besides, there were no guarantees that Michigan State would conquer top-ranked Duke in the semifinal nightcap.

"The thing that was on my mind was, I was hoping for us to win and hoping that Michigan State would win," O'Brien said. "It would have guaranteed a Big Ten champion. I was thinking that would be great. It would have given us an opportunity to play them again, knowing we would have a chance to beat them. For me personally, I didn't mind playing Connecticut."

The Buckeyes' coaches were excited about playing Connecticut. O'Brien and his staff couldn't put together the right game plan to beat the Huskies while at Boston College. This was an opportunity, with most of the college basketball world watching, to get it right. O'Brien was convinced that the

Buckeyes' style, unlike his Boston College teams, matched up better against Connecticut.

"When you get to this point, it really doesn't matter who you play," O'Brien said after Ohio State's last full practice at Tropicana Field on a hot Friday afternoon. "You're saying to yourself you can play for the national championship. If we were going to play for the national championship, it didn't matter who it was going to be against. All I cared about was getting my team to the championship game.

"In the back of our minds, we [Ohio State's coaches] knew we had a major history with Connecticut. Deep down, none of that stuff mattered. It was not about the ACC or the Big East or the Big Ten. It would have been nice to play Michigan State, but we had to get by Connecticut."

The Buckeyes hung tight early, keeping the Huskies in their sights. Center Ken Johnson and forward Jason Singleton provided most of the offense. They muscled their way inside, hitting layups and short bank shots around the basket.

Singleton, who survived O'Brien's housecleaning and three years of mediocrity, was a defensive stopper throughout the postseason. Singleton had his shot working against Connecticut, scoring 12 points to keep Ohio State within a single point, 36-35, at halftime. Singleton turned his attention to defense in the second half and would be limited to only two shots.

Curiously, Singleton did not draw the streak-shooting Richard Hamilton, an angular 6-foot-6 swingman who often brushed off picks to create mismatches against the 5-10 Penn and 6-1 freshman guard Brian Brown at the perimeter. Hamilton needed little spacing to release his soft jumpers, except when Singleton was forced to take him on a defensive switch. Singleton tried playing head games with Hamilton. He stuffed Hamilton's shot emphatically just before the halftime buzzer. The two exchanged pleasantries, then smiled as they left the floor. In the heat of battle, neither could concede an inch.

"When I got the ball, they were trying to take away my three-point opportunities," Hamilton said later. "So I knew I could shoot over the guys guarding me. One thing I tried to do was get as close to the basket as possible. I was open. I saw the screen. I made the shots."

Penn and Redd could hardly see the basket. O'Brien had to rely primarily on his coaching instincts to manufacture some points. He turned to sophomore small forward Jon Sanderson, but Sanderson's confidence had taken a beating, especially after he was benched in favor of Brown prior to the first-round game in the South Regional in Indianapolis. O'Brien deployed a three-guard offense to create more balance in the open floor. Brown gave them better defensive balance at the perimeter, so Sanderson was rendered ineffective.

Every time O'Brien looked down the bench or on the floor, he turned his attention back to Penn. O'Brien and Penn were philosophically insepa-rable. That's why O'Brien felt good about his team's chances in the final min-utes of the game. He knew Penn would orchestrate the offense perfectly, find the open man, or make a shot that would at least have Connecticut thinking of its past last-minute tournament failures.

However, the Buckeyes were tormented by the mind games. They had become a superstitious team. Everything had to be in its proper order and place. They ran onto the court in the exact same order, ran the same pregame drills, sat in the same seats, whether on a bus or a plane. They traveled with the same musical collections.

When Penn jogged onto the court at Tropicana Field with a different jersey number, some wondered if the Buckeyes would be at a psychological disadvantage. Penn couldn't find his No. 12 jersey and had to wear No. 35. He never looked comfortable. He dismissed it, but he made only three of 17 shots from the floor in the biggest game of his collegiate career.

"When I went to put my shirt back on, I couldn't find it," Penn said. "But I don't think that had anything to do with the game that I didn't have my jersey."

As the crowd settled into Tropicana Field, and with a nationwide tele-vision audience perched in front of their screens for the national semifinal doubleheader, the Buckeyes were scrambling about their locker room, trying to solve the "Great Jersey Caper."

It was hard to piece together a game plan for a team that had haunted O'Brien during most of his 11-year tenure at Boston College. Now, the Buck-eyes were confronted with an unwanted distraction. Yet, O'Brien knew Penn to be mentally tough—that a little thing like a change of number wouldn't affect his play.

"I was thinking it wouldn't have bothered me," O'Brien said. "I don't think it bothered Scoonie. We didn't have any time to really worry about it. It happened so fast. He said he hung it up, and his pregame routine is to leave his uniform hung up when they go out for warm-ups. He just had a T-shirt underneath his warm-up jersey. With about 10 minutes to go before intro-ductions, he came back in to use the bathroom and put his uniform on. When he came back in, it was gone. We started looking for it; there was only about six minutes to go before the game was about to start. We were in the locker room looking in bags, in lockers and under stuff. We had to get every-body in the locker room to look around.

"Then it got to the point when we had to get going. Now, we had to break out what we call the blood jersey – No. 35. One of the managers had to run out to the bus to get this jersey, and we were all waiting while the clock is winding down for the game. We were all looking for Scoonie's jersey. Now,

I'm saying, 'Fellas, we've got to go. You guys got to get out, and Scoonie will be right out when we get this extra jersey.' It was kind of chaotic. The kid brings the jersey in, and Scoonie puts it on so we could get onto the court in time for introductions. It was a little bit bizarre. Once Scoonie got out there, I think he probably forgot what number he was wearing. It never dawned on some people that he didn't have the right number.

"I know for myself, everything has to be in order," O'Brien said. "My socks had to come up to the right length and they had to feel right. You want things to be the way you want them to be. Ken Johnson had a thing about his sneakers."

Penn may have been just fine psychologically, but he couldn't shake Ricky Moore, whose reputation as the nation's best defensive player was further enhanced during the NCAA Tournament.

"OK, the guy got inside my shirt," Penn said later, trying to add levity to the situation. "He really had nothing else to do out there but guard me. He just stayed with me. He didn't have to worry about scoring. He just took me right out of my game. The truth is, he got into my head."

That, of course, was O'Brien's biggest fear in the days leading up to this semifinal game. Moore, overshadowed by Richard Hamilton and Khalid El-Amin, felt he had something to prove. He hadn't quite gotten over being snubbed by the Big East coaches, who left him off the all-conference first team. If Moore could rattle Penn, he would accomplish something that would certainly get everyone's attention.

"I just wanted Scoonie to shoot tough shots," Moore said. "I was taking away the drive to the basket first. The second option was stopping him from shooting jump shots. Although I was screaming and yelling at my teammates, they did a terrific job of helping me out."

The 6-foot-2 Moore had struggled some with his shot during the regular season. He never struggled with his defense. Calhoun could have used him on Redd, but the strategy was to tie up Penn. Calhoun instructed Moore to shadow Penn from baseline to baseline, from start to finish. "Ricky just makes up his mind that he's going to play 40 minutes worth of defense, and that's that," Calhoun said.

Redd, who became the first freshman to lead the Big Ten in scoring, wanted the ball. He had been the go-to man before Penn's arrival. The Huskies were more concerned with Penn possessing the ball than they were with Redd shooting it. Admittedly, it was a blow to the Columbus native's ego. He did get his looks—albeit blurred, partly because he had no one hitting an outside shot to help loosen Connecticut's double teams.

Redd didn't mind pulling his trigger finger. He matured as the season progressed, finding other ways in which his incalculable talents could help Ohio State. Calhoun feared Redd, particularly in man-on-man situations, when even the narrowest of gaps were created in the seams of the Huskies' defense. No way could Kevin Freeman and Hamilton match his quickness and acceleration. Yet, whenever Redd beat Freeman with a crossover dribble, the Connecticut defense collapsed, forcing Redd to give the ball up or take a hurried, aimless shot.

The Huskies doubled up on Penn and Redd whenever the ball swung their way, and the Huskies left the baseline unchecked. The Buckeyes couldn't counter offensively because they were without a consistent perimeter shooter. Sanderson and Brown sat next to O'Brien trying to rub the rust off their shooting hands, while Penn and Redd were on their way toward a combined 10-of-31 shooting night. In the second half, Moore held Penn to 1-for-10 shooting from the floor. Penn finished with 11 points, six below his season's average. Ohio State made only 8 of 33 shots after the break.

O'Brien tried senior guard Neshaun Coleman, who had been an inspirational leader all season. But a slightly strained hamstring and the lingering effects of a viral infection had weakened Coleman's stroke. As a result, most of his corner jumpers were frozen ropes that barely grazed iron.

Finally, O'Brien waved to freshman guard Boban Savovic, a former Yugoslav junior national player who migrated to New Jersey to play high school basketball in 1996. Savovic's first shot, a 20-foot jumper, was perfectly stroked from the corner. But the 6-1 freshman wouldn't take another shot. He lost his confidence and concentration. It seemed his mind was a world away—in Kosovo, to be exact.

This was a perplexing time for O'Brien and Savovic. Savovic wanted desperately to play in the Final Four. This was the one weekend in March that he and his fellow Serbs gathered around the television to watch America's finest amateur athletes compete for the national championship. Now, here he was in St. Petersburg, playing before an audience of millions. But no one in Yugoslavia was watching, except the privileged few, who avoided the NATO bombings in Kosovo.

"I wanted my family to see me play," Savovic said. "I can remember us sitting around watching the Final Four and thinking how the players in America had it made. I never really thought they appreciated how special it was to play in the Final Four. I was wrong. I don't know if anyone appreciated playing in the tournament more than my teammates."

On the eve of this national semifinal, O'Brien met with Savovic in hopes of comforting him. Like Savovic, his American teammates read the headlines in the *Tampa Tribune* and *St. Petersburg Times*. They tried reassuring Savovic that everything back home was fine—and that he wasn't deemed an enemy of the state because President Clinton had ordered the strikes against his native Serbs. Savovic had trouble reaching his family by phone during the bombings. He would have to call his friends, who would then check to see if his family was safe.

For all the complicated game strategies, handling Savovic's delicate situation was more challenging, said O'Brien. This, though, would not be a memorable Final Four for the 19-year-old Savovic. If his fear of flying from Columbus to St. Petersburg weren't enough, he didn't touch the ball much in the second half. He was out of it mentally and emotionally. O'Brien didn't want to press him. O'Brien was sticking to his principle that basketball may be a way of life for some student-athletes, but it doesn't imitate life.

"It had to be difficult for Boban," O'Brien said. "We needed him in the game, but we also needed him to have some peace of mind. The fact that he played at all is a tribute to the type of young man he is."

O'Brien had run out of options. He had no other choice but to put the Buckeyes' fate in the usually competent hands of Redd and Penn. He could only hope that their aimless floaters and off-balance jumpers would find the basket. They had weathered similar storms all season in thrusting themselves into the national spotlight and earning the respect of every Big Ten opponent they faced.

O'Brien, the Big Ten Coach of the Year, believed that playing the supposedly invincible Duke Blue Devils in the championship game would fulfill his team's destiny. Besides, this Ohio State team had dug itself out of the college basketball gutter to find itself at the doorstep of an improbable coronation as national champion.

The seconds ticked to a precious few as Ohio State and UConn countered blows. Finally, the Buckeyes were without an answer. Their tired legs betrayed them as their shots rimmed in and out or targeted nothing but air.

O'Brien, his tie still knotted perfectly, kept on fighting. He was like a cut man in a fighter's corner, patching and nursing the Buckeyes' bruised egos and battered confidence, imploring them to fight on. O'Brien doesn't know how to quit. If the Buckeyes were going down in the semifinals, they would do so by scratching, clawing, and running themselves ragged until the very end. It was like that even when O'Brien was a high school star at St. Francis Prep in Brooklyn. He sharpened his inherited gung-ho mentality on the mean outdoor courts of his youth. O'Brien was the skinny, but hard-nosed white kid who assimilated without airs into the cliquish society of inner-city basketball. His father had taught him to fight—even when the fight was lost.

"That's what it's all about," O'Brien said.

The Buckeyes had become their coach. They kept hammering away at the Huskies, methodically chipping away at their second-half deficit. While Calhoun was hoping the Huskies wouldn't collapse, O'Brien was like a fighter pinned in the corner, as he threw everything at Connecticut, trying to get Ohio State into its first championship game in 31 years.

"You can never give up," O'Brien said. "Almost anything can happen in basketball. Sometimes the games are over. There might be a minute to go, and you're down by 10, and people in the stands ask, 'Why do they keep fouling?' The game is over, but we try to get some kind of practice out of it. We might be in that situation again where we have a chance to win. This is what we want our kids to understand. So you keep working at it, even though that particular game might be lost. I don't think you ever sit back and let it go or accept defeat—even if it appears inevitable."

O'Brien put an arm around the broad shoulders of his prized guard, Scoonie Penn. He whispered words of encouragement. Penn smiled. O'Brien smiled. Neither coach nor player seemed flustered in the final, exasperating 2:53, with Ohio State trailing 59-55. Yet, most players around them were drying their sweaty palms or drinking Gatorade to douse their flames of anxiety.

Penn and O'Brien had come within a victory of advancing to the Sweet 16 with a similarly overachieving Boston College team in 1997. This scenario was ghostly familiar, yet familiarity didn't breed poise and confidence. That was a product of their player/coach relationship. O'Brien and Penn knew exactly what to expect of each other as time slipped away with UConn clinging to its precarious four-point lead.

O'Brien's nerves were battle-tested from his Big East Tournament clashes at Madison Square Garden. Always, his path to the Final Four was full of roadblocks, but now he had maneuvered his way past every obstacle on the road to St. Petersburg. It was reaffirmation of his coaching method, if not madness, in his acquisitive aspirations for perfection. It's what Rollie Massimino accomplished in leading Villanova to a shocking conquest of mighty Georgetown in the 1985 title game. It's what Don Haskins achieved when his all-black Texas Western (now University of Texas at El Paso) team stunned Adolph Rupp's all-white and presumably invincible Kentucky Wildcats 20 years earlier in helping to narrow the great racial divide in college basketball—except, of course, in Lexington, Kentucky.

Penn, who grew up in Salem, Massachusetts, thrived under pressure. All season he had rescued the Buckeyes almost single-handedly in leading them to wins over eight Top 25 opponents—including Indiana, Minnesota, Wisconsin and Purdue. The Big Ten's co-Player of the Year routinely made the momentum-shifting three-pointers and game-clinching free throws that propelled Ohio State back into the Top 10 for the first time since 1992.

Now, he was put on the spot again. Penn and Redd were expected to take the big shots. So much more was demanded of Penn, whose confidence and bravado energized the Buckeyes. The Buckeyes were most vulnerable when Penn was either out of rhythm or physically worn, as he was in Ohio State's loss to Penn State in the regular-season finale. A bruised hip had left him lethargic in a setback to last-place Illinois in the Big Ten Tournament semifinal at the United Center in Chicago.

Even though Penn's options were limited, particularly his daring drives toward the basket, the Buckeyes had positioned themselves to upset No. 2-seed Connecticut in spite of their uneven play. They were atrocious at the free-throw line, shooting 50 percent for the game. Somehow, Ohio State had made it this far despite finishing last in the Big Ten in free-throw shooting.

"The fact that we didn't shoot balls well from the free-throw line and still won really reinforces how well we played in other areas," O'Brien said. "We were efficient on offense and good on defense, which helped offset something as important as free throw shooting."

The Buckeyes were like John Thompson's Georgetown teams in the early 1980s. The Hoyas couldn't hit a free throw if the rim had a honing device attached, especially after the Hoyas had exhausted themselves.

"Georgetown was nonstop, in-your-face pressure," O'Brien said, recalling Boston College's Big East battles with the Hoyas. "Their games weren't real artistic. They were nasty, sloppy games, and it's the environment they created because that's what they did defensively. We joked at Boston College that Georgetown's offense started on their first miss. They would just throw it up, then the mayhem would just start, and that's when you had to really get tough. There was always action on the glass. Thompson's teams were about toughness and intimidation. They would guard you, get on the glass and get on the floor for every loose ball. I don't think that was us. We played hard, but we could never abandon the finesse plays."

The Huskies looked more like the Hoyas as they chased relentlessly after the Buckeyes. Moore did most of the hard-hat work, casting a shadow over Penn, keeping the Buckeyes' offense off stride. The Buckeyes appeared flustered at times, as they committed countless uncharacteristic mental errors. With every turnover or long rebound, Ohio State often failed to defend the Huskies in the open court. The Buckeyes had been among the best in denying teams easy hoops in transition; it was a defensive strength that enabled the Buckeyes to limit the fast-break opportunities of St. John's and Auburn in the South Regional.

"We were just doing things we wouldn't normally do," said forward Jason Singleton. "We were taking bad shots, turning the ball over, not getting back on defense. Connecticut played a good, solid game for 40 minutes and we didn't match it."

O'Brien had talked all season of how disciplined his team had become. He wasn't nearly as angered over the missed shots in the paint as he was with the Buckeyes' carelessness, particularly on defense.

While most of the Ohio State faithful were still bubbling over their team's success, O'Brien was still at an even keel deep into this Final Four semifinal. He tugged at his coat, gently caressed his tie, and calmly ran his fingers through his perfectly groomed silver hair. After coaching in relative obscurity at Boston College for 11 years, O'Brien had stepped into the bright lights that usually shine on Krzyzewski, whose Blue Devils were playing in their 12th Final Four. O'Brien, though, looked as if he belonged.

"The feeling was indescribable," O'Brien said. "I always imagined myself being in that situation. I never imagined it being so overwhelming. You have to hold yourself together, especially when things are tight. I think the players believe, as long as their coach believes. We had come too far to give up on ourselves. We had worked so hard the last two years just to earn some respect for the program.

"I was thinking to myself just enjoy the atmosphere. We knew we had good guards; and we knew Connecticut had good guards. It was going to be a real good test between some outstanding players who did not know each other. But once it all started, you wouldn't even know there was anybody else in the building. We were so tuned in to what was happening on the floor, it just became another game. We were thinking about the mind-set of our team. I couldn't tell anyone about anything that was going on in that place at that point.

"I was sitting there, and I'm saying, 'Oh, my God, this is unbelievable.' When you see the ref throw the ball up, now it's a game again. I remember them making a couple of major runs early, and we used timeouts, and it was about keeping the lid on, keeping it close until halftime. When we were down by one at the half, I was thinking we were only 20 minutes away from getting to the next game. We were right there."

As a young head coach at St. Bonaventure, O'Brien sometimes lacked patience. Surely, his patience was being severely tested in this national semifinal. He didn't want to come unglued, as his players had, during a critical stretch that enabled the Huskies to take a 61-51 lead midway through the second half. So he turned to assistant Rick Boyages, who motioned with his palms downward for his boss to watch his blood pressure.

The Buckeyes rallied whenever Connecticut appeared ready to run them out of the Tampa Bay Devil Rays' baseball park, an architectural oddity that is transformed into a makeshift college basketball playground.

The Huskies had sometimes succumbed to tournament stage fright throughout the 1990s. Now, they were putting on a magnificent performance down the stretch. The Huskies' frenzied fans had been teased like this before, however. So often, they had been left knocking at the Final Four front door.

This time, however, the Huskies were a much deeper team. They had two proven stars in El-Amin and Hamilton, who were complemented by an experienced supporting cast, including Moore, a defensive specialist, and Kevin Freeman, a perfect role player who seemingly scored only when necessary.

For Ohio State, an encore of its South Regional performance didn't appear likely as the clock ticked inside the final minute. The Buckeyes were desperately trying to throw off their albatross: bad free-throw shooting.

O'Brien had refused to characterize his team as a Cinderella outfit. His Buckeyes were legitimate title contenders, he insisted. But as countless loose balls slipped through their hands like pumpkin seeds, the Buckeyes' joyous, fantasy-filled postseason appeared destined to strike midnight.

The Buckeyes' talented backcourt mates, Penn and Redd, struggled with their shots at the charity stripe and the perimeter. They didn't have the horsepower to finish the last furlong. El-Amin and Hamilton did all they could to will the Huskies into the national championship game by making dazzling, acrobatic, highlight-reel shots in the clutch while enlisting the game clock as an ally.

O'Brien, seemingly unfazed by the clock, summoned his players to the sideline one last time for one last sermon with 45 seconds remaining and the Buckeyes down by seven. He looked into the attentive eyes of each player. The players stared back and hung on every word. They believed that somehow victory was within their grasp. They believed in O'Brien.

O'Brien had faith in every player in Ohio State's nine-man rotation. He could depend on someone else making a game-clinching play or shot other than the Big Two: Redd and Penn.

Johnson, his rail-like legs wobbling some, had slapped away shot after shot in the South Regional, including a record-tying seven in a regional semifinal win over Auburn. Against UConn, though, Johnson couldn't get his half hook to fall, partly because Voskuhl wouldn't let him spin toward the baseline.

As time expired, O'Brien stood still. He glanced at the scoreboard, but not with a look of disbelief. The Buckeyes weren't supposed to win. He was reflecting. He was praying. He was remembering how the road to the Final Four was paved with ominous potholes that threatened to lessen his drive and ambition. It was the most unlikely of journeys—one that began when he was assistant coach at, of all places, Connecticut, and ended with this 64-58 loss to Connecticut in the national semifinal on March 27, 1999.

O'Brien, with Penn at his side, hardly blinked an eye as the Huskies' jubilant faithful spilled onto the court in a wave of blue and white to celebrate their first-ever trip to the championship game. Two days later, the Huskies upset the supposedly unbeatable Duke Blue Devils, 77-74, to capture their first national championship.

As Duke and Michigan State prepared for the semifinals nightcap, O'Brien and his players walked slowly down a long corridor leading to the Tropicana Field dressing room. Oddly, there wasn't a sad, long face among them. The Buckeyes had learned to lose gracefully, partly because many of them had experienced so much defeat during the pre-O'Brien years.

First, they had to learn to win. They didn't make it to St. Petersburg by using tricks, gimmicks, and mirrors. O'Brien chipped at the loser's image that haunted Ohio State, then rebuilt the Buckeyes by reshaping his players' attitudes and aspirations. He had to make men of them before polishing their raw skills. In the aftermath of their semifinal loss, the Buckeyes were still standing tall.

"I think it was a great opportunity for, you know, the ride we had," Penn said. "I feel we have nothing to hang our heads about. I feel it's a great experience. We played some very tough games. I think this just gives all the guys on our team that are coming back a tremendous amount of confidence."

"We had nothing to cry about," Redd said. "We did our best. We've come a long ways from just trying to be competitive. We wanted to win the national championship. We were bummed out, but not depressed. It wasn't the end of the world."

During the previous six seasons, when the Buckeyes lost 81 of 96 conference games, many of the fans had turned their backs on them. Their illustrious alumni—including John Havlicek, Jerry Lucas, Clark Kellogg, and Jimmy Jackson—seldom frequented their antiquated home gym, St. John Arena. This time, some 6,000 Ohio State fans had made the trip from Columbus to St. Petersburg. As the Buckeyes gathered in their dressing room after their semifinal loss, Havlicek, Lucas, Kellogg, and Jackson were there to comfort them.

"It made you feel as if you were a part of this team, just being at the Final Four," said Havlicek, who played on nine championship teams with the Boston Celtics. "It reminded me of the old days, when Ohio State was one of the most respected programs in the country."

"I couldn't believe we were in the Final Four," said Kellogg, a CBS Sports analyst, who predicted a Connecticut victory over his alma mater. "It was so unreal. It was like a dream come true. It still seems like a dream."

For O'Brien, it was a dream realized. Even without the championship trophy, the Buckeyes still felt like winners. The Buckeyes—with Scoonie Penn and Michael Redd engineering their magnificent March Madness ride along the NCAA Tournament trail—had completed an improbable journey to the Final Four. In a crowded corridor of Tropicana Field, with the eye of every camera focused upon them, Redd and Penn embraced for one of the few times during this incredible comeback season. Together, they had helped rebuild the Ohio State basketball program and rekindle the enthusiasm of a basketball coach.

15

PENN AND REDD

Coming Together

Scoonie Penn knew his heart was in the right place. It hardly mattered that in his head, he sometimes felt out of place in Columbus. This is a college town where football is practically a way of life—and had been long before Woody Hayes became a larger-than-life campus icon.

The scarlet-and-gray banners, with an "O" and buckeye leaves stamped upon them, wave furiously in the wind from cars, homes, and buildings from one end of Columbus to the other. They are as much a tribute to the football program as they are symbols of university pride.

So, how was this basketball fanatic from New England going to thrive in football country in the Great Midwest? At Boston College, the football team—save for a Doug Flutie wing-and-a-prayer, Hail Mary touchdown pass to Gerard Phalen that enabled the Eagles to stun the Miami Hurricanes—was usually average at best.

Penn was The Man at Chestnut Hill. Maybe he couldn't run for mayor, but he certainly would have gotten his share of votes. He had become one of the most popular and beloved players in school history in only two seasons. Now, in 1997, it would be hard to walk away; yet the atmosphere, with O'Brien gone, had changed.

With most Eagles fans anxiously awaiting his decision, Penn had to decide whether he would stay or leave. In reality, his decision could have a tremendous impact the future of both men's basketball programs at Boston College and Ohio State. It wasn't long after his return home to Salem, Massachussetts, that Penn was learning the Buckeyes' fight song.

Penn, who prides himself on being a student of the game, had to take a crash course in Ohio State basketball history. He didn't have to worry about failing, mostly because O'Brien would teach him. Penn got his first lesson the day he met with the team's equipment manager. He asked for his usual jersey —Number 11—which he had always worn. It wasn't some superstitious thing. The number had become a part of him. It was, in essence, an identifiable character trait.

Penn was surprised when he was asked to make another selection. It was just a number. The way he figured, "The guy who wore it before must have been a Hall of Famer or something."

Jerry Lucas is more than a Hall of Famer. He is an Ohio State legend. He remains perhaps the most visible link between Ohio State's present and past glory. Lucas, along with two other Hall of Famers—former Indiana basketball coach Bobby Knight and former Boston Celtics great John Havlicek—helped lead the Buckeyes to three consecutive Final Four appearances in the early 1960s, including a 75-55 win over California in the national championship game in 1960.

Still, O'Brien had to explain to his new point guard that No. 11 was as sacred a jersey number as the No. 45 won by two-time Heisman Trophy winner Archie Griffin. Griffin's number was the first ever to be retired by the university, but only after All-America linebacker Andy Katzenmoyer had worn it for three years.

"Here, Scoonie wants No. 11, and that's one of those numbers—even though Ohio State didn't retire numbers at the time—no one wears," O'Brien said, his eyes wandering in amazement. Somebody told Scoonie he couldn't wear that number, but he didn't understand. He knew Havlicek's name because he was in Boston.

"We told him Jerry Lucas wore No. 11, and he shrugged his shoulders and said, 'All right, I guess he must have been pretty good.' I said, 'Scoonie, they say he is the best player to ever play in the Big Ten.' "

Again, Penn shrugged his shoulders. "Jerry Lucas?" he asked, still trying to place the name.

Finally, Penn conceded, "OK, he must have been pretty good."

O'Brien laughs softly. All the time he is thinking to himself just how much today's young players, whether at the high school or college or professional level, know little about the game's history.

"Scoonie didn't know Jerry Lucas from George Lucas," O'Brien said. "If you mention a guy named Lucas, he'd probably say, 'Oh, yeah, that guy made some good movies.'"

If you ask the average Ohio State fan who was around to watch Lucas play, he or she would argue vehemently that Lucas created more excitement than any *Star Wars* flick. He was the Buckeyes' leading man, playing a controlled, disciplined game that made him a headliner wherever Ohio State traveled.

"When I first got the job at St. Bonaventure, Bob Lanier was just retired for a couple of years," O'Brien recalled. "Guys kept suggesting I use Bob Lanier to help in recruiting. So I got Lanier to make a couple of phone calls to some recruits. You could do that back then, and it wasn't an NCAA recruiting violation. He called a couple of kids, and I swear to God, some kids didn't know who *he* was."

Lanier had been an All-American at St. Bonaventure in the early 1970s. He spent most of his 12 seasons in the NBA with the Milwaukee Bucks, where he had the unenviable distinction of replacing Hall of Fame center Kareem Abdul-Jabbar, who would eventually become the league's all-time leading scorer.

O'Brien was never comfortable asking Lanier to walk the recruiting trail. He was embarrassed to ask, and he was embarrassed when he discovered that most of the recruiting prospects knew little or nothing about Lanier. O'Brien had preferred to make the calls, anyway, so he spared both him and Lanier the embarrassment.

"Kids just don't know," said O'Brien, who admits it's rare to find a recruit who knows anything about his days in the old American Basketball Association. "They all think that basketball started with Michael Jordan. They don't even know Julius Erving [the former Philadelphia 76ers great]. You ask them about him, and they'd ask, 'Oh, is that the guy with the big Afro?' "

At least, Penn knows of Jerry Lucas. With Lucas's number still hanging from the rafters at St. John Arena, Penn settled for the next best thing— Number 12.

Penn had chosen to come to the Midwest, uplifting his roots from a familiar Boston, to help O'Brien turn around Ohio State's basketball program. It wasn't a move reflective of his feelings for Boston College, but rather his unyielding loyalty to a coaching staff that had entrusted their fate in his capable hands while playing with the Eagles. "I liked the idea of being in a place where I was comfortable with the coaches, and that made the transition easier," said Penn, who immediately became one of the premier point guards in the Big Ten along with Michigan State's Mateen Cleaves. "I didn't want to start over with coaches I didn't know and had no idea what they were about."

Like O'Brien, Penn became an integral part of the program almost immediately at Boston College when he arrived in the fall of 1995. He became one of the best players in the Big East, if not the entire country. There was perhaps no more recognizable face on campus during a time when the school was trying to devert attention from a scandalous betting ordeal involving its football program. Penn provided a much-needed positive image.

No one, however, appreciated Penn's presence more than O'Brien. Even when he was a high school sophomore in Salem, Penn had few doubters that some day he would become an impact player. His talents notwithstanding, Penn possesses a charming personality and a winning attitude.

More important, Penn was the missing piece of a puzzle that would ultimately elevate the Golden Eagles among the Big East elite. O'Brien and his staff worked overtime to find the right mix of players to complement their 5-foot-10 guard. They found most of their talent near their own backyard, getting verbal commitments from three blue-chip prospects—Elton Tyler, Sean Connolly, and Michael Bradley.

Now, Penn's hopes of a national title didn't seem so farfetched. This was one of the top recruiting classes in the nation. O'Brien had kept his promise of luring more talent into the program, hopeful of giving Boston College a legitimate chance to contend in one of the toughest conferences in the nation.

Then, suddenly, but not unexpectedly, the championship dream faded when O'Brien left for Ohio State only a month after leading the Eagles to their first Big East Tournament title in the winter of 1997. With O'Brien shipping out to Columbus, his recruits began a mass exodus that left Penn in the unenviable position of having to choose between Boston College and Ohio State.

"We had to re-recruit Scoonie," assistant coach Paul Biancardi said. "The second time was more of a pure trust of him with the coaching staff, but mostly his trust of Coach O'Brien. He knew he had a coach that would push him to be a better basketball player. He was going to be pushed academically as well. Scoonie's degree became a priority. Jim would make sure that he graduated and help him reach the next level [professional basketball].

"When Scoonie came to Boston College, he was Rookie of the Year. To be honest, I didn't think he would be Rookie of the Year in the Big East."

Penn had led his high school to an undefeated season and the Massachusetts state championship. He was the state's player of the year. He was voted MVP in nearly every AAU tournament he competed in. Yet, not every Big East coach came knocking at his door.

"Scoonie has a lot of talent and a lot of heart and determination," said Biancardi, who recruited Penn in 1995. "It's what separates great players. He has a desire to push himself beyond his own limits. We knew he had the ability to distribute the ball. We knew he could score. But we didn't know what a special player he would become."

It was not an easy decision for Penn to stay or move on. He liked the fact that his family had a short drive to watch him play. There was a part of him, too, that wanted to stick it out at Boston College, if only to prove that he could help piece together what remained of a once-promising future for the Eagles.

But something was missing at Chestnut Hill.

"We were a family," said Penn, who ran OSU's scout team during the 1997-98 season. "I just felt as if the family was being split up. We were all going our separate ways. I knew I would only feel comfortable at Ohio State, because there, I knew I would be in a family-like environment again."

Penn had come from a broken home. His father wasn't around during his impressionable years, so O'Brien and his staff became, in effect, his surrogate fathers. They picked up where his mother had left off after his high school graduation. They talked to him about drugs. They talked about girls. They even scolded him about his bad taste in music. They insisted, too, that he didn't wear his cap backwards.

He had heard it all before from his mother and grandmother. They were tough disciplinarians. Penn rarely stepped out of line. Besides, he had a younger brother and sister at home, watching his every move. He became their hero, but more important, their role model.

"It wasn't easy for Scoonie, because his dad was never in the picture," O'Brien said. "Scoonie never had much to do with him. He had a lot of people helping him, and they were very kind to him. Everyone understood that his mother was struggling to make it while raising a couple of kids."

So nothing Penn was about to experience at Ohio State could equate. He appreciated his God-given talents to perform magically on a stage before thousands. Yet, his patience would be tested during the 1997-98 basketball season. As Ohio State drifted aimlessly through O'Brien's first season, Penn's loyalty never wavered. No matter how ugly the losses, he wasn't going to change his mind. No matter how blurred his vision for his new team's future, the end of the clouded rainbow always seemed bright.

Yet, there was a time when Penn wondered what in the world he had gotten himself into. He may have been disillusioned by O'Brien's departure from Chestnut Hill, but the Eagles had to be having more fun. He could have been playing, instead of watching helplessly as the bewildered Buckeyes were being slapped silly night after night after night.

This wasn't good for the ego. It was downright humbling. Yet, Penn hoped his teammates had learned something in defeat and that they had developed mental toughness after getting their heads bashed by even middle-of-the-road Big Ten teams."

Penn had seen better days. He had been MVP of the 1997 Big East Tournament. He had been the 1996 Big East and ECAC Rookie of the Year during his freshman season at Boston College.

Now, here he was in street clothes. He didn't like being a fan. Besides, he hadn't sat on the sidelines since he was a diminutive grade-schooler, back when the bigger kids ignored him when it came time to choose sides in pickup games on the outdoor courts of Salem.

As deep as his love was for basketball, Penn wasn't all that interested when not playing. This situation was different, however. If he was going to earn the respect of his new teammates, then he had to share their pain of losing 22 of 30 games. He hadn't seen that much losing in four years of high school and two years of college basketball combined.

If only he could handle the rock, he would make Ohio State a better team. He would make the Buckeyes' energetic freshman guard Michael Redd better. He would create ways to get the ball to an agile, but unpolished 6-11 center, Ken Johnson. But his hands were tied tightly behind his back. He could only watch with a sense of hopelessness.

The most damaging blows of this particular season were delivered before the home crowd at St. John Arena. In early February, Michigan State and Purdue simply humiliated the Buckeyes within a span of four days. The Spartans won 84-58, and the Boilermakers beat them 107-75.

Incredibly, a combined 58 points separated the Buckeyes from two of the Big Ten's best. It seemed such an insurmountable deficit to narrow. Most of the Buckeyes thought so, too. Penn never had such doubts. He was confident the worm would turn and that Ohio State would rebound.

As the Buckeyes left St. John Arena after the Purdue game, Penn joked with guard Neshaun Coleman. He promised the Toledo native that the Buckeyes had nowhere to go but up. There wasn't much room left at the bottom, not without crawling under the hardwood.

"It couldn't get any worse," Penn said. "We couldn't possibly play with any less confidence than we did in those two games."

Redd was confident in his ability to score off the dribble. Coleman had a confident stroke from the perimeter. Forward Jason Singleton missed more layups than he could remember, but he was developing into one of the conference's best defensive players.

What the Buckeyes lacked most of all was leadership. But how was Penn going to assume the role of leader without stepping on some toes or without appearing somewhat overbearing to his new teammates when practice began for the 1998-99 season.

Penn's greatest challenge was finding a way to get along with Redd. After all, this had become Redd's team. He had put the Buckeyes on his shoulders and practically carried them to eight wins the year before. This, though, was going to be a delicate balancing act for a coaching staff that knew all along that Penn would be its floor general.

Again, Penn would be The Man.

Only this time, Penn would have to share the spotlight. If the Buckeyes were going to have any success, their backcourt mates would have to broker a détente. The sparks, admitted Penn, were in the air. There was little doubt that these two strong-willed basketball players weren't going to hit it off immediately as Ohio State gathered for its first practice session in mid-October.

Penn and Redd were the oddest of couples. They had come from different backgrounds. Their taste in music and clothes was different. Penn would sit in front of his locker listening to rap. Redd, who has a more conservative taste in music, preferred jazz and contemporary hip-hop. It would take them awhile to warm up to each other. They sized up one another the way a hard-throwing pitcher such as Nolan Ryan would size up slugger Reggie Jackson and vice versa. They were also like a baseball battery on different pages. Penn would throw a curve. Redd would look for a slider. The task facing O'Brien was to create some sense of syncopation for his guards.

"I don't mind telling anyone, there were some incidents during the course of the season when they would be short with one another," O'Brien said. "Scoonie would want to do one thing and Michael another. But a sign of kids being mature and of coming together is recognizing they each have their own things they want to do and willing to back off a little for the sake of the good of everybody.

"Anytime you would sit down and talk to both of those guys about that situation, they would say, 'OK, fine, that's a good idea.' You have to talk about it. You have to address it."

Penn and Redd had bumped heads a few times during the regular season. But their tempers flared during the 1999 Big Ten Tournament in Chicago. As the Buckeyes struggled to hold off the upset-minded Fighting Illini, Penn and Redd had a heated exchange in the locker room at halftime.

It was clear in the second half that the two weren't on the same page. They glanced at one another only briefly. Somehow, they had managed to violate a trust that had taken an entire regular season to nurture. As they tossed up an array of bad shots, Illinois pulled away to eliminate the Buckeyes from the conference tournament with a 79-77 win in the semifinals.

Now, Penn and Redd weren't only in the spotlight. They were under the microscope. The media predicted OSU's demise in the NCAA Tournament, citing the poor play of their backcourt. But Penn and Redd reached a compromise before the Buckeyes headed to Indianapolis for the first round of the South Regional at the RCA Dome.

"If it were two different personalities, where Scoonie demanded he was the man, and Michael didn't want to accept the fact that they could coexist, it could have been a headache," O'Brien said. "Fortunately, it was just the opposite.

"It was Scoonie not forcing his personality on anybody. He didn't force his leadership on anyone. Michael accepted the fact that there is another good player here, and it doesn't all have to be about him. They could be good together."

They were scintillating sometimes. They learned to feed off one another. They leaned on each other, too. Amid all the clamoring for concession and compromise, O'Brien would later admit that Redd "is still our go-to guy."

The incident in Chicago illustrated perfectly how Penn and Redd couldn't tolerate defeat. They were, Redd said, not the best of losers. Yet, neither pointed a finger publicly. This was a crisis in the making, with the NCAA Tournament selection less than 24 hours away. They didn't want to enter the postseason having to walk on eggshells.

On Monday morning, as O'Brien and his staff began putting together their game plan, Penn and Redd were determined to iron out a solution. An avoidable distraction wasn't going to adversely affect the team's efforts during March Madness.

"There was a little bit of friction at the start, because they were feeling each other like a couple of prizefighters," Biancardi said. "They love the game. They love to win. They both had to give up something to get something, and that's where the bond came. They both respect the game. They both believe in their coach.

"Scoonie and Michael understood they could help each other. The lesson from day one was that 'Michael, you can help Scoonie, and Scoonie, you can help Michael.'"

O'Brien's coaching staff understood that if Penn and Redd went their separate ways, then the Buckeyes would be destined to continue their slide. Ultimately, the coaches hoped the team would follow their lead. If so, according to Biancardi, "the team would prosper."

Redd, though, had spent a long freshman season getting it done by himself in so many games. At times, he was the first, second, and third scoring options. The Buckeyes rode him like a rented mule, and he plowed through the 1997-98 season without complaining about the heavy burden he carried. He was only a season removed from playing high school basketball at his father's alma mater, Columbus West.

Redd had always wanted to wear the Buckeyes' scarlet and gray. He wanted to be the next Jimmy Jackson or Dennis Hopson or Havlicek—maybe the next Jerry Lucas. If only by osmosis, he knew of Ohio State's tradition. He knew the ceiling was high, but that wasn't going to stop him from trying to make a name for himself at Ohio State.

In 1997, in his first game as a Buckeye, Redd showed no fear. He came out of the locker room shooting. He thrilled the crowd with his crossover dribbles. He would put the ball between his legs almost effortlessly, but occasionally some quick-handed defender would swipe him clean as he made his move to the basket. So often, Redd would frustrate O'Brien by deviating from the game plan.

For Redd, it was important to show he had no fear. He wanted to show everyone in Columbus that he had game. He was still miffed that he wasn't given serious consideration as a *Parade* All-America prospect. The Associated Press' panel of sportswriters made Redd only a second-team All-Ohio. There was something, it seemed, about his game the media didn't like. He was too flashy, too expressive—too Michael Redd.

Redd scored 25.7 points per game as a senior at Columbus West High School, including a season-high 40 points. He was consistent, averaging 25.1 points as a junior. Some scouts were critical of his shot selection, yet he shot 63 percent from the floor in leading his team to an 18-4 record in his final year.

Some considered him a ball hog. He couldn't shy away from a shot, no matter the degree of difficulty. He always believed in his shot, and that's why O'Brien's predecessor, Randy Ayers, recruited him. The Buckeyes had recruited plenty of players who could run the floor, but Redd opened eyes with his ability to finish in the open court. At the end of his first two seasons in Columbus, only Lucas had scored more points.

Admittedly, by the time Redd showed up at St. John Arena for his first practice with the Buckeyes, the chip he carried on his shoulder was the size of a boulder. He resented most everyone who questioned his game. He couldn't rid himself of the shadow cast over him by another Columbus native, Kenny Gregory, who turned down Ohio State's overtures for the talent-rich Kansas Jayhawks.

Kansas coach Roy Williams had seen Redd play. So had Minnesota's Clem Haskins, Michigan State's Tom Izzo, and Cincinnati's Bob Huggins. But none offered Redd an athletic scholarship. So, when Ayers came calling, he committed without reservation.

Redd's ego had been bruised. He wanted to win, but he was driven mostly by his desire to prove his skills were as good as any Dapper Dan or *Parade* All-America player.

"I guess that was part of it," Redd said. "But I had a lot to learn."

O'Brien would teach him, too. Yet, he was hesitant to keep Redd from expressing his creativity. He admired the freshman's daring approach and intensity. To tone him down might do more harm than good. If nothing else, he possessed confidence. Redd would set six Ohio State freshman records: most points (658), scoring average (21.9), field goals (241), free throws (130), three-point field goals (46), and steals (61).

Unlike Penn, Redd had a much more stable family environment. His father, Wes Redd, had always been there for him. He taught his son the game. He talked to him about everything—school, drugs, girls, and music. He convinced his son that there was nothing he couldn't do either on or off the basketball court.

"I remember Wes Redd in my first year, and I would see him and would tell him Michael is doing OK and that Michael is a great kid," O'Brien said. "His father would say, 'You don't have to worry about us, and if he steps out of line, crack him.' But not in a hundred years would I do that, but it was that mentality that was evidence he was supporting us. 'You have my son; treat him like a man and don't baby him. He knows the difference between right and wrong.' When you hear that from a parent, you're thinking this is great.

"As coaches, we are used to hearing parents ask, 'What are you doing, and don't you know he needs to be getting more shots?' or 'Don't you ever think about treating my son like that.'

"If the roles had been reversed, that would be my father talking to my coach. It was like this concept of our generation. Now, you see teachers with kids, and the parents are over them about their kids. I know that if I had a problem with the teacher, I would have a problem with my father for having a problem with the teacher. If it ever came down to the teacher and me, then I would be the one who got whacked. My father would say the teacher is right, period. He might ask me, 'Who the hell do you think you are? You better get your ass in gear.' It's why I like Wes Redd so much. He demanded a great deal of Michael, especially the way he carried himself at the university. Obviously, his parents did a wonderful job of preparing him for college. All I had to do was teach him the game."

O'Brien and Wes Redd taught Michael Redd an invaluable lesson— that of humility. He would have to adapt to his changing role. He didn't have to take every shot or do something spectacular off the dribble. In their season 1997-98 opener against Kent State, Redd dribbled the ball between his legs at the top of the key, looking for room to drive. He ignored the shot clock— and an open Neshaun Coleman. The ball bounced off his foot as he made his move, and the Flashes scored an easy layup on the turnover. Penn didn't mind Redd's school-yard moves, but the senseless turnover rubbed him the wrong way. Penn had seen enough of that while he sat on the bench the year before.

It was time to have a heart-to-heart with his backcourt mate. This couldn't wait until halftime. It had to happen now, while it was fresh on his mind and while his blood was boiling. Penn, with his cold eyes shifting left and right before locking into Redd's eyes, demanded a more disciplined game. Redd stared back intently, nodding in agreement. Redd put the ball between his legs again. Only this time, he gave the ball up to an open Coleman, who drained a 20-footer to spark an Ohio State run that halted the charging Flashes.

"Scoonie has been a tremendous asset to Michael in showing him how he should act sometimes and how he should handle himself," O'Brien said. "I think on the floor it took a lot of the burden from Michael. He didn't have to score all the points now. I think that made him slow down and made him a much better player. There wasn't going to be the frustration of him having a bad day. There was going to be somebody else to take up the slack. In Michael's first year, if he was having a bad day, it probably wasn't going to be pleasant."

As the Buckeyes began their march toward their first NCAA Tournament appearance since 1992, it was clear that Penn and Redd were a magical success formula. The Buckeyes were good, even when only one of them had it going. They were almost unbeatable when both played well. They offered different things at different times for the Buckeyes during the course of the season. In a home game against rival Michigan in early February, Redd kept the Buckeyes within striking distance and finished with a game-high 22 points. Penn was limited to six points in the first half, but responded midway through the second half in leading a late surge that enabled Ohio State to gain a 74-69 come-from-behind win.

For the coaching staff, the win over the Wolverines helped build character. For Penn and Redd, it proved, once and for all, that they could both share the spotlight. The 13th-ranked Buckeyes, playing before a crowd of 18,645 at Value City Arena, sealed the win in the last 11.1 seconds as Penn made four free throws. "We had to fight back from behind," Penn said. "We didn't shoot well throughout the game, but for the most part, we showed a lot of guts."

It was a gutsy effort by Redd, who spent much of the week fighting a 102-degree fever and the flu. He gathered a second wind, slashing fearlessly through the Michigan defense for a layup to narrow Ohio State's deficit to 60-57. Center Ken Johnson swatted away two Michigan shots in the paint, which led to two fast-break baskets - a Redd slam dunk and a Penn layup - to put the Buckeyes ahead 61-60 with 6:55 to play.

The Buckeyes were the worst free-throw-shooting team in the Big Ten. But when they needed them the most, Penn and Redd delivered. "In a game like that, you have to tighten up all the screws," Penn said. "Michael and I knew it was up to us to find some way to win that game." Most everyone knew that Redd was the likely choice to take the shots that mattered most. The Wolverines, like most other teams in the Big Ten, knew that, as well. By now, Penn was taking crucial, game-clinching shots down the stretch, too.

This was Penn's game to win. Or Redd's game to win. They were leaning on each other, as O'Brien hoped they would. The Wolverines didn't know how to react. They double-teamed Redd, only to have Penn burn them from the perimeter. When the Wolverines collapsed on Penn as he sliced through their zone defense, he kicked it out to Redd, who either made good on a jumper or tightroped the baseline for a layup or a dazzling slam dunk.

"Without question, you go with the flow," O'Brien said. "We never went into any game thinking we were going to highlight Scoonie or that we had to really feature Michael. We decided how we were going to play and what things we have available in our offense, and this would be good for us.

"Game by game, you try to exploit the things you think would be better against certain teams. Obviously, you go into every game thinking Michael and Scoonie will be featured more than anybody. They were going to get the majority of the shots. It was no secret that Michael was our first option when the game was on the line. Scoonie understood that, and it's one of the things that made him such a great floor leader.

"A lot of times at the end of games, it's about who can get his own shots. Michael does that as well as most. Scoonie bought into that because he knew Michael was very good at that. Scoonie was mature enough to understand that, yes, I'm one of the guys, but in this instance, it has to be Michael. We would go to Scoonie at times. Michael accepted that, and Scoonie accepted Michael for his talents.

"There was mutual respect on both sides. We were very fortunate that their personalities meshed. It could have been ugly—and they did have a few disagreements earlier in the season. They could have gotten to the point where they didn't like each other and they didn't want to share the spotlight. If that had happened, guys on this team would have been going in different directions."

If not for Penn's late-game heroics during the second half of the season, the Buckeyes could have easily gone into a tailspin. Penn's clutch free throws and three-point shots were what the Buckeyes had been missing during six straight losing seasons.

Despite an uncharacteristic slump at midseason, Penn averaged 17.2 points, 4.1 assists, and 3.4 rebounds in sharing Big Ten Player of the Year honors with Michigan State guard Mateen Cleaves. In the Buckeyes' final push toward the postseason, Penn averaged 24 points and shot 53 percent from the floor in leading Ohio State to four road wins—Indiana, Purdue, Illinois and Wisconsin.

"I can't imagine anyone meaning more to their team than Penn does to Ohio State," former Wisconsin coach Dick Bennett said. "They can't win without him."

O'Brien couldn't agree more.

"I shudder to think what our season would have been like without [Penn]," O'Brien said. "I think Scoonie helped our other players get better. But his unselfishness certainly helped Michael mature on the court."

Penn and Redd had come together, if only reluctantly. When the Buckeyes were assured of at least a National Invitation Tournament bid with their win over Michigan, the two began to demand more of themselves and their teammates. They were sometimes unforgiving, scolding their teammates for committing mental errors.

Redd, it seemed, became even more inspired when he was chosen only as a second-team All-Big Ten player by both the media and the coaches. Again, he was determined to prove he belonged among the elite players. His point production was down some, but his 19.5 points per game led the Buckeyes. He grabbed fewer rebounds, averaging 5.6 per game, but his defensive skills had improved.

Redd was disturbed by the snub, but not discouraged. He spent hours working on his baseline moves and free throws. He said the big picture had finally come into focus. He was at Ohio State to win a national championship. This wasn't an audition to impress the NBA scouts. Redd had matured. He had come to realize that sacrificing shots and points was good for the team.

"When the season began, I just wanted us to have a winning season," Redd said. "Then, as we began to win more and more games, I wanted more. I wanted to win a national championship. It felt good to be where we were, especially when you consider where we were during my first year."

O'Brien, like Redd, couldn't shake the memory of 22 losses in his first season at the helm. It bothered him that perhaps only he and his assistant coaches fully appreciated Redd's efforts. O'Brien had always told his players not to pay much attention to the numbers and not to take much stock in personal recognition. He thought the Big Ten selections were an outrage, so he encouraged Redd to move on, to put it behind him.

Redd had always had to do that since coming to Ohio State. Despite becoming the first freshman ever to lead the Big Ten in scoring, Redd was mired in relative obscurity, partly because the Buckeyes finished at the bottom of the Big Ten standings. The media and coaches reasoned that he should have averaged 21.9 points per game because he was the team's only consistent scoring threat. Redd took 550 shots while averaging 39.3 minutes per game —the most of any player in the Big Ten.

Redd was angry. The 1999 NCAA Tournament, he promised, would be the appropriate stage for redemption.

"It's not that big of a deal, and you try to rationalize what happened," O'Brien said. "We reminded Mike that he was only a sophomore and there are some other very good guards in this league. So don't take it personal. But making second-team All-Big Ten, I bet not a lot of sophomores have done that.

"So you just try to get him focused from something he was upset about. He could have easily been a first-team player. Through all of it, he handled himself with grace and a lot of class. It was about our team now. He was driven to do better."

Redd wanted to add to his resume a national championship. He also was fascinated by the idea that someday his jersey—No. 22—would hang from the rafters alongside Lucas's No. 11.

Ultimately, it appeared that Redd and Penn had forged the partnership that O'Brien sensed they would. They laughed together and teased each other during the shoot-around sessions before most Big Ten games. The philosophical and ideological gap that separated them closed considerably, enabling Ohio State's backcourt to become perhaps the best in the country.

"It's the common bond and common goal that you strive for when you put kids together in this environment," O'Brien said. "Just think about the task of a coach to bring together this wide range of personalities and backgrounds and family situations and religious and political beliefs. When you bring it all together and coach them to play together, that's coaching. It's part of the joy of winning and the heartache of losing. When you see it all come together, the kids buying into one thing, that's coaching."

In a remarkable, indescribable season, Penn and Redd did more than learn to live together. The Penn-Redd years will probably be best defined as a turning point in Ohio State's men's basketball history. For a program that was struggling to stay afloat, Penn and Redd rescued it, keeping the Buckeyes' heads above the hostile waters of the Big Ten until others—namely, Ken Johnson, George Reese, Jason Singleton, and Neshaun Coleman—found their confidence and developed well enough to compete.

"Phil Jackson had a lot of talent in Chicago, but how about bringing those guys together and meshing all those egos?" O'Brien asked. "Then, bringing Dennis Rodman into the mix? I would ask myself, 'How is he managing these guys?' How can you get Michael Jordan to buy into and accept these others guys like Scottie Pippen and Tony Kukoc?

"Kukoc is from Yugoslavia and he doesn't even speak English when he first comes over here. He comes to Chicago as the Great White Hope. Right away, Pippen and Kukoc don't go for that action. Then Rodman has all of his stuff. Whew!

"The Zen master [as the media dubbed Jackson] must have been at work big time," O'Brien said jokingly. "You ask yourself, 'How am I going to do this?' It's a constant selling job to get them to understand. And we all do that as coaches. Not so much in high school, because most kids come from the same area. But once you get into college—and you start bringing kids from all across the country—it's a difficult adjustment for some of them.

"You may have some well-to-do white kids from a rural, affluent, stable two-parent home. You might have a kid off the street, a black kid, who doesn't have a pot to pee in. He has nothing going for him. How do you get those two kids on the same page? It's not the Xs and Os, but bringing these guys together is the responsibility of a coach.

"Jon Sanderson became a very spiritual guy. We have some guys who aren't nearly as tuned into that. How are you going to mesh that? Sometimes, it doesn't work. There's a lot that goes into this stuff. You take Scoonie from a broken home and you take Michael, who has two parents. Somehow, they just jelled—but it wasn't easy. It's interesting when you think about how Scoonie and Michael have become good friends. I know they will be friends for the rest of their lives."

After leading the Buckeyes to the Final Four, Penn and Redd did most everything together during the summer. They hung out in Spain together, playing for the U.S. national team. They were rarely apart in Indianapolis during the tryouts. They worked out together, trying to strengthen each other's game.

They did draw a line that neither crossed. Penn wasn't listening to Redd's music. And Redd wouldn't be caught dead in some of the threads Penn would dare to wear out for the evening. "We're nothing alike, but that's OK now," Redd said. "We can say we shared in what might be the greatest thrill of our lives—playing in the Final Four."

The Penn-Redd collaboration probably wouldn't have happened if not for O'Brien's patience and the unique manner in which he transforms a group of individuals into a team.

"The best-case scenario is that everyone gets along," O'Brien said. "But we know that's not reality. You don't have to like each other, but we have to play with each other. That doesn't always work, either. If you get guys who like to spend time together, it helps. I think that's one of the things that contributed to our success.

"We all got along. I would love it when we were on the road, and I would hear they all went to a party. Everybody, including Sanderson would be invited. I thought that was great.

"You can be successful if guys don't get along, but it's not as easy. As long as they understand what the common goal is and what we're striving for, they can put away their differences. We have a situation where the Croatians and Serbs are fighting against one another. You have some of those guys trying to play on the same basketball team. Those guys were friends for years before their country split."

It was one thing trying to bring Penn and Redd together, but it would have been even more complex if O'Brien had tried to get Serbian and Croatian players to coexist in Columbus. He had already recruited three Serbians— guard Boban Savovic, forward Cobe Ocokoljic, and Slobodan Radojovic. Radojovic, though, was declared ineligible soon after the Final Four because he had played 19 minutes of professional basketball for a European club team.

"Part of the deal was that they were all friends," O'Brien said. "So that was never an issue with us. There's no question you have to approach that subject, because with the growing number of Serbian and Croatian players competing at the collegiate level, it's inevitable that it's going to happen. We would have asked Boban if he would have a problem. But we didn't have to deal with that question.

It was inevitable, though, that O'Brien would soon have to deal with the loss of his backcourt, which had helped the Buckeyes string together back-to-back 20-win seasons for the first time in eight years. Penn and Redd had one more chance to complete their unfinished business. So, despite overtures from NBA scouts, Penn decided to return for his senior season.

The Buckeyes would be wiser, better, and more experienced. They entered the 1999-2000 season as co-favorites to capture the Big Ten title along with Michigan State. But the Buckeyes stumbled on the road to the Final Four in Indianapolis, losing their second-round game to the Miami Hurricanes in Nashville.

Most NBA insiders had projected Penn as a first- or second-round draft pick. The draft prospectus for Redd appeared even more promising. Some expected he would be a first-round pick during the league's annual draft in June 2000. O'Brien wanted to talk Redd out of entering the draft. He wanted him to return for his senior season, but he wanted Redd to decide for himself.

Despite criticism concerning the drop in his draft stock, Redd was convinced his skills were advanced enough to legitimize his being a lottery pick. There was no shame, however, in being a first-round pick. Either way, the money was good—and he would have a chance to make his dream come true.

So nearly a month after his junior season, Redd opted to enter the NBA Draft. This news came on the heels of center Ken Johnson being given an extra year of eligibility to make one last run at a national championship (in 2000-01), a run he was sure he would make with Redd. It wasn't too late for Redd to change his mind. The Buckeyes offered a caveat—the chance to become the school's all-time leading scorer, thus making it a realistic possibility that his No. 22 would never be worn by some starry-eyed blue-chipper who in 50 years wouldn't know the difference between Michael Redd and Redd Foxx.

"I never considered pulling out of the [2000 NBA] draft," said Redd, who led the Buckeyes in scoring in all three of his seasons. "I've felt all along that I'm one of the best players in the country." He felt that way coming out of high school. Even then, no one would listen. O'Brien had hoped Redd would listen to him and opt to return to Columbus, if only to ensure that he would graduate.

"I was a little bit disappointed in how the whole thing played out," O'Brien said. "Frankly, we were not involved as coaches in the decision-making process. We were never consulted. He had already made up his mind. We went out of our way to do for him what we did for Scoonie. We gathered all the information we could to make his decision a rational one.

"But how do you blame young men like Michael, who in their minds, there is a pot of gold at the end of the rainbow? The only thing I wanted him to make sure of is that he got the right information."

While O'Brien opposed Redd's leaving, he was quick to defend the player who helped lead him to his first Final Four as a head coach. He took exception to comments made questioning Redd's loyalty to the university.

"I think the people who look at his loyalty are missing the boat," O'Brien said. "I never thought I would leave Boston College. Every kid I recruited at Boston College—including Scoonie—I told them this is my school, and that Boston College is where I would be. When I said that, I truly believed it. But things do change.

"I'm sure in some circles, some of those kids I recruited, there were some questions as to my loyalty. All they knew was that I was gone, and that I left for a job where I'm making more money. The fact of the matter is, I did leave. Why did I leave? Because I thought it was the right thing to do. You can't have it both ways.

"Michael had to take care of himself. Most anyone else in his position to hit the jackpot would do the same thing. How do you challenge that? I think that it was the right thing for him to leave, after I had a chance to speak with him. I do think his reasons for being here would have been different.

"Initially, I didn't think it was the right thing for him to leave. I'm not convinced if he had returned that his eye wouldn't have been on the NBA. For that reason, it was a good thing for him. It's not a criticism, but it's the reality of how it works today. He was constantly saying my goal is to play in the NBA. It wasn't about we can win the national championship or we can win the Big Ten again. It probably would have been a waste of time for him to come back. It was probably the best thing for him and the best thing for us. I can see Michael being in the pros for a long time, but he could have gone down in the annals of Ohio State basketball as one of the top three or four players.

"It's important to understand that Michael Redd doesn't owe me or the university anything," said O'Brien. "He came here during a difficult time and helped bring the program up. Michael never gave us any trouble. I hope the people who gave him advice gave him the right advice."

Redd wasn't invited to Minnesota to participate in the 2000 NBA draft proceedings. It was clear then that Redd was tumbling down the draft chart. Ultimately, the Milwaukee Bucks made him the 43rd overall pick in the second round. Penn was the next-to-last draft selection in the second round, going to the Atlanta Hawks.

Penn and Redd were lucky, really. There were a number of players—including St. John's Bootsy Thornton, Temple's Pepe Sanchez, and Miami's Johnny Hemsley—who were ignored on draft night. Like Ohio State's former backcourt duo, they imagined themselves as lottery picks.

"There are so many guys coming out as underclassmen, so they all think they're not going to be the ones hurt by this process," O'Brien said. "Somebody has got to be hurt. I just hope it's not Michael. I think he can play in the NBA, but that's not the issue. The question is, will he be guaranteed something?"

16

ALL THE WAY BACK

M ost Ohio State fans could not have envisioned that they would be gathering on March 28, 1999, to toast their once-downtrodden men's basketball team. As the team buses turned into the arena entrance, the fans welcomed the Buckeyes home with roaring cheers. It was just the beginning of a three-day celebration. Considering how many Ohio State fans had abandoned the men's basketball program after a string of losing seasons and embarrassing moments, this was a time for reconciliation.

Four days after their return, more than 3,000 fans showed up on campus again to express their appreciation to the Buckeyes. Gov. Bob Taft and Columbus mayor Greg Lashutka dropped by to salute O'Brien and the Buckeyes. Ultimately, this would become more than just another that-a-boy celebration. It became a forum for the Ohio State fans to make an emotional plea to Penn to bypass the NBA draft. The crowd chanted, "One more year!"

The Ohio State fans were now expecting even greater things from their basketball team. They figured their championship hopes could not be fulfilled without Penn's leadership. Penn provided the leadership. Penn inspired a still relatively young team that sometimes wobbled down the stretch, but had straightened itself just in time to make a run at the national championship.

Penn, blushing at the applause, stepped up to the microphone before a resounding ovation. He looked uncomfortable. Even though he spent the entire season in the spotlight along with Redd, Penn was somewhat of an introvert. He shared most of his thoughts with O'Brien and his teammates; but now the fans were demanding he share with them his intentions.

Would he stay in Columbus? Or would he opt for the NBA?

The crowd, standing in a light, misty rain, waited impatiently. They listened intently to Penn, but were anxious for his answer.

"I'm leaning toward staying," Penn said.

The crowd roared its approval. Penn, a native New Englander, was welcomed as if he was a native son of Columbus. He was an immensely popular figure, but his comment about possibly bypassing the NBA draft endeared him even more to Ohio State followers.

"Once you look at the type of team that will be coming back and how close I am to graduating, that was when I decided to come back," Penn said moments after the rally. "The coaches and I spoke about it. They were very helpful. They didn't try to sway me one way or the other to make a decision. They let me do what I felt was right and stuck behind me on whatever I did. I talked to family members. They did the same thing when I decided to come here from Boston College. I didn't get too many people involved. I talked to my coaches, knowing that they would have the connections and sources that have helpful information. I spoke to Coach O'Brien about it, and he said do what is best for you and your family. He knew that I was not in the situation or need to rush it. My teammates were supportive. They told me that they wanted me back, but they didn't hound me.

"When an opportunity like [the NBA] presents itself, you can't help but to seriously think about it. I can't make any predictions about next year. What gets me excited is the potential this team has. Right now, I can't say if we are going to make it to the Final Four or be on top of the Big Ten, but we have the potential. Last year, we knew we had the potential, but we were not so sure. This year, we know what we have. I look forward to it, and I know Columbus does, too."

"We didn't have much involvement in the decision," assistant coach Rick Boyages said. "We gave him some information that we had received from our contacts, but we left him alone this last month, letting him decide on his own. We have been with Scoonie for four years. He is a special person for us. When you get to this point in this business and a kid is as good as Scoonie, you just wish him his best and hope that you can give him the best information."

With Penn safely in the fold, O'Brien knew the expectations would be greater for the 1999-2000 season. While he thought the preseason polls might have overstated his team's chances of returning to the Final Four, O'Brien felt confident that Ohio State would prove that its 19-win turnaround wasn't a fluke and that the Buckeyes were back to stay among the Big Ten elite.

"I was trying to emphasize that because we returned a lot of the major guys from the year before and finished as a Final Four team, there was a misconception that these guys were one of the top five or six teams in the country," O'Brien said. "What [the media] didn't understand was that for the last three weeks of the 1998-99 season, we played like one of the best three or four teams, but we were not. We got on a roll.

"We could not have played any better than we did against Auburn and St. John's. Of those 80 minutes in Knoxville, we played as well as we could for 79 minutes. The last minute of the St. John's game was just kind of like holding on. To think that we would be able to play at that level the next season wasn't accurate. We went through a stretch of playing great, but we tried to temper everybody's enthusiasm."

O'Brien's enthusiasm was tempered some in early May, when the Buckeyes lost three players—including a coveted recruit—who were expected to play significant roles during the 1999-2000 season. Sanderson, who lost his starting job to Brown prior to the NCAA Tournament, decided to leave Ohio State to pursue his academic and playing career elsewhere. Center Shamar Herron decided to leave because he was used only sparingly. "Shamar asked me if he was going to play next year, and I had to be honest," O'Brien said. "I told him, 'I don't think so.' I could have told him he would play, but it would have been misleading him or getting his hopes up too high. He was good for our team, and we tried to help him find another school."

The biggest blow to the Buckeyes came when the NCAA declared prized blue-chip recruit—junior college All-America selection, 7-foot-3 center Aleksandar Radojevic, ineligible. Radojevic was unable to play with any member institution because he had signed a professional contract with a club team in Yugoslavia. Radojevic, who played two years at Barton County Community College in Kansas, played a total of 19 minutes in four games for the Yugoslavian professional team. Ohio State appealed to the NCAA to reinstate Radojevic, but the appeal was denied.

"If Alex Radojevic had been eligible, I would have gone along with the preseason polls," O'Brien said. "That would have changed a lot for us. Without him we were missing a serious scoring threat inside that could have taken some of the pressure off Penn and Redd. Radojevic would have earned the respect of everyone with his ability to score inside. The problem we had in not getting Radojevic was that we didn't get anybody else. If this had happened earlier in the year, we would have recruited somebody else. We went through the whole season thinking we had him. Therefore, there was no reason to recruit another player. We really hurt ourselves by not having a guy of his caliber. With Radojevic, we could have been one of the best teams in the country.

"I don't think the result was fair, because Alex was an innocent player in all of this, especially in view of all of the kids who have been guilty of taking money from AAU guys. There were guys paying for kids' prep schooling. So for this kid to be banned for life because he made an innocent decision, I thought was a little bit unjust. I was shocked when they came out with their findings. It was a very innocent thing."

Radojevic, with his appeals exhausted, entered the NBA draft. He was the 12th overall pick in the first round by Vancouver, which later traded him to Toronto. Radojevic, along with the 6-foot-11 Johnson, would have given Ohio State an intimidating twin-towers presence in the paint. In addition, with probably the best backcourt in the country in Penn and Redd, the Buckeyes' No. 5 ranking in the Associated Press preseason poll would have appeared more legitimate.

"I think it's a reach to think that we would have had Alex for more than one year," O'Brien said. "Now, college coaches are competing with the NBA. However, I'm not sure if it fits with Alex. He had the opportunity to go into the draft, but he kept reassuring us that he wasn't ready. It's why we kept making our plans around him. The club team in Yugoslavia sent Ohio State a letter stating that Alex was under contract with them and that they were going to expose him. They wanted him to go back and play with them. We told Andy Geiger and the NCAA about it. We wanted to be straight up about it. The club team wanted him to go back, but he didn't want to go back. The feeling was that if you don't come back, you won't play with anybody. He was in this country for two years at a junior college. He told them he wasn't leaving, but he accepted $13,000—all of which he gave to his father.

"There are no colleges or other organizations for him to compete with in Europe. He didn't know anything about the NCAA. He didn't know what that was all about. We get involved with him, and it was aboveboard. He was taking care of his grades and he didn't take any more of the European team's money. He abided by all the NCAA rules. It's why the NCAA really needs to revisit their antiquated rules as they pertain to the changing landscape with foreign basketball players. The atmosphere surrounding European basketball players is drastically different from 10 to 15 years ago, when these rules were put into place. The NCAA looked at it as if Radojevic was a professional basketball player. He offered to pay the money back and make restitution. Our idea was to have him miss 10 games and pay the money back. But he had no means to make any money."

The Buckeyes were expected to challenge Michigan State in the Big Ten. Johnson was clearly among the most dominant defensive players in the conference, but with Radojevic, O'Brien said, teams could not afford to leave Redd and Penn alone at the perimeter. O'Brien was confident, too, that Reese could provide some offensive punch, yet Radojevic's impact could have been great enough to brighten the Buckeyes' postseason future.

"We would not have been as perimeter oriented with Radojevic," O'Brien said. "We would have a viable guy whom we could throw the ball to, and he would have been ready to score. Ken Johnson is getting better, but he's not as advanced as Alex offensively. Having a 7-3 guy in the middle to catch, pass, and score changes everything. It really did affect us on both ends of the floor—especially on the offensive end."

It didn't take long for O'Brien's point to sink in with Ohio State fans. The Buckeyes were favored to beat Notre Dame in a first-round NIT game at Value City Arena on November 16, 1999. As Penn and Redd struggled to find their shots, particularly from the perimeter, the Fighting Irish nipped at the Buckeyes' heels and trailed only 27-24 at halftime. Johnson blocked five shots, but could get off only four shots against Notre Dame's zone defense and finished with only four points.

O'Brien sat on the bench shaking his head. He kept demanding that Johnson fight for position in the low post. O'Brien tried beefing up his lineup by inserting 6-foot-8 freshman forward Slobodan Ocokolijic to play opposite Johnson, along with 6-foot-7 senior small forward George Reese. With Redd and Penn shooting a combined 10-for-33 from the floor, O'Brien and his staff could only wonder what might have been with Radojevic on the floor.

However, O'Brien had to live—albeit painfully—with the hand dealt him by the NCAA. It was harder to live with David Graves's 15-foot baseline jumper at the buzzer, which broke every heart in the arena. Graves's shot gave the Fighting Irish a 59-57 victory and denied the Buckeyes a second-round meeting with Siena. Ohio State would have secured a trip to New York for the NIT semifinals with a win over underdog Siena. O'Brien was disappointed by the loss to Notre Dame, but he was bitterly disappointed knowing the Buckeyes wouldn't play another game for 13 days.

Ohio State began the Big Ten season on Jan. 6, 2000, at Illinois. It was a rematch with a Fighting Illini team that defeated Ohio State in the 1999 Big Ten Tournament. Again, the Buckeyes were beaten at the buzzer. Guard Frank Williams netted a three-pointer to give Illinois an 80-77 victory. The Buckeyes, with Corey Bradford scoring a game-high 20 points, withstood a furious Ohio State rally.

"I didn't think we were as good as everybody thought we were," O'Brien said. "We wanted to keep everybody's feet on the ground. We had to stay on them about keeping their hunger and humility. What you try to look for is consistency. When you've gone from the basement to the penthouse in a year, that is an extreme situation. We are trying to find a comfortable middle ground, and for us, that is being in the NCAA Tournament on a regular basis. It's something we can strive for. We can challenge for the Big Ten championship. I don't know if people who say we can make it back to the Final Four truly understand how hard that is. When you look at some of the premier programs in the country, only a handful can make the claim of doing that. When you think of the number of Final Four teams Duke has had, it's remarkable. If Kentucky and North Carolina aren't doing it consistently, then who is? You have to have success-oriented goals, and for us that's being in the NCAA Tournament every year. We want to get into the tournament, and maybe every other year you can get to the final eight or knock on the door of the Final Four.

"We have the potential to achieve a little bit more at Ohio State than at Boston College. It's not a reach for us to have the Final Four as a goal. There are 13 teams in the Big East Conference, and usually about five teams get into the NCAA Tournament. It was hard for us to be among those five schools. I thought we were going real well in our last stretch there, making it into the tournament three out of four years. We believe we can do it on a more consistent basis at Ohio State because it's not unusual for seven of the 11 teams in the Big Ten to get an NCAA Tournament bid.

While the Illinois game was perhaps the most thrilling game of the 1999-2000 season, the most critical stretch of the season occurred between January 20 and January 22. It was a 48-hour span in which Ohio State would face No. 10 Michigan State at Value City Arena and No. 19 St. John's at Madison Square Garden in New York City.

This test, of course, would be a chance for the Buckeyes to prove they were real—again.

"That was a critical stretch because all you needed to know was that Michigan State was coming," O'Brien said. "That in itself made it big. It was going to be on national television. Dick Vitale was here. It was a great crowd. The two supposedly premier teams in the conference were playing—and two teams that had made it to the Final Four the season before. It was Penn and Redd vs. Cleaves and Peterson. It was as good a night atmosphere-wise as you could have in college basketball. We thought it was going to be a very important game. We had to hold our home-court advantage. They had beaten us the only time we played them in East Lansing last year. We played one of our better games.

"When Michigan State arrived, you could tell it had a big-game atmosphere. You could sense this was going to be one of those special nights. There are a lot of those nights in the Big Ten, but this was more than a normal big-game atmosphere."

The 13th-ranked Buckeyes, coming off conference road wins at Wisconsin and Northwestern, ended Michigan State's 21-game Big Ten winning streak, as Reese scored 19 points to lead Ohio State to a 78-67 victory. The Buckeyes seized control early, sprinting to a 42-33 lead at halftime by, surprisingly, beating the sluggish Spartans in transition.

In a tournament-like atmosphere, the Ohio State fans rushed the Value City Arena floor to celebrate. "I've never seen anything like that at Ohio State," Redd said. "You would have thought this was the ACC or something. I think this shows that people are getting very excited about basketball in Columbus. This is great, but we know their fans are going to be excited when we get to East Lansing."

Penn, who had a difficult time with an outside shot for much of the season, tallied 16 points. He made only three of his 11 field-goal attempts, but compensated at the foul line by making eight of 10 free throws. The Spartans, with Cleaves appearing in his first game since a preseason injury, played a sloppy game, as their 18 turnovers were double the number committed by Ohio State. The Spartans closed within 71-65 with 2:11 to play after a 6-0 run. Ohio State thwarted Michigan State's comeback effort when Redd drove the lane for a layup and Johnson sank two free throws in the final 60 seconds.

"It was a great win for us," O'Brien said. "We were looking to get respect against one of the quality teams in the country. We beat Michigan State, and then less than 24 hours later you got to forget about that game. We had hoped not to play St. John's so soon because you would like to have a week to let it all soak in and appreciate this win.

"On Friday, guys were tired and sore. They had to practice, go to school, and get on a plane to New York. Then we had to play an afternoon game the next day. There was no time to think about beating Michigan State on national television. The unfortunate thing was we didn't talk about Michigan State. We had to talk about St. John's. That was disappointing, but that's the way it was. Now, it's national television on CBS. We knocked them out of the Final Four a year ago. Now, it's not Penn and Cleaves. It's Penn and Erick Barkley. It's like here we go again.

"I'm thinking we're going to find out what Scoonie is all about because they are gunning for him. He got Cleaves; now, Barkley was there waiting. Then there was a letdown. We were a little bit lethargic. St. John's played well and we were kind of treading water."

In fact, the Buckeyes were drowning in a sea of mistakes. They had 15 turnovers, including several in the first half that allowed the Red Storm to take a 29-23 lead at halftime. Unlike the teams' prior meeting in the South Regional final at the Thompson-Boling Arena at the University of Tennessee the year before, the Buckeyes rolled slowly out of the starting blocks. The Buckeyes didn't hit their stride until they trailed 64-54 with 2:49 remaining.

O'Brien, with his patience tested, yanked Redd from the game midway through the second half in hopes of getting his attention. Redd encouraged Penn to get the Buckeyes back into the game. This was a fitting stage for Penn, who led Boston College to the Big East Tournament championship at Madison Square Garden in 1997. Penn kept the Red Storm from pulling away by knocking down half of his eight three-point attempts. He kept them afloat, too, by making guard Erick Barkley, his South Regional adversary, work extremely hard for his shots.

No one, however, kept the Buckeyes upright more than Johnson. No, he didn't possess Radojevic's offensive skills. No, he didn't have a physically intimidating presence. Yet, he ruled the day in the post. Johnson, who made only two of his shots from the floor, set a career single-game record with 11 blocked shots. "Kenny started to get more and more confident as the year went on, especially with the shot blocking, which became his signature. I sensed that all the talk about Radojevic, in some small way, was part of Kenny's motivation."

Johnson repeatedly put shots back into the faces of Lavor Postell and Anthony Glover, which helped limit the Red Storm to 29 percent shooting. St. John's coach Mike Jarvis had seen enough of Johnson in the 1999 NCAA Tournament. The pregame strategy, Jarvis said, was to saddle Johnson with foul trouble. The strategy backfired, as Johnson played 34 minutes and picked up only three fouls.

The Buckeyes had hoped, particularly with Singleton and Sanderson gone, that Brown would elevate his game. Brown, a Brooklyn native, was inspired by a contingent of family members. As Redd and Penn warmed up their cool shooting hands, Brown quietly scored a career-high 16 points.

Redd returned with St. John's leading by 10 points. Savovic scored on a layup, and Redd scored on an outlet pass from Penn with 2:21 remaining to cut the deficit to 64-58 to ignite an 11-0 run. For Jarvis, this was a nightmare revisited. Penn, Johnson, and Redd had made the plays that spoiled the Red Storm's title hopes 10 months earlier. Redd stole the ball and made two free throws when fouled. Then, a suddenly revitalized Redd knocked down a three-pointer to cut the St. John's lead to 64-63 with 1:14 to go.

Penn and Barkley had waged a grueling one-on-one duel in Knoxville the previous year. Penn had won that battle when he forced Barkley into a game-clinching turnover that sent Ohio State to the Final Four in St. Petersburg. Penn, beating Barkley to the spot, drew a foul and went to the line with a chance to give Ohio State the lead for the first time in the second half with 23.9 seconds to go. Penn calmly dropped both free throws to give the Buckeyes the lead, 65-64. The Red Storm had two chances to beat Ohio State in the last seconds, as both Notre Dame and Illinois had earlier in the season.

Glover put up a 12-footer with five seconds left. Johnson rejected it. The Buckeyes fell all over themselves on the bench, waving towels and jubilantly pumping their fists.

Barkley picked up the loose ball, and with Penn shadowing him, dribbled toward the left baseline. Barkley jump-stopped and released an off-balance, 18-footer a split second before the horn sounded.

Jarvis stood on the sideline, holding his breath. O'Brien was up on his toes, as if he was defending Barkley.

The Buckeyes' bench stopped celebrating. The Red Storm's bench was empty, as every player watched anxiously as Barkley skied above the courtside seats.

Penn rejected Barkley's shot.

There was no whistle, no foul, and there were no complaints from Jarvis. The Buckeyes had held on for a 65-64 victory.

The Buckeyes, with defeat seemingly unavoidable less than three minutes earlier, had scratched back like an angry, cornered cat to successfully complete the most challenging 48 hours of the 1999-2000 season.

O'Brien hadn't gotten this worked up during the NCAA Tournament. Admittedly, he felt his heart rate speed up. He was a nervous wreck. Of his many collegiate victories, this was a special one, considering the native New Yorker had returned home—and to Big East country—to conquer a familiar foe.

"We had gone into Madison Square Garden for years for the Big East Tournament," O'Brien said. "We played St. John's on campus. I had a long history against St. John's. Our guys were excited because we were in New York. Billy Packer and Dick Enberg were doing the game. We were all motivated. I was prepared to accept the loss, then just take your beating, walk out, and go home. Our guys had given us a lot that Thursday night against Michigan State. How much more could we ask of those guys? We couldn't get mad. This was hard. However, with them, it was like we can still do this. The last sequence was incredible, especially Scoonie's block. My initial reaction was get away from him. What are you doing so close? It looks like he has his hands on the ball, but I'm looking around at the officials waiting for a whistle. I do not hear a whistle; something has to be wrong. You mean to tell me he blocked it, and we win this thing?"

As the Buckeyes circled the Madison Square Garden floor, some of St. John's fans doused the Buckeyes with beer. O'Brien enjoyed the frenzied scene. If this had happened three years ago, no one in Columbus would have cared if Ohio State had lost.

"I thought it was terrific," O'Brien said. "We got splashed a little bit. We kept talking to them about this being an NCAA Tournament situation where you got to play Thursday and Saturday. If you are a good team, you can do it. Afterwards, I'm thinking about all the unbelievable irony involved. We are playing them [in 1999] for the Final Four. Scoonie's guarding Barkley. Barkley is coming down to win the game. Scoonie bumps him off the ball, and we win. Here we are a year later on their floor, and Barkley has the ball to take the shot that would win the game. Scoonie blocks it. What's the chance of this happening?

"It was the same two guys and the absolute same scenario. We have the lead. They have the ball with a chance to win, and both times Barkley, who is such a good player, didn't get the ball to the rim.

"I remember sitting there saying to myself it may not be happening this game," O'Brien said. "I had to understand what we were facing there. How much could we ask of them? I had to understand there were some games you have to accept. It's not like they don't care. It's not like it's not important. The circumstances of the game make it hard. The timeouts weren't about getting on them. I kept telling them come on guys, we can do this; come on fellas, stay with it. Just keep it close. Hang in there. I know you are tired. It was one of those deals. It was obvious it just wasn't working for us until the end. We changed our lineup. We started pressing and trapping for the last two minutes. We played four guards to get back in however we could.

"It was one of the most incredible comebacks in my mind that I've ever been involved in. It doesn't get a whole lot better than this. It was a character-building two days. We would have been happy coming out with a split against Michigan State and St. John's. We could have easily lost both. Winning both established the fact that we were back again.

"It was a satisfying game in terms of how balanced the contribution was from everyone on the team. Savovic had the game of his life, and Brown was getting garbage baskets after we had pulled Michael Redd, who was out of it mentally. Michael was like everyone else, playing like he was in snowshoes. I just took him out and told him, 'Unless you are going to change, you're not going to play again. You are not into it.' I made similar comments to all of them. As a coach, you know you have to do something to give yourself a chance to win. I told Michael, 'You need to go in and get something done.' It wasn't about burying him on the bench. We could have sat there and said I'm really pissed at him, and I'm not putting him back in. Alternatively, you can say if we have any chance in this game, he has to be in the game. Frankly, we took him out to get into his head. I hoped that he would respond. He responded like a champion. He had five points in 35 minutes, then scores seven points in one minute.

"Scoonie shot a couple of threes that were bricks, but in the last minute and a half, he makes a big three to help our guys tough it out. St. John's got careless with the ball and a little scattery. We were prepared to play the foul game. We started trapping, and they got a little tentative."

The St. John's win boosted the Buckeyes' confidence. It also gave them a lift in the national rankings, as they moved up to No. 10 in the Associated Press poll. As they had during the 1998-99 season, Ohio State was no longer surprising anyone. For those 3,000 fans who had rallied around the Buckeyes after the national semifinal loss to Connecticut, their high expectations were being realized.

With St. John's behind them, the Buckeyes continued the race for the Big Ten championship. They beat Purdue on January 29 and then won a battle against eventual Final Four participant Wisconsin, 51-48, at Value City Arena on February 2.

"We thought we were good enough, and we were at the stage, especially playing at home, that we could beat anybody," O'Brien said. "We were in a good frame of mind. It was one of those games where we toughed it out. We were the tougher team for that game. We had the crowd and environment favoring us."

The crowd booed the Buckeyes unmercifully when they arrived in Ann Arbor to play Michigan. The Buckeyes didn't feel the Wolverines out; they went for the knockout early and then cruised to an 88-67 victory. To exemplify the emotional ups and downs of college sports, Iowa upset Ohio State 67-64 at Value City Arena. Again, the Buckeyes were victims of a buzzer-beater—a three-pointer by guard Dean Oliver.

On February 16, the Ohio State-Michigan State rematch had arrived. Inside the Breslin Center, the Spartan fans were ready. Some had made their way to the arena long before tip-off. It was clear from the start that the Buckeyes didn't have the emotional edge this time around. The Spartans frustrated the Buckeyes on both ends of the court.

The Buckeyes were forced to play such a ragged game that O'Brien finally snapped. For only the second time in his career, O'Brien was ejected after putting his hands on an official in an effort to make a point during a timeout. O'Brien, who had been booted from a game against Seton Hall in a hotly contested Big East game several years before, lodged only a mild protest. The Michigan State crowd cheered as O'Brien made the long walk back to the dressing room. As Boyages took a knee in the huddle, O'Brien glanced quickly at the scoreboard behind the Ohio State basket. Unlike some coaches whose teams struggle on the road, this ejection was not a calculated move by O'Brien.

"I did not want to get kicked out," said O'Brien, who hesitantly came out of the locker room to conduct a postgame interview. "I didn't mind the first technical foul. It gave me a chance to act up a little bit. When I got the first technical, something needed to be done. There had to be some kind of diversion to the way the game was going. We were just hanging in there by a thread."

O'Brien was barely hanging onto his pent-up emotions. He was careful not to scold his players too much, fearing their confidence had been severely shot already. On almost every possession in the last 10 minutes of the first half, O'Brien debated with the officials. He sometimes berated them when he felt they were too liberal with their whistle, particularly when Ohio State was on defense. Occasionally, one of the three officials would stare back —an unspoken warning of sorts.

As the Spartans began to stretch their lead, O'Brien's jaw tightened as if he were grinding his teeth to the gum. He couldn't counter the heavy blows thrown by Michigan State. He deployed a zone. He changed to a man-to-man defense. The Spartans solved both defenses. The Spartans, with Cleaves hitting consecutive three-point shots, put together a 17-2 run that left Ohio State trailing 26-13 with 8:45 remaining in the first half. O'Brien was hot enough to have an egg fried on his face. It wasn't going to take much to rub him the wrong way. He called for a timeout in hopes of calming the Buckeyes' rattled nerves. Before he could chat with his players, O'Brien saw the official out of the corner of his eye. He voiced his objections calmly, but his reach for the official was the last straw.

"I didn't think I did anything to get the second technical," O'Brien said, looking genuinely puzzled. "The way that it happened is that I tapped him on the shoulder. The game was on national television, and both teams were in first place. I didn't want to bail out and not be a part of it. I didn't think I should have been kicked out. I was not happy that I was kicked out. When you go into that kind of place, winning is the exception; losing is the norm."

The Buckeyes losing to Michigan State in East Lansing was nothing out of the ordinary. The Spartans, avenging their 78-67 loss in Columbus, would not lose a game at the Breslin Center all season. Penn scored a season-high 30 points, but it wasn't nearly enough to keep Michigan State from rolling to an 83-72 victory. The Buckeyes simply didn't have enough fire-power to contain Michigan State's 1-2 punch, forward Morris Peterson and Cleaves, who combined to score 50 points. Up to this point, Ohio State had achieved much of its success with balance, but on this forgettable night, O'Brien's usually reliable bench didn't produce a single point.

The Spartans were easily the best team in this rematch. They figured out every trick the Buckeyes had used in Columbus. They beat the Buckeyes in transition. They beat them on the boards. They got to every loose ball and aimless shot—at least it appeared that way to an aggravated O'Brien.

"The general feeling was that we were kind of playing with house money in East Lansing," O'Brien said, looking to find an easy way to digest the defeat. "We got them at our place, and if you're going to get them at their place, you better hit a home run. You do not go into East Lansing and Bloomington and win very often. Those kinds of games make it easier to accept that you lost that game. You know the difficulty of playing one of the best teams in the country on their home floor. You have to have an exceptional performance to win games like that. We played OK, but not good enough to win there."

The Spartans hadn't lost a home game all season. Although that was slight comfort to O'Brien, it was still little consolation to his players. They had been confident that they could escape the Breslin Center with a victory. Besides, they had gained some measure of redemption against most every other team in the Big Ten. More important, the Buckeyes had gotten everyone's attention. At the beginning of the season, a Michigan State conquest of Ohio State didn't seem all that significant. This win, though, was a big one for the Spartans, who secured the No. 1 seed for the Big Ten Tournament.

Even though the Buckeyes came up short in East Lansing, O'Brien figured that this was a meaningful defeat. If nothing else, beating Ohio State was suddenly a big deal. The Buckeyes were no longer conference pushovers who could be taken lightly.

The Spartans were coming off a loss at Indiana before Ohio State paid them a visit. Michigan State coach Tom Izzo said before the game that beating Ohio State would be critical to his team's success. That, O'Brien reasoned, was affirmation that the Buckeyes were being taken seriously by the conference's title contenders.

"If we could make them feel that way, we knew we were as good as any team in the country," O'Brien said. "It was a sign of respect. The fact that they looked at their game with us as a big game showed respect for our program. We didn't want them to run away with the Big Ten championship. There was nothing else on our plate but finishing first in the conference."

Still, the Buckeyes had to put this disappointing loss behind them. There was little time to sulk, considering their next stop was Indiana, where they were to face the Hoosiers. In the days leading up to this important two-game stretch, O'Brien admitted that a split was a realistic goal. Yet he and the Buckeyes realized the odds were stacked heavily against them. The Spartans were perfect at home, and the Hoosiers had never dropped two games in a row to Ohio State on its home floor.

"If you come out of playing consecutive games at Michigan State and Indiana with a split, most guys would say, 'Take it right now, forget the game, let's do it,'" O'Brien said. "We don't even want to mess with playing. We would love to get a split out of those two.

"We had to change gears after the Michigan State game. At least in football, you have all week to prepare. In basketball, you have the next day sometimes. We had 12 days after our season opener against Notre Dame and then no time for Michigan State. It was over and done."

In fact, the Buckeyes had three days to prepare for their Feb. 19 showdown against Indiana at Assembly Hall. The Buckeyes stepped onto the Hoosiers' court with glowing confidence. The Hoosiers exchanged blows for much of the game, but Ohio State prevailed 82-72, after leading only 36-35 at halftime. Redd scored 26 points to counter A.J. Guyton's game-high 27 points.

"We went in knowing we were a better team," O'Brien said. "We went in with the attitude that we can win. You're always looking for ways to get an edge. Psychologically, we convinced our guys not to go into the game sitting back on their heels. We had to go after those guys, knowing full well it would not be easy. We had played some tough games against some tough teams, so there was no reason for us not to believe that we could win."

Despite their loss to Michigan State, the Buckeyes felt at least a share of the Big Ten title was within their grasp. They had finished second to Michigan State during their Final Four run in 1999. The Buckeyes finished with a strong kick down the stretch, ending the regular season with five consecutive wins—including an impressive 64-51 win over an Illinois team that had upset them in their Big Ten opener on January 6. Ohio State completed the regular season with a 22-5 overall mark (13-3 in conference play) and earned a share of the Big Ten title for the first time since 1992.

O'Brien was taking his team to the Big Ten Tournament in Chicago feeling confident the Buckeyes would play Michigan State for the third time in 1999-2000, preferably in the title game at the United Center. The scenario was similar to what occurred in the 1998-99 season, when Michigan State and Ohio State were favored to meet in the title game—before Illinois eliminated the Buckeyes in the semifinal round.

"I think anytime you can win a championship of any sort, it's big," O'Brien said. "The Big Ten isn't some run-of-the-mill conference. In most people's minds, it's the best conference in the country. I think, at times, that is what was lost on everybody. It was not lost on us. I made sure we told our guys this was an unbelievable accomplishment. What was impressive about these guys is that in two years they won a Big Ten championship, went to the Final Four, and won 50 games in two years. It didn't hit them until they realized that this program once went four years without winning 50 games.

"I didn't want them to dwell on it, but appreciate the level of their accomplishment. Reese, Redd, and Penn left an impressive mark. I'm asking myself, 'What is Brian Brown thinking? Will Brown and Boban think it's like this all the time? Is this what always happens?' Then you look at Michigan State. Then you realize Duke does this every year. That's why those programs are where they are. You have to tip your hat to them.

"We really have gotten some things done here. Far too many times in this business it's like you have survived something. The unfortunate thing about coaching is, there are only a handful of games you play where you sit in the locker room and say what a great win. Most of the time, you say, 'Whew, we didn't lose.' It should be the joy of winning instead of the relief of not losing. When we got to the Final Four and won twice in Indiana, you remember those games for a lifetime."

Somehow, despite the team's successes, there wasn't the same kind of bubbly enthusiasm in Columbus that existed in 1999. Even the Buckeyes approached games in a more businesslike fashion. Now, they were expected to win. The vociferous crowds at Value City Arena sometimes sat back on their hands, assuming victory was assured. O'Brien, though, was constantly telling his players to remember how bad things had been. He wanted them to appreciate every victory—no matter the opponent or the venue.

"The two seasons were so drastically different," O'Brien said. "We went from the first year, winning eight games, to the second year, where any game you won was good. Now, in our third year, we were expected to beat the Indianas and Purdues. We just kept winning. Every single win was like cause for happiness. Then we came back, and there's this sense that our fans are thinking, 'Yeah, they won, but by only eight points.' It got to the point, at times, where it seemed like the winning wasn't enough. We weren't winning right. We weren't winning by enough points. I think that kind of became a burden."

The Buckeyes weren't happy with themselves, either. Their faces were often long in the players' lounge during postgame interviews. However, as the 2000 Big Ten Tournament neared, the Buckeyes appeared more focused and determined. They won their last five regular-season games—including road games at State College, Pennsylvania; Minneapolis, Minnesota; and Bloomington, Indiana.

"We were on this innocent climb last year [1999]," O'Brien said. "Everything was instinctive. Everything we did was fresh. We totally lost our innocence in 2000. We had become spoiled and tainted a little bit. It really was different. You could sense that winning wasn't a big thing. You could sense people saying, 'Yeah, they should have beaten those guys.' We played a Coastal Carolina team that shot a lot of threes. We struggled, but we won the game. I said to the guys in the locker room that it seemed as if we had lost the game. It was like, come on, fellas, we don't have to apologize for beating anyone.

"I remember asking them, 'Who do we think we are when we're not happy about winning a game?' It's hard to win games. I didn't want to see anybody coming in hanging their heads after we had won a game. We'll fix what we have to fix tomorrow. Be happy tonight. They were standing around with their heads down. It was almost as if we escaped. It was the same way when we played Toledo. I had to remind them that those guys beat us last year.

"There was this underlying current that we weren't doing well—that we weren't doing what everybody thought we should be doing. "I used the analogy a lot about our football team. When the football team is 10-1, there's a feeling that they didn't get it done. They lost to Michigan. They didn't win the national championship. I think that's the burden those guys go through every year. We went through it one year. Regardless of who you lose or regardless of what happens, you'd better be pretty good this year. That's what everybody is expecting. Yeah, Duke gets the best players every year. But they still have to go out and get it done. So I give them credit."

The Buckeyes will remember that for the second year a row, they were unexpectedly ousted from the Big Ten Tournament. They lost to Penn State in the quarterfinals 71-66 at the United Center in Chicago. Only nine days earlier, the Buckeyes had beaten the Nittany Lions 79-73 at Penn State. Again, they wouldn't get a crack at Michigan State in the tournament title game.

The Buckeyes were felled by their shooting woes from the perimeter. Penn made only three of his 16 shots—including a miserable 2-for-14 from beyond the three-point arc. The two-time All-Big Ten point guard also committed an uncharacteristic seven turnovers. O'Brien had insisted that Penn would find his shot. Penn believed it, too. So he kept firing away, hoping something would eventually drop. At some point, the Nittany Lions peeled back to double-team Redd whenever he touched the ball inside 12 feet, partly because they no longer feared Penn's perimeter shooting. It was a strategically brilliant move by Penn State coach Jerry Dunn, who insisted before the game that Redd and Reese would not dominate this game—if Penn's late-season shooting slump continued. And it did. In fact, Penn finished the regular season by making only 16 of his last 55 shots during the Buckeyes' five-game winning streak.

Redd and Reese got their points, combining for 41. Reese, despite averaging 13.2 points per game, was largely overlooked. He was efficient from 12 to 15 feet, which was good enough to pull the opposing defense out of the paint to give Penn room enough to drive and Redd room enough to slash through the paint. It was Reese who demanded the ball after Penn State went ahead 37-35 at halftime despite Ohio State's 11-1 advantage on the offensive boards. He played all but two minutes to net a game-high 22 points on 9-for-13 shooting and a team-high eight rebounds.

"I had been saying all along that our team wasn't so physically dominant that there was a fine line between us winning and losing," O'Brien said. "Our team was predicated on playing skillful basketball—not by physically dominating somebody. There was a delicate balance between being good or just average. I think that was the case with Penn State. I don't think our guys didn't come to play. We had struggled with Penn State since I've been here. That game Joe Crispin [13 points] and Jarrett Stephens [21 points and 12 rebounds] had was very good. They had two of the top three scorers in the conference. They had guys who had the ability to hurt you."

Whether the Buckeyes were ready or not, they once again had trouble dealing with one of the tournament's lower-seeded teams. The Nittany Lions entered the game at 14-14 overall and 5-11 in the Big Ten, leaving them with the No. 9 seed. This was a particularly tough loss for O'Brien. The door had swung wide open for Ohio State to secure a No. 1 seed in the NCAA Tournament when both No. 1 Cincinnati, which had lost Player of the Year Kenyon Martin to injury, and No. 2 Stanford suffered late-season upsets two days earlier.

"I think the loss impacted our seeding tremendously," O'Brien said, repeating almost the same line as the year before, when Illinois sent the Buckeyes packing. "If we had taken care of business, we would have gotten a No. 1 seed."

O'Brien, looking from one corner of the interview room to the other, appeared to be lost in thought. The Buckeyes had seemingly gathered enough steam in time to make a serious postseason run. As Penn and Redd answered a volley of questions, O'Brien was already trying to figure out how he was going to prepare his team for the NCAA Tournament. There was nothing more he could say about this defeat, so he left the podium.

O'Brien may have struggled to find the right words to describe Ohio State's performance, but his cocaptains, Penn and Redd, knew exactly what happened. "They had nothing to lose," Redd said. "We had everything to lose."

Even though Ohio State came into the tournament riding a five-game winning streak, O'Brien knew the team's wheels were slightly off track. Only then, said O'Brien, did everyone realize how valuable Jason Singleton and Neshaun Coleman were to Ohio State—if only psychologically.

Only then did the Buckeye faithful come to grips with O'Brien's reality—that competing with the likes of Duke and Kentucky on a yearly basis is a monumental task. It's easy, O'Brien said, to go from a college basketball darling to an ugly duckling. Like their fans, the Buckeyes wanted to win the Big Ten Tournament; but with a conference as balanced as the Big Ten, winning isn't easy. If there were any doubts about the conference's strength, Wisconsin and Michigan State erased them by advancing to the Final Four in Indianapolis. The Spartans would eventually prevail in the NCAA Tournament, beating the Florida Gators 89-76 in the national championship game. Michigan State won the title for the first since Magic Johnson led the Spartans to a win over Larry Bird and the Indiana State Sycamores in 1979.

"It was always too easy to say we weren't motivated or they didn't get up for the game," O'Brien said. "There are other times when the other guys are just better. We look for reasons why we didn't win those kinds of games, but most times it's counterproductive. We just didn't make enough shots. We had already won the conference championship and we knew we were going to the NCAA Tournament. We prepared for the Big Ten Tournament. We wanted to go to Chicago and win three games. It just didn't happen."

The eighth-ranked Buckeyes wanted to go back to Indianapolis, but the RCA Dome was the site of the 2000 Final Four. This time, the Buckeyes couldn't fire up their engines to make a run at the national championship, as they had 12 months earlier in St. Petersburg, Florida. There wasn't nearly as much drama this time as there was when the Buckeyes sat inside the Schottenstein Center waiting anxiously to see where they would begin on the road to the Final Four. The Buckeyes' share of the conference regular-season championship all but cemented a top five seed. The 22-6 Buckeyes were seeded third in the South Regional in Nashville. They had been the fourth seed the year before in the same regional tournament.

Because the Buckeyes had stumbled in the conference tournament, they had to make a statement in their first-round game against Appalacian State at the Gaylord Entertainment Center. O'Brien, still believing that Penn would rediscover his shooting touch, promised everyone during the pregame press conference that his backcourt would bring its A game. Besides, Penn couldn't possibly shoot the ball as poorly as he had against Penn State a week earlier. As O'Brien predicted, Penn and Redd stepped on stage, then delivered an awe-inspiring performance. They combined to make 18 of 27 field-goal attempts, including a magnificent 9-for-11 effort by Penn, who led all scorers with 23 points in 36 minutes.

"I had a good night tonight, and hopefully it will continue," said Penn, who looked as if the heavy burden still hadn't been lifted. His eyes revealed nothing, just like O'Brien's. He had to be excited about finding his shot, but Penn was unmoved and unimpressed with an outstanding effort that carried the Buckeyes to an 87-61 victory over the Mountaineers—the Buckeyes' eighth consecutive first-round NCAA Tournament win.

This, of course, was one of those businesslike victories. It was efficient, precise, and somewhat of a clinical, systematic spanking of Appalachian State. The Buckeyes were supposed to win. So they weren't nearly as impressed as Appalachian State's players, who gave the Buckeyes a four-star review. "I think they deserved at least a No. 2, or even a No. 1, seed," said guard Tyson Patterson, who led Appalachian State with 15 points.

Redd, palming a bottle of spring water, said unequivocally that the Buckeyes wanted to prove a point. "A lot of people doubted us since the Penn State loss," said Redd, who supplemented his 21 points with five rebounds and four steals. "We were in a groove."

On this groovy Thursday evening, the Buckeyes were singing some sweet music in drumming Appalachian State, a team coached by Michael Jordan's former North Carolina roommate, Buzz Peterson. Yet, in the shadows of Opryland, the Miami Hurricanes—Ohio State's next foe—were hoping the Buckeyes would wind up singing the blues after their subregional final on a cold, wet March 19.

The Hurricanes were far more athletic and skillful than Appalachian State. Guards Vernon Jennings and Johnny Hemsley presented better matchups against Redd and Penn. Miami, the No. 6 seed, decided long before tip-off that Johnson and Reese were not going to beat them. The Hurricanes had to limit their looks at the basket and hope that Redd and Penn couldn't hit the high notes that carried the Buckeyes to victory in the first round. Reese and Johnson totaled 13 shots and made six. Ohio State's heralded backcourt took 31 shots: Penn was 7-for-17, while Redd was 5-for-14, including 3-for-13 from three-point range.

Again, the Buckeyes' flawed perimeter game and inconsistent free-throw shooting came back to haunt them. Ohio State, which was 18-for-26 at the foul line, shot 25 percent from the arc as Miami opened a 36-31 lead at halftime. The Buckeyes were within striking range, but their body language inspired the Hurricanes to go for the jugular. Hemsley scored a game-high 24 points, but it was one of O'Brien's former Boston College recruits, Elton Tyler, who made the deepest cut.

Tyler, a 6-9 forward, had been at the center of an admissions controversy that ultimately influenced O'Brien's departure from Boston College. For O'Brien, this was a bad dream. Tyler had been part of a blue-ribbon recruiting class that would finally make the Eagles a national power. Tyler, Jonathan DePina, Sean Connolly, Michael Bradley, Billy Collins, Adam Allenspach, and Penn were expected to do something special at Chestnut Hill. They were supposed to rid the Boston College basketball program of its second-class status, elevating it to the same level as the school's tradition-rich ice hockey program.

Instead, here was Tyler spinning past and gliding over the Buckeyes. It's exactly what O'Brien told the Boston College director of admissions to expect from Tyler. It's why he asked the school to reconsider its stringent admissions policy. Tyler scored 20 points on 7-for-13 shooting and perked up his Miami teammates after Ohio State took an early lead and increased it to 24-18 midway through the first half when Redd took the ball the length of the floor for a layup following one of Johnson's four blocked shots.

Tyler altered the course of the game by shutting down the low post, effectively using his eagle-like wingspan to redirect the Buckeyes' shots in the paint. Tyler sliced the Ohio State lead to 27-26 when he banked a 10-footer off the glass to ignite an 18-7 scoring spurt that gave Miami its halftime lead. The Hurricanes blew away the Buckeyes in the second half, cruising to a 75-62 victory. The game had been tied at 50 with 10:56 remaining, but Hemsley canned a trey to give Miami a 53-50 lead.

On the one hand, O'Brien was disappointed that the Buckeyes' tournament run came to a screeching halt in Nashville – only an hour drive from Knoxville, where Ohio State had completed the most unlikeliest of journeys in advancing to the 1999 Final Four.

On the other hand, O'Brien was happy for Miami's Tyler. Tyler was the quintessential O'Brien recruit: disciplined, genial, unselfish and talented. He did not make the grade to gain entry into Boston College, but on this night, Tyler, unlike Penn and Redd, brought with him his A game. "You always want to see nice kids do well," O'Brien said during the postgame interview session. "Tyler is special. Michael is special. Scoonie is special."

Penn and Redd had forged a unique bond during their two years together. In the aftermath of their defeat, they sat in the locker room consoling each other. They cried together. There was as much joy in their tears as pain, considering the sweat they shared in helping O'Brien rebuild Ohio State into a national power.

EPILOGUE

When Jim O'Brien returned from Nashville, Tennessee, he had little time to dwell on the Buckeyes' early exit from the 2000 NCAA Tournament. He and his assistant coaches had to throw themselves back into the recruiting wars. Even though three prize recruits had verbally committed to Ohio State in 2001, O'Brien wanted to focus his attention on scouting Ohio's high school underclassmen. He wanted to get ahead of the game, hoping not to lose the state's most promising talent to rival Big Ten schools like Michigan State. The Spartans had defeated Florida to capture the national championship and two Ohio natives— forwards Andre Hutson and A.J. Granger—made significant contributions.

O'Brien, though, had to take care of his bad back before going on the recruiting trail. He had grimaced in pain for much of the 1999-2000 season. During games, he would lean more on the scoring table instead of standing tall near the coach's box. He would often sit on the bench because it was sometimes too painful to get down on his knees to shout out instructions, as he was accustomed to doing. He had to deal with the aggravating, annoying pain caused by a herniated disc, partly because, for O'Brien, there was no other option. It was not an easy season for him in more ways than one. After watching him awkwardly negotiate his way up and down the stairs of the Schottenstein Center, the team trainers provided him with a chair during practices. He didn't feel it was necessary, but finally conceded.

"The players teased me a little bit," said O'Brien, who missed one practice and a preseason game in October 1999. "I did sit down more doing practices. My back just went out on me when I picked up a pair of pants. The pain was more intense when it started going down my leg. All that activity took its toll after every single game. I was taking medication to alleviate some of the pain. It was a long couple of months. It was uncomfortable the whole time."

The summer of 2000 was even longer for O'Brien, in part, because he couldn't play golf. He did, however, feel good enough to make it out to the Memorial Tournament in Dublin, Ohio, to watch Tiger Woods win the event for the second year in a row.

O'Brien has a history of back problems. He first ruptured a disc while playing softball in Boston seven years earlier. O'Brien had been a good in-fielder in high school, but one day in 1993, as he chased down a ground ball while playing softball, he keeled over on the infield dirt. He couldn't straighten himself up. He couldn't even pick himself up as he lay there with the ball dangling on the tip of his glove. "They carried me off the field and took me away in an ambulance," said O'Brien, who healed quickly enough to return before the start of the basketball season. "My back has been stiff for a long time. I spent a month in rehab in Boston."

Initially, O'Brien's doctors gave him the option of undergoing back surgery soon after Ohio State's loss to Miami at the South Regional. After another series of X rays, surgery was ruled out as an option. In reality, O'Brien never considered it. He had already made up his mind that he was going to spend a month in Miami at the clinic that specializes in the treatment and rehabilitation of the back. He knew the healing process after surgery would definitely have kept him from traveling to see some of the country's top high school players at various AAU tournaments.

O'Brien had considered some form of treatment before the start of the season. However, there was a strong possibility that he might have to miss a significant number of games. He opted to delay any extensive medical treatment. Instead, he spent most of the season taking different medications to remedy or at least numb the unrelenting pain. With the Buckeyes having a legitimate chance at competing for the Big Ten title, O'Brien wasn't going to let anything like a bad back thwart Ohio State's effort. But his back didn't hurt him nearly as much as the buzzer-beater that Notre Dame's David Graves hit to knock the Buckeyes out of the first round of the preseason National Invitation Tournament.

"My back did not affect our team at all," O'Brien said. "It was just a matter of going to work every day, then dealing with the discomfort. In January, the doctors told me I had to have surgery, but I told them it was out of the question. They told me if I had the surgery, I would probably be laid up and miss the remainder of the season. I said to them just do what you can to help me get through the rest of the season. I figured if I was still having the same problem, I would have surgery after the last game."

Inexplicably, the pain in O'Brien's leg dissipated two weeks before the Big Ten Tournament in Chicago in early March. For the first time in nearly four months, he was dressing without much pain. He didn't lean on the scorer's table nearly as often at the United Center, but Penn State put a hurt on Ohio State in an upset that left the Buckeyes still searching for their first conference tournament title-game appearance.

In early February, that stinging feeling that ran from his back through his right leg was sharp enough that O'Brien could not make the three-and-a-half-hour drive from Columbus to Ann Arbor, where No. 5 Ohio State was to face the troubled Wolverines. "The traveling didn't affect me too much until the Michigan game," O'Brien said. "Fortunately, there are a lot of nice people in Columbus who have their own planes, and somebody took me to Ann Arbor. I flew up the night before the game. I couldn't imagine being on the bus for three hours."

That 40-minute flight to Ann Arbor wasn't the first time that O'Brien had not traveled with his team. For two years, while at Boston College, he flew on the morning of Saturday-night games because he wanted to spend Friday nights with his daughters, Amy and Erin, shortly after their mother, Christine, died. Every week O'Brien would hold a pregame strategy session with his players and assistant coaches on Friday afternoon, then go watch his daughters play high school basketball. He would get up early on Saturday to catch a commercial flight, always making it to the arena in time to supervise the Eagles' afternoon shoot-around.

"For a two- or three-year period, I would stay because my daughters were playing games themselves on Friday night or maybe we just wanted to hang out together," O'Brien said. "I could stay and go to their games, even when Erin was in college. It really gave me an opportunity to spend a little more time with them."

O'Brien didn't spend much time in his office during the summer of 2000. His doctors weren't particularly crazy about it, but he was out hustling on the recruiting trail. He didn't want to let up or give them the impression that the Buckeyes were going to be satisfied with earning back-to-back NCAA Tournament bids. O'Brien, along with assistants Dave Spiller and Paul Biancardi, had worked hard in the months after Ohio State played in the Final Four in St. Petersburg. Then, on November 8, 2000, the Buckeyes signed perhaps their most impressive recruiting class as O'Brien prepared to begin his fourth season with the Buckeyes. Ohio State signed 6-7 forward Matt Sylvester of Cincinnati, 6-9 power forward Terence Dials of Youngstown, Ohio, and 6-foot point guard Brandon Fuss-Cheatham of Beaver Falls, Pennsylvania. The Buckeyes secured most every recruit they wanted, except the state's top prospect, Jawad Williams, who accepted an offer from North Carolina after O'Brien informed him that OSU had received its last commitment.

Sylvester, who led Cincinnati Moeller High School to a state championship, was the blue-chip prize in a recruiting battle that included Cincinnati, Xavier and Michigan State. In the previous seven years, the Buckeyes could not secure signatures on the national letters of intent from Ohio's best players—except Michael Redd. This time, O'Brien lured two of the top three players.

"We eyeballed this class a couple of years ago when those guys were sophomores," O'Brien said. "What we experienced this past year [2000] is the efforts of what we've done since we first got here. It's the first year of being a part of the Ohio recruiting landscape. The first couple of years, we were recruiting from not having real good seasons. We were relatively new; but now, we have started to focus in on many younger kids, which allows us to establish some relationships. This is one of the best recruiting classes we have had since we've been here.

"In our first two years, we couldn't get anywhere with guys of this caliber. This year there were many good players in the state. We feel very comfortable now going after the good kids in Ohio. There is a lot of interest in playing at Ohio State, and getting these kids is a sign that things are improving. We consider ourselves very fortunate to have signed Terence Dials, who was hurt in high school, meaning some schools didn't know much about him. These kids are good kids, good students, and good players."

In O'Brien's first two years, he and his coaching staff had to hustle. They had to re-recruit Scoonie Penn. They also had no choice but to recruit only high school seniors and two junior college players—George Reese and Aleksander Radojevic. O'Brien's first recruiting class would form the corps of his team through the 2000-01 season.

"You take Boban [Savovic], Doylan [Robinson], Brian [Brown] and Brent [Darby]. Those kids rolled the dice big time when they chose to come to Ohio State," O'Brien said. "We didn't have anything established here. All of those guys came here without the program having any success. When a whole lot of other guys weren't interested in coming, those guys were very interested."

O'Brien had made a serious pitch for Ohio's top two blue-chippers, Eugene Land and Sam Clancy, in 1999. But Land accepted a scholarship offer from the University of Cincinnati and Clancy decided to go west, to the University of Southern California.

"We couldn't even get Land and Clancy to visit," O'Brien said. "[Land] was supposed to visit on a Saturday; then he called to cancel. At that point it was time to focus on young kids, so they would know who we are. Now, we are recruiting only sophomores and juniors."

O'Brien has made major inroads in narrowing the recruiting gap between Ohio State and Michigan State. The coaching staff has put in the time, but *Boston Globe* columnist Bob Ryan believes that O'Brien's personality has also helped to convince high school blue-chippers that Ohio State, is once again, an attractive place to play college basketball.

"My guess is when recruits encounter this guy—and I've known him for a long time—their radar tells them the last thing in the world O'Brien is going to do is lie to me or try to exploit me," Ryan said. "There is an inherent sincerity that comes through to kids who he is interested in recruiting. They find out they are right when they play for him. There is no razzmatazz and no hype. The program is going to be about them, not Jim O'Brien."

Even as O'Brien continued roaming about the country, recruiting, his doctors pleaded with him to slow down. If the recruiting wars weren't enough, O'Brien was faced with the tough task of replacing a good friend, assistant coach Rick Boyages. After more than 10 years with O'Brien, Boyages assumed the head coaching duties at William and Mary prior to the 2000-01 season, leaving a vacancy on the coaching staff that O'Brien needed to fill almost immediately. He did so before making the trip to Miami, adding former Penn State head coach Bruce Parkhill as associate head coach.

Even after his recruits made verbal commitments in July, O'Brien found himself in gyms all across the midwest, searching for young talent. He would not relent. He did not have golf as a vice. At times, he got on his own nerves. Therefore, he often relied on his friend Jack Schrom to handle many of his university-related affairs.

O'Brien, though, leans most heavily on his longtime girlfriend, Mary, an attorney who made the move to Columbus with O'Brien in 1997. Mary, a native of Greenwich, Connecticut, left a successful law practice in Boston. She had reservations about leaving the New England area. She had hoped that O'Brien would work things out in Chestnut Hill and remain as the head coach at Boston College. However, she knew that staying in Boston was never an option for O'Brien. Before meeting with Ohio State athletics director Andy Geiger in early April 1997, O'Brien consulted with his circle of friends—including his former Boston College teammates Bill Evans and Tom Veronneau; John Bonistalli; his personal attorney, Bob Richards and former Big East commissioner Dave Gavitt. They all agreed it was time for O'Brien to move on.

"The thing that is great about Mary is that she is exceptionally bright and she has her own perceptions about things," O'Brien said. "She doesn't mind speaking up about things she has an opinion about. It's good sometimes, and she helps to keep the lid on things."

In his suburban Columbus home, O'Brien has three championship rings on a display shelf. They are there to remind him—and his visitors—of the championships won in the Big East and the Big Ten, including the 1999-2000 conference title OSU shared with Michigan State. His Final Four ring is visible, too. He does not wear his rings, but they are sources of great pride for O'Brien. For Cahill, the collection of rings is a clutter.

"I'm not a big jewelry person," O'Brien said. "I don't display anything in my house at all, but I have these three rings on my shelf. Mary asked me, 'Why do you have these rings out?' I said because I am proud of what we accomplished. She said, 'You know what you've accomplished, so why do you have to show everybody?' I said, 'Yeah, you're right, but the rings are going to stay there for a while.'"

More than anything else, Mary has been O'Brien's biggest critic and, at the same time, his most vociferous supporter. On those occasions when he wraps himself too tight or pours everything into his job, she reminds him that what he does is a job and that basketball, even at this level, is still just a game. Unlike Jimmy Johnson, who led the NFL's Dallas Cowboys to two Super Bowl victories and the University of Miami to a national title, O'Brien insisted basketball doesn't totally consume him.

"It doesn't come close to that," O'Brien said matter-of-factly. "You have to separate your life as a coach from who you are away from the game. Being a basketball coach is what I do, but it's not who I am. There are people out there who wonder how some of us coaches can take time to go to a movie. They think we should always be preparing our teams for the next game. I'm not one of those guys who spends 100 percent of my time coaching. I don't think Mary would tolerate that, anyway. She made a tremendous sacrifice coming to Columbus, so I owe her more than a few minutes of my time.

"The decision to come to Columbus was a real critical time in our lives. We were at a real crossroads. She didn't want to come. Until this day, she is a little upset that I didn't include her in the decision. I really felt this is what had to be done. I said this is what I have to do. I was at a point at Boston College where I absolutely had to go. It was a hard choice for her. She is still adjusting. It was easier for me because I was coming to Columbus for a purpose. The day I showed up, I was involved. She didn't know anybody but the wives of the assistant coaches."

On September 10, 2000, O'Brien was having far less pain in his back. He woke up that morning already wondering if his team could compete for the Big Ten title in the 2000-01 season. He was going to relax for a change, though. He didn't have to go on the road. He decided to hang around the house and watch a little football. However, as he settled into his easy chair, he heard the first rumors of the impending dismissal of Indiana coach Bobby Knight, who had had an ugly run-in with a freshman student only a few days earlier.

O'Brien knew almost instantly that Knight's fate had been sealed. He knew from the start that the zero-tolerance ruling imposed earlier in the year by the Indiana administration was only a temporary stay for Knight, whom O'Brien believed was destined for termination the moment he accepted the terms of the zero-tolerance agreement. O'Brien had hoped it would not end like this for a man whom he genuinely admired—a man who also admired O'Brien.

"I was hoping that when he came back off of his hunting trip, he would resign," O'Brien said. "I wanted him to decide the terms under which he was going to leave. No one ever thought he would leave there."

O'Brien understood the awkward, uncomfortable circumstances that prompted Knight's controversial firing in Bloomington. He, too, had his share of troubles during the final months of his 11-year stint at Boston College. Fortunately, O'Brien had walked away from Chestnut Hill before matters deteriorated completely. Despite winning three national championships in 29 seasons, Knight departed unceremoniously amid mild protest from some students. O'Brien had always been impressed by Knight's ability to motivate even below-average teams and also that in all of those 29 years, he did not have a single losing season.

"I had other opportunities to leave Boston College, but I wasn't interested," O'Brien said. "I never thought it would get to that point for me at Boston College. It tells you that nothing is forever and that things change. Things changed dramatically for both Bobby and me. Did anyone really think that the zero-tolerance thing was going to work? Everyone could sense things were different. I didn't know how things were going to work out, but I was hoping he would decide his own fate. It didn't happen, and I think he deserved better than that.

"When [Boston College] beat [Indiana] twice in the NCAA Tournament, I thought he was gracious in games they probably were supposed to win. When someone treats me like that, they're going to get it back 10 times over. I feel about the young men who play for me the same way.

"I'm sure Bobby had a hand in getting me this job. He had faults like all of us, but he is someone I would want to be friends with. Forget about some of his antics. We had some success against him the last couple of years; and believe me, it is Indiana by which everyone in the country gauges his program."

The Buckeyes knew they had turned the corner after beating Indiana in Bloomington two years in a row. They had never accomplished a feat against Indiana like that before. Despite his recent success against Indiana, O'Brien still considered Knight invincible.

"I couldn't sense anything changing with Bobby's situation," O'Brien said. "You go into that place and see those national-championship banners. That's impressive. You know where you are when you go into that place. Bobby Knight is a reflection of their great history."

O'Brien is convinced that time caught up with Knight. In a country where social mores have changed without much warning, the volatile Knight may not have heard the sounds of inevitability. The warnings came long before the university's president began losing his patience with the Hall of Fame coach.

"I think, like all of us, he needs to be more flexible to deal with the changing times in our society," said O'Brien, who won his last three games against Knight's Indiana Hoosiers. "But he doesn't compromise his values. I think it's impressive that most of his kids supported him. It wasn't that big a deal there. I read how Woody Hayes would get up in a guy's face, and yet everyone loved Woody. But that was then, and this is now. The kids are different today. I remember when I was playing for Bob Cousy, and he physically threatened me a couple of times. He never put his hands on me, but he told me if I kept throwing the ball away, he would take me outside and kick my little ass back to Brooklyn. There were no more turnovers because I thought the guy was going to punch me out. Now, kids question everything. Unless you are willing to be a little more tolerant, you are going to have some headaches. It's obvious that Bobby struggled with that."

As for Woody Hayes, he was fired almost immediately after assaulting a Clemson player during the 1978 Gator Bowl. The Buckeyes lost 17-15 in what ultimately was Hayes's last game, an unfitting ending to a career for a coach who remains a football icon in Columbus.

"I try to put myself in my players' shoes," O'Brien said. "I have experienced every emotion as a player myself. I have experienced being the best player on my team, and I experienced being a guy who never got into games at another level. I understand it because I've lived it. I try to understand some of things that I know I'll never understand.

"The thing that disappoints me is I wish it could be more fun for everybody who is playing. It's not just at Ohio State. There is so much pressure on everybody that sometimes we take the fun out of it for the kids, the coaches—everybody. The only way to really have fun is to win. The kids have created some of it themselves because of this major push to get to the NBA. Unless you are winning, there is no fun for anybody. So something is missing that used to be there."

For both O'Brien and Knight, what is missing is a simpler society— one in which a coach's job can be made easier. They both have great communication skills, but an inordinate number of college athletes are speaking a language that has become increasingly difficult for coaches to understand.

"You have to let these young men have their own identity," O'Brien said. "I don't love the fact that a lot of guys wear earrings. They can wear them, but not in the gym. It's all a part of being flexible. At Boston College, Dana Barros had a rattail hanging down his back and he wore two earrings. This is how he wanted to play. I asked him to cut the tail. We had to compromise somehow. He could keep the earrings if he cut the tail. You have to give a little to get a little. One of the reasons why I love that kid even now is because he cut that tail for me. He took a huge amount of ribbing from guys in the dorm. If you get your best guy to do things for you, then the other guys will usually follow suit."

When O'Brien was running the point for Cousy and Chuck Daly at Boston College, male athletes were not making cosmetic and fashion statements. They would not be caught dead wearing rattails and earrings. For his part, O'Brien wouldn't dare question anything Cousy or Daly told him. Nowadays, too many college basketball players are hesitant to run through walls, fearing they could jeopardize their professional careers.

"I wasn't the best player at Boston College, but every single day when I would leave practice, I wanted Cousy and Chuck Daly to know I was a good player," O'Brien recalled. "Bob Cousy was Mr. Basketball, for goodness sake. I would have done anything he wanted. I just wanted to be his guy."

While many of Knight's former players have had, at best, frosty relationships with their college coach, O'Brien shares a special bond with perhaps his most revered pupil, Scoonie Penn.

"I felt that Scoonie was my guy," O'Brien said with pride. "He led by example. He inspired his teammates. He demanded something from everybody. You have to ask Scoonie if I was his guy."

Said Penn: "Coach O'Brien is more than a coach to me. I owe him a great deal. Sure, he's my guy. He helped make a man of me."

O'Brien blushed. He was touched, too.

"How can I not do for that kid the rest of his life for the sacrifices and commitments he made for me at Boston College and Ohio State," O'Brien said. "There aren't many young players willing to make those commitments today. I will never forget that."

The Ohio State fans aren't likely to forget what O'Brien has done for the men's basketball program. He practically resurrected the Buckeyes from the depths of college basketball hell to make them legitimate title contenders after years of mediocrity. Ohio State continued its ascension up the college basketball ladder by advancing to the NCAA Tournament for the third year in a row in 2001. The Buckeyes were seeded fifth in the East Regional, but suffered a 77-68 upset at the hands of No. 12-seed Utah State in the first round at the Greensboro Coliseum in Greensboro, North Carolina. It was only the fourth time in school history that the Buckeyes earned three consecutive NCAA Tournament bids. Ohio State accomplished that feat, coincidentally, with two Buckeye legends—Jerry Lucas (1960-62) and Jimmy Jackson (1990-92).

Again, the Buckeyes stunned most everyone during the 2000-2001 season. They had lost Scoonie Penn to graduation, and Michael Redd had entered the NBA draft a year early. That left center Ken Johnson as the team's only legitimate star, yet the Buckeyes compiled a 20-10 overall record—including a surprising 11-5 record in the Big Ten. The Buckeyes placed third behind cochampions Michigan State and Illinois, both of whom were No. 1 seeds in the 2001 NCAA Tournament.

The Buckeyes lost nearly 70 percent of their offense with the departure of Penn, Redd, and George Reese. They leaned heavily on Johnson, who for the second year in a row, led the Big Ten in blocked shots and was named Defensive Player of the Year. Somehow, O'Brien mixed and matched a collection of role players, whose games complemented Johnson's enormous talents.

Ohio State had a bunch of no-names on its roster—including guards Brian Brown, Brent Darby, Sean Connolly, and Boban Savovic; center Will Dudley; forward Tim Martin and two unheralded freshmen—forward Zach Williams and center Velimir Radinovic. On paper, the Buckeyes didn't look like much. Yet they upset Michigan State and Illinois at a time when each was ranked third nationally.

In taking Ohio State to the NCAA Tournament three times in his first four years—including the 1999 Final Four—O'Brien, most college basketball experts agreed, had performed one of the most masterful coaching jobs ever. In doing so, he earned Big Ten Coach of the Year honors twice (1999 and 2001) and was named national Coach of the Year in 1999.

Despite leaving his dream job at Boston College and inheriting a mess at Ohio State, Jim O'Brien had bucked the odds.